**Julius Duscha**
11   16     05

Dear Reese: I thought you'd like to see a copy
of my memoirs. If someone would like to review
them, fine of course! Also I would of course
have no objection if you wanted to excerpt
something.

I find it hard to believe that I have beem
in San Francisco 15 years. I am okay, after
open heart surgery a year ago. It's a good
way to lose weight, but not recommended.
I saw one-column-by-five-inch ads in AJR for
books by Murray Seeger and Jules Witcover.
How much does such an ad cost?
Hope all is well with you.

2200 Pacific Avenue, #7-D, San Francisco, CA 94115-1412
Tel: (415) 931-7729                    Fax: (415) 673-3512

# From Pea Soup to Politics

✦

## How a Poor Minnesota Boy Became a Washington Insider

*A Memoir by Julius Duscha*

iUniverse, Inc.
New York  Lincoln  Shanghai

# From Pea Soup to Politics
## How a Poor Minnesota Boy Became a Washington Insider

iUniverse books may be ordered through booksellers or by contacting:

iUniverse
2021 Pine Lake Road, Suite 100
Lincoln, NE 68512
www.iuniverse.com
1-800-Authors (1-800-288-4677)

ISBN-13: 978-0-595-37057-3 (pbk)
ISBN-13: 978-0-595-81458-9 (ebk)
ISBN-10: 0-595-37057-8 (pbk)
ISBN-10: 0-595-81458-1 (ebk)

Printed in the United States of America

<u>Classification of book and primary readers</u>

From Pea Soup to Politics is a non-fiction book.

The book is a memoir of growing up poor in Minnesota during the Great Depression and the story of the author's 60-year career as a national political reporter and writer.

The book should appeal to teens and adults interested in politics, presidents and presidential election campaigns, American history, and the personalities of national political figures of the last 60 years. It should also appeal to college students taking political science courses, professors of politics and history, historians and collectors of books about politics and presidents, the history of the Great Depression and Minnesota. Finally, the book should appeal to people interested in how it was to grow up poor during the Great Depression of the 1930's.

# Contents

# PART I

## Growing Up in Minnesota
## in the Great Depression

# 1

# *First Memories—And Where I Came From*

My first memories are about my Aunt Honey and Al Smith, a governor of New York in the nineteen-twenties. No, they were not romantically involved. They did not even know each other. I remember Honey, who was my mother's youngest sister and whose real name was Edith, because she was so pretty and because she smoked cigarettes. At that time—1928—women who smoked were considered scandalous, at least in our household and neighborhood in St. Paul, Minnesota. Honey was living with us for a few months while she attended classes at nearby Macalester College. She was in her early twenties. It was so unusual to see a woman smoking then that I spread the word up and down Stanford Avenue where we lived that my aunt Honey "poked," my strange version of the word "smoked." My mother was shocked and quickly upbraided me and told me I should never again talk that way about Aunt Honey. And I never did. Aunt Honey later went to Washington State to teach school.

Now, to Al Smith, the governor of New York who in 1928 was the Democratic nominee for president, running against Republican Herbert Hoover. Smith was the first Roman Catholic to run for president. And he was also from the sidewalks of New York with an accent to match. Our next-door neighbors, the McDonalds, were Democrats and Catholics. So it was not surprising that they were backing Al Smith. To show their support, they put a campaign placard in their front window. Smith's craggy face covered most of the poster.

My mother was outraged. She was a staunch Republican—and a Lutheran. How dare neighbors be for Al Smith—and broadcast their support for all of Stanford Avenue to see by putting his homely—and Catholic—face in their front window? Hoover did defeat Smith in the presidential election that year, and that was some consolation to my Republican mother.

3

Aunt Honey's smoking and Smith's candidacy happened 75 years ago when I was only four years old. I don't know why I remember those two things, but they are as clear in my mind as if 1928 were only yesterday.

I was born on November 4, 1924, on the day Calvin Coolidge, like Herbert Hoover a Republican, elected president. My mother was proud of that coincidence and frequently told people about it. As I grew up and became a Democrat I seldom mentioned my distant relationship to Silent Cal, as the uncommunicative Coolidge was called.

I guess you could call me a Roaring Twenties baby. The nineteen-twenties, I later learned, were considered to be a raucous decade. Fashionably dressed women were called flappers. Dances like the Charleston were thought to be lewd by conservatives, just fun by others. Sports dominated much of the news with baseball slugger Babe Ruth the best known star. World War I was quickly forgotten. It was after all the war to end all wars. Prosperity was back and it looked as if it would never end with the stock market reaching new heights almost daily. When he ran for President Herbert Hoover promised a chicken in every pot and two cars in every garage.

But how quickly things changed. When I grew up I called myself a child of the Depression, and I was. In October 1929, shortly before my fifth birthday, the stock market collapsed and the worst depression in the nation's history began.

In 1932, when I was eight years old, Franklin D. Roosevelt, the Democratic governor of New York, easily defeated the discredited Hoover and in March 1933 was sworn in as the first Democratic president since Woodrow Wilson left office in 1921.

I was vaguely aware of these political developments as I was of the rise to power of Adolph Hitler in Germany at the same time. My mother and father had little money and no investments in stock; so the collapse of the stock market had no immediate effect on us. My father managed to keep his job as a shoe salesman until 1937, when he was laid off, as they said then. I knew of neighbors who lost their jobs and struggled to pay their bills or even to eat.

But for the most part the Great Depression did not seem to affect my boyhood. We always had enough to eat, even when my father lost his job and was out of work for a year. I only remember once when I asked my mother for a dime for the movies and she didn't have it.

As for Hitler, he was far away in Europe and, besides, we had handily defeated the Germans in the Great War. Thoughts of another war were far from my thoughts and those of my boyhood friends.

And World War II was upon us in 1939 when Germany invaded Poland and France. I was not quite fifteen years old, but just three years away from the draft.

May you live in interesting time, says the old Chinese proverb. And I have. But little did my parents and I know that when in November of 1924 I came squealing into the world of the Roaring Twenties. How the world changed in just fifteen years.

I was born in Midway hospital in St. Paul, a hospital long since gone. I grew up in what was called a bungalow at 1431 Stanford Avenue, between Albert and Pascal streets. The neighborhood was certainly not fancy, but its streets had a lot of fancy names like St. Clair, Berkeley, Wellesley, Jefferson, Brimhall, Warwick, Hamline and Snelling.

Large, spreading elm trees shaded the streets and houses, which were a mixture of bungalows like ours and grander two-story houses, some built of wood and others of brick. Almost every house had a screened front porch and sometimes a back porch, too, where people sat on humid summer evenings to try to catch a cooling breeze. There were a few two-family houses—we called them duplexes—but only a couple of apartment buildings, and they were small with only six or eight units.

St. Clair was the business street. In the eight blocks from Snelling to Hamline that were convenient to our neighborhood St. Clair had a movie theater, three drug stores, two groceries, two gasoline stations—known as filling stations then—a bar called "a 3.2 joint" by my mother because of the alcohol content of the beer it sold, a movie theater, beauty and barber shops, a café called a "sweet shop," and some offices for doctor and dentists. St. Clair Avenue also boasted a street car—or trolley—line which ran to the downtown area of St. Paul and then on to the East Side of the city.

St. Paul is a city built on hills and has sometimes been compared to Rome because of its hilly terrain. Our neighborhood was situated on top of one of the hills, but we had no views. The city itself is always compared unfavorably with its "twin" across the Mississippi river—Minneapolis—but to me, a boy growing up in St. Paul, the city was fine. I never got to Minneapolis until I was in high school and an uncle took me to a baseball game there.

I am not sure why my parents ended up in St. Paul. My mother was born in Sauk Rapids, a small Minnesota town on the Mississippi River about seventy miles northwest of St. Paul. My father, as far as I know, also grew up in Sauk Rapids after coming to the United States as a child from what was then East Prussia in Europe and is now part of Poland. St. Cloud is across the river from Sauk

Rapids and is a larger city, which early in the nineteen hundreds was something of an industrial and railroad center.

I don't know how or where my mother and father met. I do know that they were married a couple of years before I was born and that for their honeymoon they took a trip on a ship that cruised Lake Superior, one of the Great Lakes. Excursion boats left regularly in those days in the summer from Duluth, a city in northern Minnesota, and a Lake Superior port.

After their honeymoon my father and mother settled in the bungalow on Stanford Avenue. My father was working as a shoe salesman for the Emporium department store in St. Paul when he married my mother, and had saved enough money to buy the bungalow.

My mother was 34 years old when I was born, and my father, I learned much later, was 48. She was Anna Perlowski, before she married, the oldest of ten children, four boys and six girls, and she also had a half-sister. She was an attractive woman with dark hair and always quite serious. I don't remember her laughing much. Was she unhappy in her marriage and in her modest place in the world? I don't know.

Before she married, my mother was a country school teacher. Her classroom was a one-room school house near Foley, Minnesota, not far from Sauk Rapids. As a teacher she boarded with a farm family and walked a mile or so, in rain, snow, blowing winds or heat, to her school house every morning where her first chore was to build a wood fire in the school's pot-bellied stove.

My mother had graduated at the age of sixteen from what was then called a normal school; today it is a teachers' college. The school was in St. Cloud and she walked a couple of miles each way from Sauk Rapids to her classes. But the way, don't confuse Sauk Rapids with the novelist Sinclair Lewis' town of Sauk Center, which is thirty miles up river from Sauk Rapids.

One-room country schools in those days housed students ranging from kindergarten age to eighteen-year-olds. My mother told me that some of her pupils were older, taller and bigger than she was, and not very smart. But she maintained order, did some teaching and was never attacked by a big lout.

Much later in life I learned from my mother that while a country teacher she decided one year to run for superintendent of education in her county, but was unsuccessful. Perhaps, that's where my life-long interest in politics began. After her marriage my mother devoted her life to being a housewife—or homemaker—and a mother to me, an only child.

But after I went away to the University of Minnesota, she took up teaching again, becoming a substitute teacher in the St. Paul schools, a job she loved and hated to give up when she reached the then mandatory retirement age of sixty-five.

I know little about my father's boyhood and early years. I don't even know where he was born in East Prussia or how old he was when he came to this country and how he happened to come to Minnesota. My father did not have much education and I suspect he began working when he was just twelve years old. I do know that before he became a shoe salesman at the Emporium he had worked in a shoe factory in St. Louis, Missouri, which was a center of shoe making in the early years of the twentieth century.

My father was one of six children, four boys and two girls, and was the oldest. Later in life I discovered through a beautiful old picture of a wedding party that my father had been previously married. Strangely, the picture was among my mother's effects, which I found after she died. The man at the center of the picture is unquestionably my father, and the woman next to him, a beautiful young woman, is certainly not my mother, not that that she wasn't pretty too. To whom had my father been married? For how long? Any children? Did his first wife die? Were they divorced? Where was she when I was growing up? I have no answers. Nor did any of my relatives have any answers, when I asked them about my father's first marriage. Some of them knew of the marriage; some did not. In those days eighty or ninety years ago divorce was disgraceful and second marriages were even questionable. So my father's first marriage remains a mystery, and sometimes a brooding one, to me to this day.

My father seemed to be an easy-going man, short, wiry and bald. He wore gold-rimmed glasses and was always nicely dressed in a suit and tie when he went off to work. He seemed to enjoy his job as a salesman. He sold women's shoes and his customers liked him because they always asked to be waited on by him when they came a second or third time for shoes. He was William Julius Duscha but preferred Julius, so after becoming a Julius, too, I also became Junior, a name which I hated particularly when I was still called "Junior" by relatives and friends when I was in high school and even in my twenties.

I don't think my father was prejudiced but he was always proud that he worked for the locally-owned Emporium department store and not for the rival Golden Rule store, which was part of a chain headquartered in New York City and, as my father said, "owned by Jews,"

I liked both my father and mother. As an only child I suppose I was spoiled, although there were few monetary or other resources in our household that could be used to "spoil" anyone. I also was a "late" child and that probably had something to do with the loving care I received. My maiden Aunt Emma lived with us and doted on me as if I were her child. Emma, as I always called her rather than "Aunt Emma" or "Auntie," was my mother's sister and deaf, or hard-of-hearing as we always said. She was a beauty operator, working in a neighborhood shop run by a woman named Helen. Although Emma was pug-nosed and attractive, I always thought she never married because of a shyness brought on by her deafness. Emma was in her late twenties when I was born.

The four of us got along reasonably well. If my father objected to Emma's presence in our household, I never heard him say so. Emma did contribute to household expenses from her meager earnings giving permanents, marcelling hair with hot curling irons—very popular then, unheard of today—shampooing customers and manicuring nails. (She regularly inspected my nails to check on my cuticles, whatever they were.)

# 2

## *School, Glorious School*

My small world became somewhat larger when I entered kindergarten. I was five years old in November 1929, but under the school rules had to wait until September 1930, to begin kindergarten. The Great Depression was upon the country but I was not aware of it. Nor did I hear my parents talking about the Depression. My father was working and life seemed to be going on as usual.

My school was called Randolph Heights and was located on Hamline Avenue between Wellesley and Jefferson Avenues, two and a half blocks from our house. My mother took me to school the first day, but after that I walked by myself down Stanford, across Albert and up Wellesley to Hamline where I was escorted across the street, a fairly busy one, by a member of the School Police Patrol, natty with his Sam Browne belt around his waist and over his shoulder and officious with the yellow stop sign he held in his hand and raised when he walked into the street to escort his charges to the school grounds. Maybe I could be a School Patrol when I got bigger? It was an exciting prospect.

The front of Randolph Heights school was only one story but in the rear of the sloping block on which it was situated the school became a two-story structure. It was a concrete building painted white with red-trimmed windows. A neat lawn and shrubbery surrounded the front entrance off Hamline Avenue. The first thing you saw when you entered the building was a large auditorium with a stage. On either side of the auditorium were classrooms with doors that opened directly to playgrounds with their slides, swings and parallel bars.

The kindergarten room was close to the entrance hall. The room was rather large—humongous to a five-year-old—and its walls were covered with colorful posters extolling learning and often crude drawings by the boys and girls who had just graduated from kindergarten to the first-grade classroom next door. And we neophytes soon added to the scrawlings decorating the walls.

Kindergarten lasted for only half a day, a morning for the first few months and an afternoon for the rest of the year. In the beginning of each session we sat in chairs listening to our teacher read to us and then singing some simple songs. Later we got on the floor and drew pictures. We also were required to bring a piece of linoleum with us so we could lie on it during nap time. I hated nap time, and particularly the linoleum, which was cold and smelled bad; not that it was dirty, it was just that linoleum smell.

The kindergarten year went by fast and before I knew it I was in first grade, with a desk of my own where I could store a pencil, a blue-lined notebook, a ruler and an eraser. I remember worrying whether I could remember which desk was mine, but that was a needless concern as I quickly located my place every morning. Push-pulls dominated the initial weeks in first grade. You stood at the blackboard and pushed a piece of chalk up and down a few inches. This was to get you in practice for learning the cursive Palmer Method of writing. I also learned that I must do the push-pulls with my right hand and while holding an eraser behind my back in my left hand. And I still hold my "eraser hand" behind my back when I shave.

I learned to write in the first-grade and also made some progress in learning to read. Arithmetic? I guess that came mostly in the second and third grades. I liked school from the beginning, particularly reading and writing, and I picked up things pretty fast. By the time I was finishing the third grade I was judged smart enough to skip the first semester of fourth grade. Skipping grades was an accepted practice then, but today educators frown on skipping. I liked it. It made me feel important.

I could not wait to go to school every morning and when I came home in the afternoon I often could not wait to stick my nose into a book—Tom Swift's magical stories, The Hardy Boys' adventures. I was indeed becoming a bookworm. Despite Minnesota's fierce winters of snow, wind and below zero temperatures, school never stopped. Even if it was ten or eleven degrees below zero, my mother bundled me up with a sweater, a warm coat, a fur cap and ear muffs and sent me out the door to school.

Almost all my memories of Randolph Heights are good, but some are not and some are funny. I enjoyed the trip each class made every morning to a nondescript storage room to drink from a bottle a half-pint of milk, which cost three cents. The beginning of the school-lunch program? I liked the way teachers sat children in their classrooms—the slow learners in front, the brightest in back. I was almost always in the back, which I thought was nice because I never liked to be under someone's nose. My being in the back alerted one teacher to my nearsightedness. She noticed that I couldn't read the blackboard, sent a note home with me to give to my mother, and that led to my first pair of glasses at the age of eight. But in music class I was in the front because I couldn't sing, and still can't.

I also remember Miss Buell, the stern principal who favored long dresses in dark colors like purple or a mourning gray. Miss Buell was a stern taskmaster who scared us pupils and I suspect put the fear of God into her teachers, too. Every Thursday was newspaper day. On Thursdays all school doors were locked in the morning except one which led up a flight of stairs. At the top of the stairs stood an unsmiling Miss Buell. Every pupil was expected to have the week's discarded newspapers under his or her arm; and believe me Miss Buell's steely eyes watched carefully as we slowly made our way up the stairs. Lord help the boy or girl who did not have newspapers every Thursday. After passing Miss Buell we went to an empty room where we dumped the newspapers before going on to our class-rooms. When after a few weeks the room was filled with newspapers, a huge Waldorf Paper Company truck came by and the driver and his helper dumped the papers into the truck to be recycled into cardboard boxes. The paper company paid Miss Buell for the papers and the money was used to buy books and other materials needed by the school.

Before I left Randolph Heights for junior high school I nearly disgraced myself—well, why don't I admit it—I did disgrace myself, and before the entire school body. Before the May 30 date of Memorial, or Decoration, day Randolph Heights always had an assembly in its auditorium honoring war veterans. On the stage with some teachers and Miss Buell were a few students and some veterans of the Great War—better known now as World War I—the Spanish-American War and even the Civil War. One year I was selected to recite the poem that begins "In Flanders field the poppies grow..." I spent many evenings memorizing the verses and thought I had them down but when it came time for my recitation I panicked and recited the second verse before the first. I was mortified, and so was my mother who was in the audience. My face reddened as I practically ran off the stage after finally finishing the poem. But somehow I survived and even skipped another half grade before leaving Randolph Heights for junior high school. I even became not only a School Police patrol boy with my own Sam Browne belt but in my last semester was promoted to captain of Randolph Heights' school patrol.

# 3

## *Falling in Love—With Ginger Rogers*

Grade, or elementary, school opened new worlds to me, but when it ended at the end of the first semester of the seventh grade I was eager to get on to junior high, or middle, school. Other things widened my horizons as I joyfully moved through grade school. I started going to the movies and fell in love with Ginger Rogers, when I was nine years old. I particularly liked the serialized westerns on Saturday afternoons which literally ended every week with a cliff-hanger. I began listening to the radio with my parents—the Breakfast Club from Chicago, that exciting Emerald City far away; the National Farm and Home Hour, also from glamorous Chicago at noon when I came home for lunch; Ma Perkins, Vic and Sade and young Rush and the other soap operas that were on after I came home from school. Evenings the radio was a command performance—Amos 'n Andy, two white men playing Negroes who were always getting in trouble, but were always funny—comedian Jack Benny on Sunday nights, comedian Fred Allen and singers Bing Crosby and Rudy Vallee, comedian Bob Hope, ventriloquist Edgar Bergen and his dummy Charlie McCarthy, comedians George Burns and Gracie Allen, and the adventures of One Man's Family.

And then there were the children's programs that were on the radio from five to six o'clock in the evening. Little Orphan Annie. Jack Armstrong the All-American Boy, who I was led to believe was that way because he ate Wheaties for breakfast every morning; so did I. Cowboy Tom Mix who was strong because he ate hot Ralston cereal every morning; so did I (in the cold winter months). A dilemma: Did I want to be Jack Armstrong or Tom Mix? Both, I guess. The stories, fifteen minutes in length minus a few minutes for commercials each evening, went on and on, but I never tired of them.

I didn't realize it at the time, but both talking movies and radio were so new in the nineteen thirties and still experimenting with techniques of sound and how to tell stories in new mediums. Singer Al Jolson appeared in the first talking picture only in 1928, and the first commercial radio broadcast was in 1924. Yet by the mid-thirties when I became a movie-goer and radio-listener, movies and radio were the major sources of our entertainment. They were cheap, entertaining and windows on both the rich of the world and its travesties. The movie newsreels were my first window on the real world. For me, radio was mostly for entertainment as there was little news on radio in the thirties. But as one newsreel proclaimed itself "The eyes and the ears of the world" that said it all for me.

But the movies and radio did not displace reading for me. At Randolph Heights I was introduced to My Weekly Reader, four or eight pages that summarized news in language a grade-schooler could understand. The text in My Weekly Reader corresponded with the grade you were in and consequently became more detailed as you progressed from grade to grade.

Our family subscribed to the St. Paul Daily News, an evening paper somewhat on the tabloid side in its news presentation. It competed with the more serious morning St. Paul Pioneer Press and evening St. Paul Dispatch. The Daily News was struggling as were so many papers in the thirties, and in the late thirties went out of business.

I liked the Daily News, and actually became a Daily News carrier for a short time, but more about that later. The Daily News had some good comics—Maggie and Jiggs, who were always arguing; Our Boarding House, which featured the sedentary, lazy and puffed-up Major Hoople; Mutt and Jeff, one tall, the other short and both roustabouts; Little Orphan Annie and her fabulously rich Daddy Warbucks; and the ace detective Dick Tracy. There was also Uncle Ray's Corner which was a bit of history each day written so a child could understand it, and a crossword puzzle with clues simple enough for a boy to solve. I also liked the daily poems by Edgar Guest, which were easy to understand and made you feel good. Later I learned that Edgar Guest was heartily disliked and derided by "real" poets, but he certainly was popular for many, many years and loved by newspaper readers like myself, and my mother, I should add. The front page of the Daily News featured a column every day by a man named Arthur Brisbane. It was usually too serious and complicated for me to understand, and it was not until many years later that I learned that Arthur Brisbane was perhaps the most important writer for the Hearst newspapers. The Daily News was not a Hearst paper—it was locally owned—but the Brisbane column was syndicated widely by the Hearst organization beyond its own papers.

And then there were Big Little Books, those fat little volumes with a cartoon on the right page and text on the left. First published in the early thirties, they were the forerunners of comic books. They cost but ten cents and were devoured by boys like me. Titles ranged from Little Orphan Annie and Dick Tracy to Buck Rogers in the Twenty-Fifth Century. Prairie Bill and the Covered Wagon, Pioneers of the Wild West and The Plainsman, which was based on a movie starring Gary Cooper and Jean Arthur. Each book told one story and could be read in an hour or two. I loved them and collected fifty of them. I even set up a Big Little Book lending library, with little cards modeled after the real ones used by the library downtown. My "customers" were other boys and girls in the neighborhood, some of whom had collections of their own and loaned books to me.

I guess I was about ten years old when I started to go downtown to the city library, where I loved to browse in the children's book room, checking out Tom Swift's adventures as well as those of the Hardy Boys. The library was, to me at least, a massive building with large rooms, all devoted to books or magazines and newspapers. It was nirvana for a bookworm like myself. I was a little afraid of the newspaper room, where bums—homeless, we call them today—congregated to get out of the cold Minnesota weather. They often seemed to be doing more sleeping than reading. Taking the street car to and from the library was as much fun as being in the library itself. The street cars were big rumbling, yellow machines. The motorman, as the driver was called, stood up as he turned a crank to deliver the power to propel the car and stepped on a break pedal to slow down the car. It looked like a wonderful and glamorous job to me, and as I sat in my seat by the window I twirled part of a knob used to lower the window, pretending that I was actually the motorman.

Sunday school had also become an important part of my life. We, my mother and I, that is, went to Calvary Lutheran Church, which was in a handsome brick building across the street from the Randolph Heights School. While she attended church in the sanctuary I was in Sunday school in the bare and usually chilly basement. My father and Emma never went to church. I enjoyed Sunday school, listening to the Bible stories, reading the colorfully illustrated weekly paper we were given, and day-dreaming about God and religion. I came away with a "Green Pastures" view of religion, which I am sure was not what the church intended for me to have. "Green Pastures" was a nineteen-twenties play with an all-black cast and a story about a heaven where "De Lawd" presided over a never-ending fish fry and where his male disciples were always smoking "cee-gars."

One summer I did try to read the Bible all the way through. I started on the New Testament and made it through all four gospels and other books without much trouble, and understanding a good deal of what I read. But when I got to the Old Testament, I was soon bogged down in all the "begats" and never did get to the end. It was a good exercise and even today I remain fairly well conversant with the New Testament.

I remember, too, taking confirmation lessons on Saturday mornings in the church basement. These included memorizing and understanding the Ten Commandments, the Apostles' Creed, the Twenty-Third Psalm and other icons of the Lutheran church—and all Protestant dominations. I did all right learning all these important things, but disgraced myself on the day—around my twelfth birthday—when I was confirmed. I was nervous and when I went to the altar rail to receive my first communion with the other members of my class I fainted. My mother, who was in the congregation, rushed to my side and I was soon revived. But I was as embarrassed as my mother was, and I have never forgotten that Sunday.

One other aspect of my early church-going days that I liked was Luther League. Our Luther League group met every Friday evening, again in the church basement. Part of the meetings involved religious matters such as learning to understand a particular part of the Bible. But there was also time for fun and games and a little something to eat and drink. The best part though was walking a girl or girls back home. There was no kissing but I was beginning to enjoy just the presence of girls.

After I was confirmed my Sunday School days were over, and I was allowed to go to church with my mother. I didn't mind the hour of worship, but my mind often wandered from the hymns, psalms and sermons. I liked to watch a nattily dressed middle-aged man who sat in front of us and invariably went to sleep soon after Reverend Braun started his sermon. I also liked to snoop into the collection plate to see if any five or ten-dollar bills showed up there. I don't remember seeing anything more than coins and dollar bills.

Of all the religious or patriotic events of the year, Christmas was by far the best. For us the Christmas season began in mid-December when my mother and I, towing my sled behind me, walked up to a lot on St. Clair Avenue where Christmas trees were sold. We carefully looked over the trees until we found one that suited us and was not too expensive, which meant that it could not cost more than a dollar, and preferably less. Once we made our choice we tied the tree to the sled and I, filled with excitement, carefully pulled it home.

We always set up the tree in a corner of the living room by the davenport. The decorating of the tree did not start until a day or so after we brought the tree into the living room because it was usually frozen and we had to be sure it was thawed out well before putting on the lights, ornaments and tinsel, those wonderful silvery strands of what we called tinfoil. My mother or father handled the lights and

I put on the ornaments and tinsel from the bottom branches to as high as I could reach, my parents finishing the higher branches. The first lighting of the tree was such a magical moment with the colored lights, the ornaments and the tinsel all sparkling in the darkened living room.

Then came Christmas Eve, and Madame Schuman-Heink, a German opera singer who sang "Silent Night, Holy Night," in German on the radio every Christmas Eve. My mother loved to listen to her and sat quietly and reverently in the living room as Madame's strong voice came from the radio.

Christmas morning was when presents appeared under the tree and we opened them with ooh's and ahh's. When I was small I wanted, and received, toys—cars, trucks, a steam shovel, an Erector set with which you could construct cars or even buildings. As I became older I received always-welcome books, sweaters and ties. There were never any elaborate or expensive presents because we could not afford them.

After presents were opened we had a sumptuous Christmas breakfast. There were canned peaches or pears, bacon and eggs and, most importantly, poppy-seed bread. My mother made poppy-seed bread for all the holidays, but it always seemed the best on Christmas Day. She mixed the ground poppy-seed with eggs, spread the mixture on bread she made herself, rolled up the bread and poppy-seed and baked the loaves until they were golden. Nothing was better than her poppy-seed bread, which I can still taste as I write this. Christmas dinner was at one o'clock and always featured goose, which my father loved but which I did not particularly like. We had the usual mashed potatoes and peas and pumpkin pie for dessert, which I did like. Christmas is still a wonderful time of year, but as I look back the Christmas times of my boyhood still seem the best.

# 4

## *"The Spirit of Sanford"*

As I started junior high school in 1936 the Depression still gripped the United States and Europe and Adolph Hitler had begun his efforts to conquer a Europe that never recovered from the Great War. But I was blissfully unaware of these world-shaking problems. My parents were Republicans but they seldom talked about Democratic President Franklin D. Roosevelt or what was going on in Germany, the country of my father's birth or other European countries like Poland from which my mother's ancestors came. Perhaps my parents talked about such matters as the Depression and Hitler when I was safely asleep.

Nor do I recall reading about these matters in My Weekly Reader and later in Scholastic magazine which I began reading in junior high school. I am sure the Depression and the European situation were covered, but for some reason they left no impression on me. Perhaps it was because junior high school was such an exciting prospect.

Maria Sanford Junior High School was about two and a half miles away, near Macalester College. The school was in a quite new, tan-brick building and was three stories high. Next to the junior high was an old, red-brick grade school, called Ramsey, the name of the county where St. Paul is situated.

We were told that Maria Sanford was "a pioneering Minnesota educator," and later when I moved to Washington I was pleased to find a statute of Maria Sanford—a stern-looking woman with a dress and cape reaching to her ankles—in Statuary Hall in the Capitol building where each state has placed one or two statutes honoring great citizens.

The classrooms as well as the hallways in my new school were bright and airy. We began each day in our "home room" where attendance was taken and announcements were made and then moved from room to room for our classes—English, mathematics, history, civics. Boys also went to woodworking or metal "shops" and girls to cooking and sewing classes. But things were starting to change. A few boys were admitted to cooking and sewing classes and a few girls to the shop classes. The boys who were trying to learn something about cooking and sewing were teased, as were the girls in shop classes.

I did not like woodworking, where I did succeed in making a small end table and a magazine rack, or metal shop where I managed to blow a fuse when a lamp I made was plugged into a socket and when I tried my hand at soldering the teacher looked in dismay at my efforts and derisively asked whether I had used an icicle as my soldering iron.

Both the woodworking and metal shop teachers seemed to me to be mean men, unhappy in their work and state in life. For whatever reason, I did not take very well to making things even though my father loved to work with wood.

But what I really hated were gym classes. I was never athletically inclined and I always thought that gym teachers liked to bedevil "sissies" like me. I was big for my age and thought myself terribly clumsy.

The gym teacher at Maria Sanford seemed to take a certain delight in pushing boys around, particularly clumsy boys like me. In the winter months we had to go outside in the coldest weather and run around in our under shorts and a T shirt. It's surprising that none of us caught pneumonia.

Inside the gym he insisted that someone like myself try and try and try to do somersaults on the parallel bars as well as try to do a high jump. I hated it all, and the teacher in particular, whose name I have long since forgotten.

I don't want to be overly negative here, because there was much I liked about Maria Sanford Junior High, which I guess you would call a middle school today. I liked to be able to move from room to room and have different teachers for the different subjects. I liked to be able to bring my lunch, eat with the other students in the cafeteria and not have to go home for lunch. The sandwiches my mother made for me were always good, particularly the cold meat-loaf sandwiches. I can still taste them.

And what did I learn in junior high? Grade school was devoted mostly to the basics—reading, writing and arithmetic with some art, music and hated gym classes thrown in. A lot of the reading and writing I learned by rote, but however much rote learning is decried these days it certainly bangs the basics into your head. My basic learning time was way ahead of the Dick and Jane books and their sophisticated take on reading. I never thought I was very good at arithmetic, but I am able to balance a checkbook.

But back to junior high. What I most remember from my first year at Maria Sanford is the diagramming of sentences, another lost art. You wrote out a sentence and then, in today's parlance, deconstructed it. First you separated out the subject and verb, then you drew a diagram indicating the modifiers and finally the participles.

There were dangling participles and modifiers and you had to differentiate between adverbs and adjectives. I am sure I have forgotten other in's and out's of diagramming sentences, but I hope you get the idea from what I have remembered. The diagramming exercises helped make me a better writer by learning to keep subjects and verbs close together and by not dangling participles and modifiers. It was all taught by a nice but demanding English teacher who made sure we were learning and understanding what we were learning. I am still grateful to this eighth grade teacher.

Another teacher whose name I have also forgotten presided over a ninth grade Latin class. He was a short man, with not much hair but too much stomach who wore an almost threadbare suit and vest. His ties were often stained, probably from the soup he had for dinner the previous night. But oh how he knew and loved his Latin.

We immediately learned to say, behind his back, "Latin is a dead language, dead as dead can be, first it killed the Romans, and now it's killing me." But I enjoyed Latin, and there is no question that it helped me to become a decent writer. Latin is so well organized that its declensions and other attributes cannot help but aid someone wanting to be a writer. I can still see and hear our Latin teacher leading us in reciting Latin verbs and phrases.

But I suppose the most important thing that happened to me in junior high school was the "Spirit of Sanford," a newspaper put out by students four times a year. I was a member of the paper's staff in the ninth grade and knew immediately that I wanted to be a newspaper reporter when I grew up.

The paper was somewhat smaller than a tabloid and each issue ran to eight pages. An English teacher supervised us neophyte journalists in a kindly and understanding way. The paper stuck to school matters—new teachers, new students, Maria Sanford sports events and a little something about the neighborhood surrounding the school. It was a neat and readable publication that I was proud of, and that my mother and father were proud to have their little boy involved in.

In my attic room I had drawn tiny, make-believe front pages, but here at Maria Sanford I had actually written real articles for a real newspaper and had even composed some headlines for the "Spirit of Sanford." I couldn't have been happier.

As I settled into junior high, I found the class work—academic work?—easy, perhaps too easy. Our teachers seated us pretty much according to how they perceived our learning abilities, smart ones in the back of the room, the duller ones in the desks in front.

I almost always was in the back row, and the learning came so easy to me that I took to bringing magazines with me to while away empty moments after I had completed assignments. My favorites were "Boy's Life," published by the Boy Scouts of America, and "Open Road for Boys," a commercial magazine filled with adventure stories. I also was reading the "Saturday Evening Post," the premier weekly magazine in the nineteen-thirties, and "Liberty," another popular weekly known for the "reading times" it posted at the beginning of each of its articles which were short and snappy.

I was always busy. I left home for school at about seven-thirty every morning and was not back home until close to four o'clock. There was always some homework and during the winter months skating three or four times a week at Mac Rink, Luther League on Friday nights, confirmation classes on Saturday mornings and Sunday School or church on Sunday mornings. There were radio programs to listen to in the evenings and perhaps a movie to go to on the weekends.

My junior-high school days were now coming to a close. But before I leave junior high I should mention yo-yo's, those toys that spun on a string and if you were good enough you could spin them under an arm, between your legs and over your head. Every spring a couple of young Filipino men would come to a corner by the Maria Sanford building and demonstrate Duncan yo-yos. Duncan was the most famous brand. I don't know why Filipinos were chosen to demonstrate the toy, but they were. And were they ever good at spinning yo-yos, between their legs, over and around and around their heads, spinning together and in tandem, never missing or entangling their strings. And of course they had yo-yos for sale. You knew spring was here when the yo-yo men appeared outside school, and it was hard to resist their sales pitch. A yo-yo cost twenty-five cents, a considerable sum in those days, but a lot were sold on that corner. I bought one and kept it for many, many years even though I was not very good at spinning it.

# 5

## *From Tragedies to Pea Soup*

My first brushes with tragedy came during my junior high days. The first tragic event was the death of my grandmother—my mother's mother. I can still vividly remember the look on my mother's face when the telephone call came from one of her sisters telling my mother about my grandmother's death. It was in the fall, she had been raking leaves and suddenly collapsed. I guess it was a heart attack. It was the first time I saw my mother cry.

My mother and Emma took a bus to Sauk Rapids where their mother's funeral was held. My father and I stayed in St. Paul and life soon was back to normal. I don't remember whether I had any thoughts about my grandmother's death. I did not really know here, having seen her only a few times. And I did not understand death.

I was three or four years old when my grandfather—my mother's father—died and have no recollection of his death. I guess if as a boy I ever thought about death it was in terms of moving on to a better life in the place called heaven. My mother and father never talked to me about such things as life and death. And the subject of death was never mentioned in school.

The other tragedy of my junior high years was my father's loss of his job as a shoe salesman at the Emporium department store. He was a casualty of the Depression, another subject I did not understand or know much about. I just remember my mother telling me one day that "Dad" had been "laid off," as the language of the day had it. Why? I asked. Because of the Depression, she said. I looked at her as if I understood, but I am not sure that I really did.

What I remember most about those out-of-work days was seeing my father sitting in his chair, smoking a cigarette and just staring out into space. He said nothing, even stopped reading the newspaper and just looked across the room or out the window. I was frightened as I tried to understand what was happening. Somehow we survived, but I have wondered how.

I do remember a man coming from Michaud's, the grocery store where my mother placed orders that were then delivered to us, sitting down with my mother at our dining room table where they went over bills that were owed and discussed how they might be paid. I was sure this man spent a lot of time doing just that as jobs and lives collapsed into the Depression.

How the debts to Michaud's were taken care of I simply do not know. I have often wondered how my mother and father made it through the Depression even when my father worked. How much did he earn? Maybe twenty-five dollars a week? Sure, everything was cheap, and we ate simply but well. Still, life must have been a struggle. So far as I know, our little bungalow was paid for before we ever moved in. It had to be, because in those days there were no thirty-year mortgages. You had to save up to buy a house and pay for it before you moved in.

But somehow we came through it. At times my mother did not have a nickel to give me so I could get an ice cream cone or a dime for a Saturday matinee at the St. Clair theater.

I was organized, but never felt over-organized. I am sure my organization came from my mother, as did my neatness. Everything was always in its place in my pigeon-hole desk and in my bookcase and closet.

The part of my mother's organization I most remember is the sequence of our dinners. Every Monday we had round steak, every Tuesday meat loaf, every Wednesday pork chops, every Thursday Polish sausage, every Friday leftovers from the week, and every Saturday wieners. Sundays, as I noted earlier, were chicken days. The food was simply prepared and always good. During the week my mother would bake custard and apple pies, a flat chocolate cake and cookies. Every Saturday she made cinnamon rolls and bread. We had the rolls with our hot dogs on Saturday night and the bread with our Sunday breakfast of fried eggs and bacon. If I was home when my mother was baking I always got to lick the pan. Chocolate was my favorite. I never saw my mother look at a recipe. She had learned how to cook from her mother, and kept it all in her head. She never made a mistake, and everything was always delicious.

I should not leave a discussion of my mother's cooking without mentioning her pea soup. Every week or two she made pea soup flavored with what she called a ham hock, a large bone from a piece of ham. The soup was wonderful and was a meal in itself. Often we had pea soup for Friday dinner rather than the leftovers from the week's cooking. Again, my mother did not have a recipe; it was all in her head.

There was never a speck of dust in our house; everything was always in its place; once you used something you put it back exactly where she had decided it belonged.

Everything my mother did was done in an organized way. Every Monday, rain or shine, was wash day. The washing was done with an old-fashioned machine with a wringer attached. After the clothes were washed my mother put them through the wringer to squeeze out all the water and in the summer took the clothes out of our basement where they had been washed and hung them out to try on our clothes lines in the back yard. The clothes always smelled so good when they were dry. In the cold Minnesota winters she hung the clothes in the basement where they eventually dried but never smelled the way they did in the summer.

The rugs were vacuumed every Tuesday, Wednesday was the day for changing sheets and cleaning the bedrooms, Thursday for washing the kitchen floor and spiffing up the kitchen cabinets. My mother worked hard and often complained about how tired she was at the end of the day. But I think in a way she enjoyed the housework, and she certainly was unhappy when things were not in apple-pie order.

I learned early to keep my room in order, hanging my clothes neatly in my little closet, emptying my wastebasket when it became full, keeping my pigeon-hole desk just right and never leaving a mess behind me anywhere in our house.

I also learned a certain thriftiness that has stayed with me throughout my life. You had to be thrifty in the Depression years because there was little money available for the necessities and none whatsoever for anything frivolous. You ate everything put before you because, as my mother used to say, "Remember those starving children…." Wherever they were, sometimes they were Armenian, other times they were Bohemian. Nothing was wasted. Even string was saved, wrapped into a ball. Clothes were worn until holes appeared. Children's clothes were handed down to friends or neighbors who could use them.

If something broke, like a radio, or an iron, it would be taken to a repair shop to be fixed, not thrown away. Sometimes all this saving and fixing would be carried to extremes, but that was the way life just seemed to be when no one was earning much money, when many men were in constant fear of losing their jobs when there were no other jobs available.

Despite our lack of money or resources we always dressed neatly and had enough sweaters and coats to keep warm in the icy Minnesota winters. My mother wore what she called housedresses most of the time, simple dresses some of which she made herself on the sewing machine in my parents' bedroom. It was an old machine, powered by a foot pedal that my mother pushed as she fashioned the clothes.

I suppose my father only had a couple of suits but he always looked nice when he went off to work, cigarette in hand. The picture in my mind of my father always has him smoking. He probably started smoking when he was a boy and did not stop until he was seventy-eight years old and had a heart attack. Four years later he died.

Occasionally my mother and I visited my father at his job in the shoe department of the Emporium department store. I liked the big store with all its goods ranging from shoes and clothing to furniture and beauty supplies for the women. I also remember the floor-walkers, nattily-clad men with handkerchiefs in their breast pockets. They walked importantly around the first floor checking to see if everything was in order and helping customers find the departments they were looking for. My father did not like the floorwalkers, though, because he thought they were snooty—they were—and that they had an easy job just walking around all day. Also, the floor-walkers were paid more than he was.

What I also remember from the Emporium was the machine that showed you an x-ray of your foot when you placed your foot in a hole at the bottom of the machine. The machine was used to see whether the shoes you were buying fit you well. The machines were later taken out of shoe departments because of the danger of x-rays to both employees and customers.

During visits downtown to see my father we often would go next door to the rival Golden Rule store which I particularly liked because it had escalators, the only ones in St. Paul. I was a little afraid of getting caught in the rather fast-moving stairs, but that did not keep me from riding up and down while my mother did some shopping.

# 6

## *From Knickers to Cod-Liver Oil*

I have decided to call these random jottings Sidebars—Youth. A sidebar is an old journalistic term for a secondary story related to a major story. For example, a sidebar might be a mini-profile of a person suddenly making news and the sidebar would be placed next to the spot news story in which the person figured. So here we go.

When I was eight or nine years old I started wearing knickers, or plus-fours as they were sometimes called. Knickers were a kind of pants that reached just below the knees and were fastened there by a sort of a string wound around your leg. Golfers as well as boys sported knickers, and I think the fad, if that is the right word, was begun by golfers in the nineteen-twenties. The knickers I wore were woolen and sometimes scratchy. I like to say I was a cute kid in knickers, but by the time I was twelve I was eager to graduate to long pants, which I did in a year or so.

Smells are an important part of my memories of growing up. To this day, when I smell cigarette smoke I think of my father. When he was at home and sat in his favorite easy chair his cigarettes and ash tray were always next to him, and a cigarette was often in his mouth. My picture of him going off to work always included a cigarette in his hand as he walked up the street to catch the St. Clair street car. In those days the rear platforms of the street cars were open and men stood on the platforms smoking their cigarettes. I never smoked but I still like the smell of burning tobacco. I also remember the smell of witch hazel, which my father used as his after-shave lotion. Witch hazel is a plant, and the fluid that is squeezed out of it has a rather pungent but nice smell. Then there was the smell of tar that was poured onto our streets every spring to keep down the dust. That was a strong smell. The streets were packed down dirt and the tar kept them quite hard. The fresh tar was covered with sand but the streets were still a mess for some time after the tarring, and woe to anyone who tracked tar into the house.

As a boy my favorite stores were drug stores and dime stores. There were three drug stores on St. Clair Avenue, and all were an easy walk from Stanford Avenue. All three had soda fountains where a freshly made Coca-Cola cost only a nickel, even if a little cherry flavoring were added. An ice cream soda loaded with vanilla or chocolate ice cream was a dime, as was a root beer float, which consisted of root beer and two or three scoops of vanilla ice cream. Ice cream was the real thing in those, with a high butter-cream count. Drug stores also had racks full of magazines, and you could usually thumb through a magazine or two before a clerk would ask what you wanted to buy. Dime stores were downtown, on Seventh Street where there was a Woolworth's as well as a Kresge's. They had lunch counters where you could buy a hot dog for a dime. I liked to troll the aisles of the dime stores where you could see and finger everything from pencils and pens to screwdrivers and hammers. The dime stores also had machines in their windows that made salt water taffy. It was always fun to press your nose against the window and watch the wheel on the machine stretch and stretch the taffy. I didn't really like salt water taffy, but I did enjoy watching it being made.

It seemed that about the only visitors we had were delivery men and salesmen. Elsewhere I have mentioned the milk man and the ice man, but we also had regular visits from a bread man whose wares included cakes, pies and cupcakes; the Jewel tea man who sold coffee and other packaged goods in addition to tea; and the now legendary Fuller brush man. Another man I will never forget was the Metropolitan Life Insurance agent. My mother had taken out a $1,000 policy on my life and every couple of weeks the Metropolitan man came by to pick up a premium of a dollar or so. I remember him because he was a small and friendly man who lugged around a large and heavy book containing information on all his clients. When he came to our house he always sat down with a sigh and laboriously paged through his book to find our account. I thought, day after day he does the same thing; how bored he must get.

I guess I was twelve years old when I began to feel whiskers growing on my chin. When my father noticed me scratching my chin, he said he had something for me. He went up to the attic, rummaged around, and came back with a beautiful black case. Inside was a shining gold razor, which had been given to him long ago. Here, Junior, my father said, it's yours. To the end of his life my father shaved with a straight razor. Safety razors, as the razors like the gold one that used blades were called, became popular about the time of World War I but many men like my father who had started shaving with a straight razor never switched to blades. I still have the gold razor, which is no longer shiny but still quite serviceable.

I also got a typewriter when I was twelve years old. Most boys were given bicycles at that age, but my mother thought it was better for me to have a typewriter. And I was happy with the typewriter, an Underwood portable that I used for close to fifty years before it finally wore out. I tried to teach myself to touch type, but without much success and to this day I am still a two-finger typist, but a pretty fast two-finger person. At about the same time that I was given a typewriter my mother also bought an encyclopedia set for me. It was called the Book of Knowledge and was written simply so that children could understand the articles. I used the encyclopedia some, but not all that much. I always wondered how much the encyclopedia cost and how my mother had to scrimp and save to pay for it so that her boy could become smarter.

Childhood diseases were serious matters as I was growing up. I remember having measles, mumps and chicken pox, particularly chicken pox with the scales that never seemed to disappear. Fortunately, I escaped diphtheria, whooping cough and the dreaded infantile paralysis, as polio was then called. These childhood ailments were considered so contagious that if you had one of them you had to call the city health department and a man was sent to your house to tack a yellow sign on your front door warning people to stay away.

Thinking about illnesses, colds, sore throats and fevers were quite common, particularly in the cold Minnesota winters. A spoonful of cod liver oil was prescribed by my mother for me every morning. It tasted terrible and was hard to get down your throat. As I write this I can still feel that awful tasting and smelling cod liver oil reluctantly sliding down my throat. The cod liver oil was supposed to ward off colds and sore throats, but they came anyway. That meant cups of steaming tea—I still think of being ill as a boy on the few occasions when I drink hot tea today—and having my chest smeared with Vicks Vapo-Rub before going to sleep. It smelled too but it was a rather pleasant medicinal odor. Whether tea or Vapo-Rub did anything I don't know but it was not for me to question the treatments.

Roomers were a part of the Depression. With so many families struggling to make ends meet, it was not uncommon to have children double-up in a room so that another room could be freed-up for a paying roomer. I remember two or three families in our neighborhood who took in roomers who would pay five or ten dollars a week for a place to sleep, or more if breakfast and dinner were included. Times were tough.

Alley-ways divided the streets in most neighborhoods of St. Paul in the thirties. Trash cans and worn-out furniture were placed by the alleys to be picked up by garbage collectors and "sheenies". Garbage consisted of food waste—meat

scraps, bones, apple cores, stale bread, etc.—and it was taken by the trash collectors to hog farms where it was dumped onto fields and fed to the hogs. A most
unsanitary practice, and one which ended by the time of World War II. The
"sheenies," which I think was a synonym for Jews, collected anything else that
was placed in the allies. Both the garbage men and the "sheenies" drove up and
down the alleys in wagons pulled by horses. The "sheenies" often called out as
they made their rounds, alerting housewives to their coming so that junk could
be brought to the alleys.

A nicer memory is the White Castle on Grand Avenue. It was indeed a small
castle-like building that served tiny hamburgers and soft drinks. The hamburgers
usually cost a dime, but every month or two a coupon would appear in the papers
advertising a bag of five hamburgers for a quarter—two-bits, as we used to say.
We kids clipped the coupons and made our way to the White Castle. On the way
home we pulled the burgers out of their sack and happily munched on them. You
can still find White Castles in the Midwest, and for a time you could find the
hamburgers in the frozen food sections of supermarkets as far away as California.

Another happy note was Christmas windows. By the day after Thanksgiv-
ing—then the official beginning of the Christmas season—both the Emporium
and the Golden Rule department stores decked out their windows with holiday
scenes ranging all the way from Santa Claus climbing into a chimney and the
manger where Jesus was born to sleighs charging over fake snow and the bearded
old year giving way to the infant new year. You made a special trip downtown
just to see the windows. Each store tried to outdo the other, and smaller stores
like Schuneman's and Field and Schlick joined in the competition. Some of the
windows would even have a stuffed reindeer. It was said that we all got into the
Christmas spirit once we had seen the windows. And there was something to
that.

For me, life growing up was mostly fun, but as I look back on the Depression
years I realize how tough life was for my parents and most other adults on Stanford Avenue. Every day my mother cooked "from scratch." So much of the day
was spent preparing meals—peeling potatoes, shelling peas, making soup, pounding meat to tenderize it, baking cakes, pies and cookies. Then there was the
weekly washing of clothes, tending to the decidedly non-automatic washing
machine, laboriously putting clothes through the hand wringer, hanging the
clothes up in the backyard in the summer or in the basement in the winter. Keeping the house clean, sweeping and mopping the kitchen, running a noisy and
heavy vacuum cleaner. Canning in the summer, peaches, pears, crabapples, toma-
toes, jar after jar after jar. For my father there was the furnace to be tended before

going to work in the morning and before going to bed at night, shaking out the ashes and clinkers, shoveling in the coal, "banking" the fire at night in the hope that the fire would not go completely out by morning.

# PART II
## First Jobs

# 7

## A *"Junior Salesman" Makes Good—After Stumbling*

My first job, when I was in junior high school, was as a magazine salesman, not a very successful one, but I did try hard.

It all began when a man from the Curtis Publishing Company canvassed Stanford Avenue looking for what he called "junior salesmen," by which he meant young boys willing to go door-to-door to try to sell the company's three magazines, the weekly Saturday Evening Post and its two monthlies, Ladies Home Journal and Country Gentlemen. When the man stopped by our house he talked to my mother and me and I was immediately enthusiastic about becoming a "junior salesman," probably because as an avid reader it meant that I could read the magazines free before I trudged out to try to sell them to neighbors. My mother wasn't so sure I should do this, worrying that it would take time from my all-important school work. But after some pretty persuasive talk from the magazine man about how being a "junior salesman" was excellent training for life's work, my mother said all right Junior will give it a try.

Before the nice man left he gave me a pristine white bag with the words "Saturday Evening Post" emblazoned on it and showed me how to put the bag over my shoulder when I went out to sell the magazines. Everyone loves these magazines, he told me, and went on to assure me that I would have no trouble at all making sales. He was convincing me that I was a born salesman bound to make good in life once I had learned the ropes as a "junior salesman."

I was excited and could hardly wait until the first bundle of ten Saturday Evening Posts arrived on our front stoop on the following Tuesday. After school that afternoon I carefully slipped the magazines into my white bag, slung the bag over my shoulder and was off down the block on my first day as a "junior salesman." I was full of optimism as I looked forward to filling my pocket with nickels as I quickly sold out my ten magazines. And I could always order more, as the man so helpfully told me.

Well, I didn't have to order more magazines. I didn't sell a single copy that afternoon. As I knocked on doors and timidly asked if you'd like to buy a Saturday Evening Post, I was told either that my neighbors already subscribed to the magazine or simply didn't have time to read and weren't interested. I was in tears when I returned home with my white sack by then burdening me down with unsold magazines. To try to cheer me up my mother gave me a nickel for a magazine she could ill afford and probably would not read much.

I continued to receive magazines every Tuesday for a few weeks and managed to sell two or three a week, but as the weeks went on I began to dread Tuesdays and sometimes did not even page through the magazine before setting out to try to sell some of the magazines. I was a failure, a big failure. The Saturday Evening Post was the most popular magazine in the United States, full of good fiction, including mysteries and Westerns, and articles about important matters like the Depression, goings on in Washington and the tragic developments in Europe, none of which I had an understanding of but I somehow knew were significant. And I, a budding "junior salesman," could not convince the people of Stanford Avenue to pay just a nickel for so much information every week. And I had no better luck trying to sell the Ladies Home Journal, the premier magazine for women, or Country Gentlemen, which was filled with articles about the good, rural life.

Finally, and not too reluctantly, I told the nice man who was recruiting "junior salesmen" that I longer wanted to try to sell his magazines. He said he understood and I could keep my magazine bag.

Fortunately, I did not have to pay for the magazines I was unable to sell. For every magazine I did sell I could keep two cents out of the nickel and three cents out of the dime for which the monthlies sold. And I kept the white magazine bag, somewhat soiled by now, for many years afterward.

But despite my bad experience selling magazines I was still eager to earn some "spending money." So when a year or so later when I was in my last year in junior high school and a St. Paul Daily News paper route opened up in our neighborhood, I applied for the route and was selected as a "paper boy."

I didn't know it at the time, but the Daily News, which was the paper we received, was on the verge of shutting down. It was an evening paper and its circulation was much smaller than its evening rival, the St. Paul Dispatch, which had a sister paper, the morning St. Paul Pioneer Press, the oldest paper in Minnesota which traced its beginnings to the beginning of the state in 1849.

I liked the idea of having a paper route because unlike my ill-fated magazine-sales venture I did not have to sell the papers, at least I didn't think I did. I found out differently later. But in the beginning I had my list of subscribers and delivered the paper to them every day.

I had about 40 subscribers, or customers, as I referred to them, spread over three blocks of Stanford, Berkeley and St. Clair Avenues. Hurrying home after school, it took me about forty-five minutes to deliver the papers. I had to collect fifteen cents every week from every customer, and I didn't much like having to do that, but I pocketed a nickel out of every fifteen cents, and that came to two dollars a week, which was a lot of money for a thirteen-year-old boy. I spent some of the money on frivolities like ice-cream cones and some on Big Little Books, comic books and Western and detective pulp fiction magazines. And I tried to save a little each week in a Mason jar.

But the Daily News route did not last more than a few months.

Despite constant exhortations delivered personally to carriers and at Saturday morning meetings of carriers at the paper's office downtown on Fourth Street to ring doorbells and seek more subscribers, circulation declined until one day an announcement on the front page proclaimed the end of the Daily News and the beginning of the St. Paul Shopper. The Shopper was to be published every Thursday and distributed free to every household in the city. It would be full of advertisements—and bargains! We Daily News carriers would distribute the new paper.

Shoppers, which are so common today, were a new concept in the Depression years of the thirties. Lots of people did not subscribe to daily papers—even though they sold for only three cents on a street corner and cost but fifteen cents a week delivered to your door. People had little money and saving just three cents a day or fifteen cents a week was important.

The St. Paul Shopper lasted only three years. It simply did not attract enough advertising. Fortunately, I had left my route before the paper's demise; I had not much cared for delivering the paper. I had to deliver a copy to every house on my blocks, which meant that my sack of papers was quite heavy as I started out on my rounds. And I earned only a dollar a week for my efforts.

As I struggled with the Shopper route and entered Central High School as a tenth-grade sophomore, a Dispatch and Pioneer Press paper route opened in our neighborhood. I immediately asked my mother and father if I could apply for the route. They were not so sure about such a route because it meant I would have to get up very early in the morning to deliver the Pioneer Press and then hurry home from high school in the afternoon to deliver the Dispatch. But they finally said, okay, see if you can get the route.

I quickly discovered that it was not easy to become a Pioneer Press and Dispatch carrier boy. The routes brought in enough money—about twenty dollars a month—to help pay for a family's groceries and even contribute to the cost of rent. One family in the neighborhood where the man had been out of work for some time sustained itself with three paper routes, one delivered by the man of the house and the other two by his sons.

When I indicated my interest in becoming a Pioneer Press-Dispatch carrier, the district manager for our area came by our house one evening to talk to me and my mother and father. Before sitting down in the living room he carefully eyed both the living room and dining room, which were as neat as always.

Then as he sat down he opened a notebook and started asking questions. Where did my father work? The Emporium, hmm, that's a good store. How long had he worked there? Did my mother work? No. Few women did in those days. Did I make good grades in school? Was my health good? Did I ever have trouble getting up in the morning? Did I like to walk? Could I stand the cold, cold Minnesota winter mornings? On and on the questions went, with the circulation manager carefully writing down the answers in his little notebook.

As the questioning continued, I became nervous, but I tried not to look concerned and to squirm in my chair. Finally, the district manager closed his notebook and said we would hear from him in the next day or two. Oh, I thought, I probably won't get the route. He'll find somebody much better than me and my parents.

Fortunately, I was wrong. A couple of days later the district manager was on our doorstep with the good news that I had been selected as a Pioneer Press-Dispatch carrier. He impressed upon me and my parents the honor that had been bestowed upon me. I was overjoyed. My mother and father were happy, too, but expressed concern over whether I could deliver papers twice a day and still be able to maintain good grades in high school so that I could go on to the University of Minnesota one day. I said I was confident that I could do it all, and that I would contribute some of my paper-route earnings to help with household expenses. No, my mother said, that would not be necessary; instead, save some of the money for college. And I did just that, opening a savings account in the First National Bank of St. Paul. With my selection as a carrier I received a bag in which I could carry my papers and a list of subscribers on my route, which was on blocks of Wellesley, Jefferson, Pascal and Brimhall Avenues.

I picked up my papers at St. Clair and Hamline avenues, as did three other carriers. I had to lug my papers three blocks to Wellesley Avenue where I began my route. The papers could be heavy, particularly on Fridays and Sundays, but I managed the load. And papers were not as loaded with advertising as they are today; so when I say a heavy paper I am talking about a paper weighing only a fraction of today's copies. Besides, I was so happy to have a route that I would never have complained about anything concerning my delivering of papers.

I got up at quarter to five every morning and was packing my papers into my sack just fifteen minutes later. I had to finish delivering papers by six o'clock, and once or twice a week the district manager would drive up and down the streets he was responsible for to make sure the papers were on doorsteps. St. Paul had several factories where morning shifts began at seven, and the workers wanted to take the paper with them to read on the street car on the way to work.

On some winter mornings the temperature went down to thirty degrees below zero. I still shiver when I think of those temperatures, but I managed to struggle along the snow-swept and icy sidewalks and streets to finish my deliveries by six a.m.

The delivery of the afternoon Dispatch was easier, although I did have to hustle home from high school to get the papers distributed as early as possible. And when I started working after school on the weekly Central High Times, I walked back to high school after delivering my paper route. And that meant a walk of two miles each way. Looking back, I often wonder how I did it, but I managed. When you are young, anything seems possible. I was happy to be earning some money, and just as happy with high school and particularly with being on the staff of the Central High Times.

Today most newspaper carriers are adults, many of whom are college students. But a lot are also recent immigrants struggling to make their way with two or even three jobs. But in the thirties carriers were almost always high school students like myself. Newspapers liked to call us "little merchants" and to say that our work was wonderful training for adult jobs. There was something in that, but the newspaper publishers pressed the idea that we carriers were "independent contractors" so that carriers would not be subject to the wage-and-hour and workmen's compensation laws that were part of Franklin D. Roosevelt's New Deal. The publishers obtained from Congress specific carrier exemptions from these laws.

I also must say that my fascination with newspapers, which became my life, increased with my work as a carrier. When I started delivering the St. Paul Daily News, I would read articles in the paper as I walked my route. I confess that in the beginning I skipped important articles from Washington and from Europe. They seemed too complicated for my young mind.

But when I became a Pioneer Press-Dispatch carrier I started reading the more complicated articles, trying to decipher and understand them. I loved the comics, Edgar Guest's poems and Uncle Ray's Corner of facts and stories for children—Who was Christopher Columbus and what did he do? Why do we celebrate the Fourth of July? What are whales and why are they so big? Where does milk come from? Is the earth really round? Uncle Ray dealt with these and other more cosmic matters in a way that a boy could easily understand. I also loved to try to work the crossword puzzle and to read the horoscope. I studied the pictures and sports-page cartoons and wondered how the paper managed to get them every day. Most importantly, the newspaper was one of my windows on the world, together with magazines and movie newsreels. My real world was still quite small, being just a relatively small part of St. Paul.

# 8

## *And Now, "Show Biz"*

Now comes the "boffo" part of my teen-age work life—my short but promising career in "Show Biz"!

The St. Clair theater, where my Show Biz career began and ended, was our neighborhood theater. It was located on St. Clair Avenue and near Snelling Street, an important corner close to Macalester College and where two street car lines intersected. The St. Clair line with its big, rumbling yellow cars, ran downtown, and the Snelling line, with newer, smaller and streamlined cars ran cross town intersecting with several downtown lines.

At the corner of St. Clair and Snelling were Kregel and Decker's drug store, with a soda fountain, a lending library and a free telephone in the back of the store that anyone could use; a Shell Oil Company service station; and the St. Clair Sweet Shop, owned by a Greek whose first name was Bill, with its own soda fountain and a plethora of booths where I thought often sinister things happened between the boys and girls and men and women occupying these hideaways. The Sweet Shop also had a popcorn machine and a cigar counter where men rather mysteriously shook dice to see, I guess, if they could get a free cigar.

A young man, also Greek, who worked for Bill had a crush on my Aunt Emma, but I don't think it ever got any further than an occasional chocolate soda—consumed in a booth, however.

Behind the Sweet Shop was a tiny jewelry and watch shop. Fittingly, the proprietor was a tiny man, Jewish, I am sure, who always seemed to have one of those watch maker's eyeglasses squinched in his right eye. He was a nice man, and my first watch came from him. It was a small, square wrist watch that someone had left to be fixed but had never been reclaimed. So my mother was able to buy it for only a few dollars. It was a good watch. I kept it for years, using it as a spare after I was able to buy a bigger and better wrist watch.

The theater was on the side of St. Clair Avenue just above the Shell station and adjacent to an apartment building with a small grocery store and Red's tavern on the first floor. Red's was called by my mother and others a "3.2 joint," because its license restricted it to selling only beer and the beer could not have more than an alcohol content of 3.2 per cent.

But back to Show Biz. The theater attracted neighborhood residents as well as Macalester College students. It also helped bring business to the drug store and the Sweet Shop was well as to the 3.2 joint.

I started going to the movies at the St. Clair Theater when I was six or seven years old. The Saturday matinees attracted me. They usually showed a Western, or cowboy movie as we called these films. There was also a serial, usually about cowboys and Indians, too, and ending each week with the hero in a horrible predicament. Naturally, he got out of his troubles the next Saturday.

As I got older I was allowed at times to go to an early show, starting at seven o'clock on a week night or to a movie on Sunday afternoon. By the time I was ten years old, I was a regular moviegoer and had fallen in love with Ginger Rogers. Unfortunately, she did not know about my infatuation with her, and went on her merry way dancing with that lucky guy Fred Astaire.

The St. Clair theater was built in the early nineteen twenties and I have been told featured vaudeville as well as silent movies in its first years. Rudolph and His Violin, famous on the vaudeville circuit, was an early and favorite act. The original theater had a red brick façade.

Early in the nineteen thirties the front and lobby of the theater were remodeled in an art deco style. The bricks on the front were replaced with a facing of large chunks of tan stone, a new modern sign proclaiming "St. Clair" in neon lights was put up over a canopy filled with lights. On either side of the canopy was space for removable lettering so that the title of the current movie could be proclaimed for all to see.

Most importantly, I think was the digging behind the theater of an artesian well tapping cool water deep in the ground that could be used for an early air-conditioning system. The water was piped into the theater and sprayed behind a huge fan which distributed the resulting cool air into the St. Clair's auditorium.

There was little air conditioning in the early thirties, and St. Paul—despite Minnesota's frigid winter temperatures—could be hot and muggy in the summer. So the St. Clair theater proudly advertised that it was cooled by artesian well water and I know that a lot of people went to the movies there on hot, humid nights just to get cooled off, not particularly caring what movie was being shown.

My first commercial contact with the St. Clair came when I was in high school and got a Saturday morning job distributing handbills advertising the next week's movies. They were the kind of handbills that you could hang on the knobs of front doors. I was paid a dollar for two or three hours work walking around putting the handbills on front doors. It was not bad pay and I guess you could say it was my entry to Show Biz.

The assistant manager of the St. Clair seemed to like me and the way I went about my work and when there was an opening for an usher asked me if I would like to have the job. Would I? Oh, boy, I sure would. I was finishing my junior year in high school and still had my paper route, but another job with its additional income sounded fine to me.

My mother and father were concerned that I was trying to do too much, but they finally agreed to let take the job after I assured them that I could handle it along with school and the paper route. I was delighted and could hardly wait to start work.

But first I had to get some nice pants and a sport coat. The theater did not provide uniforms for its ushers, to save money, I am sure, and I had to wear a nice shirt, tie, coat and pressed pants every night.

All dolled up, as we used to say, I began to learn the ropes as an usher. The St. Clair theater was owned by the Minnesota Amusement Company, which had about twenty theaters in St. Paul and Minneapolis. The St. Paul theaters included three downtown—the Paramount, very fancy and where the best movies started out (twenty-five cents admission before one o'clock); the Riviera, almost as fancy as its name indicated and the place for first-run movies not quite good enough for the Paramount; and the Tower, showing double features, almost always one of which was a Western, and reputed to make more money on popcorn and candy than on its fifteen cents admission price. In the neighborhoods Minnesota Amusement had five theaters. In those days a new movie would stay downtown a week, sometimes two weeks, but no longer than that. Then the Uptown theater, the classiest of the neighborhood houses, got the movie for four or five days. It then moved on to the Park theater for a few more days and finally to its last stop at the St. Clair where the admission price was only twelve cents and eight cents for children under twelve.

Minnesota Amusement was a subsidiary of Balaban and Katz of Chicago which owned theaters throughout the Midwest. Balaban and Katz was in turn owned by Paramount Pictures, hence the name of the best theater in downtown St. Paul.

There were other theaters in St. Paul and Minneapolis. The other fancy theater in downtown St. Paul was the Orpheum, which still had vaudeville shows in the late thirties and early forties. It was part of the RKO—Radio Keith Orpheum—vaudeville circuit, and I remember seeing big bands like Glen

Miller's and Tommy Dorsey's on the Orpheum stage. In addition to the stage shows, there were first-run movies at the Orpheum. Another downtown theater with vaudeville was the Lyceum, a famous theater name but in St. Paul a rather rundown place with second and third-rate acts. There was also the World theater, today the home of Prairie Home Companion broadcasts, but in the thirties and forties the home of the few foreign films that found their way to St. Paul. I still remember seeing "Four Feathers" there.

I guess I detoured from the St. Clair for a moment to show the importance of movies in the thirties and forties when people had little money and a night out at the movies was an important diversion from the uncertain and underpaid work-a-day life. Oh, by the way, St. Clair was not a Roman Catholic Saint. He was a general in the early years of the country and was for a while in charge of the Northwest Territories, which included Minnesota.

The St. Clair theater seated about five hundred people. Its staff consisted of seven people—a young woman who sold the tickets and had another job as a secretary during the day; the manager, Louis Hertle, a handsome man in his forties; an assistant manager in his late twenties who lived in the neighborhood with his mother, was not particularly good-looking, but always impeccably groomed and had his hair trimmed on his day off every Tuesday by Mike the St. Clair Avenue barber; two ushers; the man who ran the machines that projected the movies on the screen and belonged to a tight and tough union and at seventy-five dollars a week was the highest paid of the staff (the manager made fifty dollars); and a janitor who did his dirty work sometimes right after the last show ended at eleven or eleven-thirty or came in at six a.m. He too worked another job.

As an usher, I stood at one of the doors to the auditorium with a flashlight in my hand ready to guide moviegoers to their seats. In those days not everyone came to the theater at the beginning of the movie. It was not uncommon for people to arrive in the middle of a movie. In addition to the featured movie there were always a newsreel, a cartoon, a fifteen or twenty-minute comedy (often the Three Stooges) or a travelogue and some previews of coming attractions.

The St. Clair theater showed movies every evening Monday through Saturday and offered a Saturday matinee primarily for children and on Sundays started showing movies at 2 p.m. and continuing through the evening. The 2 p.m. opening time was chosen to make sure that movie-going did not interfere with church services, some of which lasted until one o'clock.

As an usher I worked six days a week. My day off was either a Monday or Tuesday, the slowest movie days of the week. On the week days I worked I reported for duty at six-thirty, and, as said, doors opened at six-forty-five. The evening began with a newsreel at seven followed by the short subjects and the movie, with everything repeated from nine or nine-thirty.

I was off-duty by nine-thirty except on the nights when we had to "change the front." What that meant was that a new movie was starting the next day and we had to move around the "stills"—pictures, that is—and "three sheets", or posters, advertising the coming movies. The pictures and posters were displayed throughout the theater lobby and in glass cases on the front of the theater. We also had to change the lettering on the marquee which proclaimed the name and sometime the stars of the current movie. I hated doing that because I had to climb up a rickety, shaky ladder while balancing the letters for the signs. And once a week I also had to haul the ladder to one side of the theater and climb up to post with white paste a "six-sheet," a large poster advertising the movie coming the next Sunday. That was a particularly difficult job on a cold and sometimes snowy Minnesota night. Ladders still scare me.

The assistant manager was usually the ticket-taker, greeting our patrons with a smile and a pleasant "Good Evening" and carefully tearing in half the tiny ticket sold by our comely "cashier" from her glass box just inside the entrance to the theater. The ticket-taker also sold candy and pop corn from a shiny glass case that was at his side.

Occasionally, I got to take tickets, a job which I enjoyed. I put on my best smile and my most sincere "Good Evening," and noticed that many people came to every movie. I can still see the faces of some of these men and women and their children as they made their way into the St. Clair for their twelve-cents worth of entertainment.

Here, I also have to make a confession. Candy was not as securely wrapped then as it is today, and I took to removing—stealing?—one piece of candy from a box of Milk Duds or a box of licorice. No harm done, I told myself, and the candy tasted so good.

I thought that in addition to earning money—twenty-five cents an hour, the minimum wage, or about ten dollars a week—I would as an usher be able to see all the movies free. Actually, I saw only bits and pieces of movies as I was going up and down the aisle seating people, taking tickets from time to time, sweeping the sidewalk in front of the theater and tidying up the lobby. Also, I would have to dash upstairs to the theater's office and storerooms to get more candy and pop corn to replenish the supplies in the glass candy case in the lobby. We did not have a popcorn machine. Our popcorn came from a warehouse in colorful cellophane packages.

Sometimes I would pop into the projection booth to chat with the man who operated the two machines through which the film was threaded and then projected on the large screen. A heated, metal-looking object called an arc lamp burning at an extremely high temperature provided the illumination for the film. In those days the film was on reels, and each reel held only fifteen to twenty minutes of film; so when a reel began to run down the projectionist had to change reels, switching from one projection machine to the other one in his booth. A small circle in a corner of the film signaled the end of a reel, and it was a rather tricky job to move from one machine to the other at just the right time.

The job as a projectionist was a skilled one, what with arc lamps to heat up, reels to change and rewind, but the projectionist also had considerable free time between tasks. Sometimes he watched the movie; other times he read a magazine or a book. But he always welcomed a visitor and liked to talk about everything from the movies to the war in Europe and what was going on in Washington. Because of the hot, hot arc lamps fire was a constant danger in the projection booth; so it was encased in steel and the door to the booth was always supposed to remain closed, but our projectionist often left the door open to get some air into his confined space.

# 9

## *Here Comes Stiff!*

The worst nights at the St. Clair theater were when our cashier opened the door to her tiny booth and shouted to whomever was taking tickets that "Stiff was on his way!" She was referring to Mr. Stiff, the manager of our parent Minnesota Amusement Company, and he inspected his theaters quite often, sometimes once a week. The cashier's cry was immediately relayed to the manager, the projectionist and everyone else on duty.

And I and the other usher left our posts at the doors to the auditorium to run a sweeper through the lobby, sweep the front sidewalk, check the posters and still pictures to make sure they were in proper position, check and clean the restrooms, and, worst of all, clean the sand in the containers near the theater entrance where people could throw their cigarettes, spit our their gum and just plain spit. We used a strainer to pick up the cigarette butts, the gum and the spit, but it was still a nasty job that we all hated.

Soon Mr. Stiff appeared. He was a short, nattily dressed man who always seemed to strut. We always knew when he was coming because as he left one theater he told the manager where he was going next, and the manager called ahead with the message that Stiff was coming.

As Mr. Stiff entered our lobby he seemed to look everywhere and sometimes even checked out the men's room—but never did he ask to be escorted into the ladies' room. We all stood at our posts, almost at attention and as if we were being looked over by a colonel. "Good evening, Mr. Stiff," each of us would say as he passed by. He would say nothing, just look at us in what we hoped was an approving way. After his tour of the lobby, Mr. Stiff would go upstairs to the office with our manager, Louis Hertle. After a while Mr. Stiff and Mr. Hertle would come back downstairs and Mr. Stiff would tell Mr. Hertle that he was going on to, say, the Uptown theater. Mr. Stiff was hardly out of our theater before Mr. Hertle was on the phone in our box office with the urgent message to the Uptown: "Stiff is coming!"

I started work as an usher in the summer before my senior year in high school. That was 1941, the war in Europe was almost two years old, Hitler was smashing through the Maginot Line in France and the talk in the United States was that we would soon be in the war. I was seventeen years old that November and would soon be old enough to be eligible for the Army. But I was so busy with high school, my paper route and my job as an usher that I put thoughts of the Army out of my mind.

But the likelihood of our entry into the war became a certainty on December 7, 1941, when the Japanese attacked Pearl Harbor. I remember the day well, as do other Americans who lived through those times. It was a Sunday afternoon when I heard the news. As on most Sunday afternoons, I was taking tickets at the St. Clair when someone entering the theater said, rather casually, "Heard the news?" "No sir, what news?" "The Japs attacked Pearl Harbor, sunk all our ships. It's war now." Over and over, people asked me if I had heard the terrible news. Fewer and fewer people came to the theater. They were staying home, sitting close to their radios, listening for more details on the Pearl Harbor disaster.

As the United States entered what was now being called World War II the movie business continued as before, and prospered as more people went to movies to take their minds off the military draft, a shortage of goods and the beginning of food and gasoline rationing. Meantime, I gave up my paper route to concentrate on my last year in high school and my job in Show Biz.

After graduating from high school in June of 1942 I was offered the job as assistant manager of the St. Clair theater. Was I interested? Was I!

Of course I was interested. Here I was not quite eighteen years old and I could become an assistant manager in a subsidiary of Paramount Pictures. This was indeed Show Biz. As it turned out there was little Show Biz glamour in being the assistant manager of the artesian well-water cooled St. Clair theater (doors still opening at six forty-five, admission now fifteen cents, ten cents if you are under twelve).

I did get an increase in pay to seventeen dollars and fifty cents a week. But I also got an increase in hours. In addition to working six evenings and two afternoons a week—Saturdays and Sundays—I had to be at the theater three or four hours every morning or afternoon to compile reports, check out receipts and make sure the theater was clean.

Being part of "big business" we not only had to report receipts daily but also had to tell Mr. Stiff's office what the nearby Randolph and Grand Avenue theaters—which were not part of Minnesota Amusement—were showing and what other events, such as a playground carnival, were going on in our neighborhood.

We also had to note when the rival theaters had "dish nights." Those were the nights you got a free dish when you went to a movie and could eventually accumulate a set of dishes. We were proud we did not have to resort to such giveaways.

Soon after becoming assistant manager—my predecessor, by the way, had become manager of the Park theater, a mile or two up Snelling Avenue from the St. Clair—I learned that manager Louis Hertle had a little secret.

It seemed that Mr. Hertle was living beyond his means. His fifty-dollar a week salary seemed munificent to a seventeen-year-old like myself. But it was not enough for Mr. Hertle who was a spiffy dresser and obviously bought good clothes and who had a perky girl friend who I am sure demanded the best when they went out for dinner or for dancing.

When Mr. Hertle ran short of money a day or two before pay day, which was Wednesday, he took to dipping into the "candy fund." We deposited receipts from the sale of candy and popcorn in the bank only once a week; so there was always candy money in a metal box in our office. Box office receipts had to be placed in the bank daily.

By the time I became assistant manager Mr. Hertle was always a week behind in his finances. So when his check arrived, he immediately cashed it and placed the receipts in the candy box. But then he had to begin making withdrawals from the candy box to finance his next week's activities.

I don't think he ever stole any money, but this monetary maneuvering went on throughout the summer that I was assistant manager. I assume that at some point he caught up with his unorthodox financing and I do know that a few years later he left Show Biz to become a hearing-aid salesman. I should mention that he had been hard-of-hearing for some time and never thought the sound for the movies we were showing was loud enough.

As assistant manager I also learned how genuinely frightened the managers were of Mr. Stiff. Once a week all the Minnesota Amusement managers in St. Paul attended a meeting with Mr. Stiff in the manager's office at the Paramount Theater. The office was nicely appointed with a table big enough to seat the dozen or so managers and their assistants.

I was invited to sit in on two or three of the meetings, and they were not very pleasant. After talking about some of the movies soon to be released—and how great they were—Mr. Stiff launched into a litany of complaints about the managers. Their theaters weren't clean enough. The ticket-takers and ushers should be better dressed. More people should be coming to the movies. Why was so little candy and popcorn sold? Why were other theaters doing better than ours? And on and on.

I never seriously thought about making a career of Show Biz, and I certainly did not after seeing these managers quiver and almost shake after the weekly lectures and litany of complaints they received from Mr. Stiff. From what I could see at the St. Clair theater, we had good crowds, sometimes filling practically every seat, sold a lot of candy and popcorn and kept a tidy lobby and a clean auditorium.

I am sure Mr. Stiff received dressing-downs from his superiors at Balaban and Katz in Chicago. I was learning that bosses are never truly satisfied with the work of their underlings, that companies never think they are earning enough money, and that the managers at Mr. Hertle's level have to shoulder most of the blame for the actual or perceived shortcomings of the business.

When I took the job as assistant manager I guess I thought I might stay with it through my first year at the University of Minnesota, where I was to begin classes in the fall of 1942. Most of the university's campus was in Minneapolis and I had saved enough money to purchase a car so I figured I could juggle the job and a somewhat reduced schedule of classes. My first car, by the way, was a two-door, maroon 1937 Ford, which I bought for two hundred and fifty dollars.

I did not know how to drive when I bought the car, but my friend Wade Lundegard said he would teach me. First I had to get a driver's license. All you had to do in those days was go by the Minnesota Highway Department office on University Avenue, near Monkey Wards, fill out an application form, hand over thirty-five cents and—presto!—the man behind the counter handed you your license.

So what did I learn from my teen-age work experience? Well, I guess I learned the importance of working hard, being on time, following instructions and being pleasant to the people you were working with and to the people who were your customers, whether they be subscribers to the Pioneer Press and Dispatch or the moviegoers who came to the St. Clair theater.

I learned too that bosses could be nice, like the Pioneer Press and Dispatch district manager and St. Clair manager Louis Hertle and mean like Mr. Stiff. But I did seem to get along with all sorts of people. And I had a drive to succeed, as evidenced by my disappointment in my failure as a "junior" magazine salesman and my subsequent success as a newspaper carrier and in Show Biz. And much greater early successes were still to come.

# 10

## Central High—and The Times

As I made the transition from junior high to high school I cemented several friendships with boys in the neighborhood. I guess my best friend was Wade Lundegard, who was a year younger than I was. He lived a few doors down Stanford Avenue from us. He had two older brothers in their twenties and a sister a couple of years younger than he was. His father worked for the Great Northern railway, which had its head office in St. Paul as did the Northern Pacific railway. Together, the two companies owned a third railroad, the Burlington. I don't think Mr. Lundegard had a very important job. I think he was a clerk of some sort processing paper work all day.

It seemed to be a rather chaotic household with two older sons frequently hung over from too much beer the night before, Wade's mother often shouting at his father—whom she called Hub, for Husband, I think—particularly when he came home slightly tipsy. Wade's mother was also a Christian Scientist. His sister Delores was a very pretty girl and an excellent ice skater. Before finishing high school she joined the chorus of the Ice Capades ice-skating show which was based in Minneapolis and put on shows throughout the country—and still does.

I particularly remember two things about Wade and his family. One summer Wade was seriously if not desperately ill and spent days lying bundled-up in a chair on the family's front porch. Being Christian Scientist, his mother would not call a doctor. My mother and others on our block thought Wade would die, but he eventually recovered and seemed as good as new.

The other remembrance concerns Wade's father. He loved the Saturday Evening Post, which he started reading when it was delivered on Tuesday evening and continued every night until he finished all the stories and articles and was ready for the next issue. Often the stories were serialized and later published as books.

Other good friends were the Anderson boys, Art and Elmer, who were a couple of years older than I was. Their father was a steamfitter but had died some years earlier. Art and Elmer had two older sisters who were working in clerical or secretarial jobs but earned enough money to support the family. The Anderson garage, where we sometimes played a shrunken version of basketball, was still full of pipes and other equipment used by their steamfitter father. The Anderson house always smelled of coffee. The Andersons of course were Swedes and I was told that Swedes drank more coffee than anyone.

Another good friend was Leo Donovan, who lived on the corner of Stanford and Albert. Leo had two younger brothers. I remember his mother well because she could put two fingers between her teeth and let out a whistle that could be heard maybe a block away. When she whistled, it meant that Leo was to get home, quickly, and he did.

Leo's father was kind of a hero to neighborhood boys. He worked for the Northern States Power Company as a lineman, which meant that he climbed up electric power poles to repair and reattach lines when they came down in a storm. It was a dangerous job, but it seemed to us boys a rather glamorous job, too. Maybe you could grow up to be a lineman!

I entered Central High School in the fall of 1939, jut as the war in Europe was beginning. Central High was located on Lexington Avenue a good two miles from our house. I walked to school and back again every day. I could have taken a street car but that would have meant two transfers from the St. Clair to the Snelling line and then to the Selby line, all of which took as much time or even more time than walking. Three or four of us walked together and talked about everything from school work to girls. None of us were dating at that age; so I suppose you could say the girl talk was rather academic. The truth is I was scared to ask a girl, say, to go to a movie or share an ice-cream soda. I was worried that I might be rebuffed or concerned that if a girl said, yes, I'd like to go to a movie, I would not know how to act or what to talk about before and after the movie.

Central High was a massive, almost castle-like building at the top of a hill. The structure was faced with red bricks and trimmed in white stone. There were three stories and a basement, with classrooms on all levels. The basement even included a swimming pool, but it was no longer used and besides I was not a swimmer.

Central was one of four high schools in St. Paul at that time and had a large enrollment of about 1,500 students. As I have noted high school began with the tenth grade—or sophomore—year and ended of course with the twelfth grade.

I was impressed but not overwhelmed by the size of Central. The size only seemed to bore down on you when you changed classes and moved through the crowded hallways, trying not to bump into people. My classes during the first year at Central included English, European history, geometry, civics—a kind of elementary political science course—and the dreaded gym classes.

Our gym teacher was a Mr. Perlt. His distinguishing characteristic was his nose which was skewed sideways. He was once a prize fighter, I was told, and his nose had been broken in a fight. As in junior high school, we were sent outside in freezing weather in shorts and T-shirts. And, again as in junior high school, our teacher seemed to delight in making clumsy, non-athletic boys like me embarrass ourselves on the parallel bars and trying to do push-ups and somersaults.

Gym classes—and geometry—were not my thing, and fortunately I only had to take gym in the tenth grade and I did not have to follow geometry with trigonometry in the eleventh grade.

But as soon as I got into Central I was intrigued by the school newspaper, the Central High Times. It was an ambitious project, a four-page full-size paper published weekly by and for the students but under the supervision of Miss Allen, an English teacher who also taught a journalism course and stayed after school to see to it that the Central High Times got out on schedule each week.

In the second half of my sophomore year I sort of sneaked into Miss Allen's classroom after regular school hours and was allowed to do some work on the paper. I had touted my experience on the Maria Sanford paper to get myself in the door. And from then on high school was the Central High Times. Schoolwork was still coming easily to me so I was able to devote many hours to the paper. And I loved it, whether I was writing an article about a particular class or program, seeking out items for what we laughingly called our gossip column, or writing headlines. This was a genuine introduction to journalism, or newspapers, as it was referred to then. From then on I knew what my life's work would be.

For me, high school was many things. There were the daily classes. My favorites were English and history, and the one journalism course I took and loved. I enrolled in a physics course rather than chemistry because I did not like the smells coming out of the chemistry classroom. How's that for a reason for making a decision about what to study?

High school was also a place to make new friends like Fred Claassen, Bill Olson and Otto Meeker. Fred's father worked for the St. Paul Book and Stationery Company and the Claassen home was always filled with new books that Mr. Claassen received as part of his job. Bill's father was a postal employee who worked in the mail cars on trains sorting mail as the trains hurtled from, say, St. Paul to Chicago. That sounded like a glamorous job. Otto's father was part owner of the fanciest men's clothing store in St. Paul.

Central high was a place, too, where I first ran into social distinctions. The hierarchy among students belonged to the Front Hall group. These students gathered between classes in Central's front hall just outside the principal's office. There the Front Hall gang gossiped and looked down at ordinary mortals whose clothes were inferior and whose families' incomes were usually lower.

Another group was made up of athletes who played on the football, basketball and other teams and actually looked forward to gym class. Still others grouped around the drama class which put on a couple of plays each year. And there was a chess club, a literary club that published a magazine once a year and other clubs ranging from stamp collectors to dance enthusiasts.

I belonged to the Central High Times group. The paper's office was in Miss Allen's room in a hallway just off the front hall. Some of the paper's editors and reporters were part of the Front Hall group, but I never was although I was friends with some of the Front Hallers. I was though definitely part of the Central High Times group in my junior and senior years at Central.

High school meant busy, busy times for me, but I loved every bit of it. Beginning my junior year, I had my Pioneer Press and Dispatch route, which meant getting up at five a.m. to deliver the morning paper and rushing from high school to deliver the afternoon paper and then going back to the school to work on the Central High Times. And then during my second semester as a junior I took on the job of being an usher at the St. Clair theater. I still marvel at how I did it all.

Ten or twelve of us were regulars working to get out the Central High Times every week. Except for one column on international affairs, the content of the paper was all about what was going on at Central high. Page one was the big news of the day—a new teacher, an interesting classroom story, plans for a special school event, a message from the principal. Page two was our editorial page, where we ran one or two editorials commenting on school issues such as deportment, proper attire—I and most other boys wore ties every day!—edicts from the principal's office and suggestions for special programs. Page three was our features page where we might display a profile of an outstanding student, a new teacher or a graduate who had made good in an unusual or spectacular way. Page four was the sports page. At the time Central was something of a powerhouse is football, winning city championships and also a kind of Twin Cities Bowl where the best St. Paul team played the best rival Minneapolis had to offer.

We even had a photographer and a couple of students who drew cartoons for us. Miss Allen was a stern, middle-aged, gray-haired woman who sat at her desk while we worked at our typewriters and our copy desk, configured in a half circle like the ones in real newspaper offices.

Miss Allen would look over our copy and paste-ups of pages, but she was not a heavy editor and the paper was truly the work of the student-reporters and editors. Looking back, I think it was a fairly good paper. Sure, sophomoric, high-schoolish stuff got in, particularly what got in a gossip column and a sports column, but what do you expect from a high school publication?

What I really liked was going downtown on Wednesdays to help oversee the make-up of the pages at the printers. To get to the print shop you had to get on a rickety elevator and pull a rope which started the elevator. When you got to your floor, you let go of the rope, the elevator stopped, and you slid open the door which disappeared above your head.

The printers were hospitable to us high-school editors in part, I am sure, because the shop relied on high school papers for much of its business. It printed the papers of all four of St. Paul's high schools as well as papers published by some of the schools in the city's suburbs.

It was always fun to watch the printers pick up type and place it in the page forms exactly where we wanted them. The forms were on what were called "stones," heavy platforms on wheels. Magically, everything came out just right week after week.

The papers were distributed free to all the classrooms every Friday. We did carry some advertising to help defray our costs, but most of the money to finance the paper came from school funds. It was a good investment. The paper contained a lot of useful information, and it provided some training for budding journalists like myself.

Another important aspect of high-school journalism at that time were trips that we would-be journalists took to the city room of the Pioneer Press and Dispatch. A couple of times a year the Central High Times editors were invited downtown to the real paper where an editor or two would talk to us about how the Pioneer Press and Dispatch was put together each day. The papers had a weekly half-page or so of stories written by high-school journalists, and it was always an event to see your name and story in the "big" paper.

I was never editor of the Central High Times, but I was features editor one semester and sports editor another. I don't know why I never made editor. Miss Allen chose the editors and I thought I always got along well with her. But my failure to become editor did not diminish my enthusiasm for working on the Central High Times.

Milt Bellis, one of my best friends and you might say a rival, did become editor in our senior year. Milt was Jewish and I must pause here to tell a story about him. As I have mentioned before, my mother and father were uncomfortable with Jews, which I guess is a nice way of putting it. I still don't think they were anti-Semitic, but they didn't like Jews even though they knew few Jews. I can't think of a single Jewish family that lived on Stanford Avenue or elsewhere in our immediate neighborhood.

Well, Milt was a handsome and very polite boy and one day I brought him home with me. He was tall, he had perfectly groomed black hair and always sported a ready smile. He talked softly and impeccably. After our visit with my mother and after Milt had left, my mother said to me, "My, Milton is a nice boy—for being Jewish."

Milt and I were also rivals for a girl who worked on the Central High Times—Dorothy Dugas. She was a pretty, perhaps a little splashy, blond. I thought I had an advantage because I had my own car while Milt had to wheedle use of his parents' car. But I soon realized that I was fooling myself. Milt was far more handsome than I, suave if you will, and knew much more about girls and dates than I did. I was shy and still uncomfortable on a date.

# 11

## *Whispers—And Charlie Brown*

To show how much times and attitudes have changed, I want to tell the story of another girl who worked on the Central High Times. Her name was Audrey, and I can still see her in a tight and a short skirt, crossing her good-looking legs and sitting on our copy desk. She was a flirt, attractive enough and always popular with boys.

One day she stopped showing up for school and in the Central High Times classroom. We all wondered what had happened. Had she done something to cause her to be expelled from school? Was she sick? Had she moved away? If Miss Allen knew what had happened, she wasn't saying.

After a few weeks there were whispers. Our girl had to drop out of school because she was going to have a baby! A baby! My gosh, a lot of us were not exactly sure how babies were produced and where they came from. This news was a huge shock to all her friends on the paper. It was a black mark, a disgrace. Why, she would be ruined the rest of her life. Poor girl.

Today high-school pregnancies are not uncommon. I have even heard of situations where high-school mothers take their babies to school with them. The world has indeed changed. For the better? I am not so sure about that.

Thinking back on that incident, I am reminded about Central High's "mourner's bench" where someone who had disobeyed a school rule was forced to sit for an hour, or perhaps two hours, as part of his or her punishment. The bench was in the principal's outer office and in full view of anyone walking in the front hall. You were disgraced. And what could get you to the mourner's bench? Well, chewing gum in class. Running in the hallways. Coming to school in an outlandish costume. Smoking on the school grounds or inside the school building. Talking back to or sassing a teacher. Absence from school or class without a good excuse.

Today most of those transgressions probably seem minor and not worthy of public humiliation on the mourner's bench. Drug use was unheard of during my high school days. Nor was there any violence that I can remember on school grounds or in the building. Maybe a minor fight now and then. Some teasing. But nothing serious like the fights and shootings we hear about in high schools today. I never heard of an incident involving a gun at Central High, for example. Times have indeed changed, and not for the better.

My senior year in high school was an exciting time. There were so many things to do in my still young life that I hardly knew where to begin. I gave up my paper route because I was just too busy. The money I earned from my job as an usher at the St. Clair theater provided enough for me to finance such things as the few dates I had time for and to continue some savings. Ten dollars a week does not seem like much money today, but in 1941 and 1942 it could be stretched a long way. Besides, I had saved enough money in the previous two years to buy a car.

At Central High I continued to spend much of my time helping put out the school paper, and in the 1941 fall semester I was sports editor. And that fall the Central football team won all but one of its games and was the talk of St. Paul. It was a good time to be a sports editor.

In December the Japanese attack on Pearl Harbor shocked everyone and the realization that the United States was now at war in both the Pacific and Europe sobered high school students as well as our teachers and other adults. Some of my friends even talked about enlisting in the Army before they graduated from high school and would be called up in the military draft. But I did not think in those terms. I was scared, but willing to wait for the draft.

As the Christmas season ended and the New Year's celebration was over I went back to Central High to find that I had been named editor of the CEHISEAN, the senior yearbook. CEHISEAN stood for Central High School Senior Annual. It was an honor to be editor of the CEHISEAN. High school yearbooks were prized possessions that graduates kept for the rest of their lives.

I continued to do some work on the Central High Times, but the CEHISEAN editorship was practically a full-time job. Fortunately, I had completed all of my high school work except for a course in English and one in American history—both subjects I liked and were easy for me. So I had a lot of time for work on the annual.

The CEHISEAN published individual pictures of the graduating class, informal pictures of students and faculty and formal pictures of the school orchestra, band, student council and such clubs as the literary, international relations, Latin, German, chemistry, bird, art, thespians, bowling, stamp, debaters, radio, aeronautics and rifle organizations. As you can see, the variety of interests of Central high students was wide and eclectic.

Sports—both girls and boys—were not neglected. For girls' sports, there were pages devoted to basketball, fieldball, volleyball and tumbling. And what was fieldball? It was a game played by two teams of eleven players each, with five forwards, three halfbacks, two fullbacks and a goal guard on each team. The object of the game is to make as many points as possible by passing the ball through a goal. It is a combination of basketball and soccer. It is more strenuous than soccer and the ball is thrown rather than kicked as in soccer.

Boys' sports ranged from football and basketball to swimming, gym, hockey, track, baseball, golf and tennis. But as it is today the emphasis was first on football and then on basketball. In those days high school basketball was a major sport in Minnesota, culminating each March with a state tournament that attracted enormous attention.

The CEHISEAN was first published in 1922; so I was the editor of the twentieth anniversary edition, but I don't remember any special commemoration activities in 1942. I guess we were too busy getting out the annual to pause to look back. Miss Borden was our advisor, and like Miss Allen with the Central High Times she pretty much left the annual staff alone.

The biggest job was getting all the pictures taken and assembled, but there was much writing to do, too. Individual pictures of the graduates were taken by a professional photographer in hopes of selling multiple copies to the individual students as an official graduation photo. The pictures of the officers and members of the many clubs and other organizations were taken by student photographers, as were the informal—or candid—shots, some serious, some funny, and a few bizarre.

As editor, I was in charge of all these activities, plus the organization of the annual and seeing it to press. The CEHISEAN was printed on shiny paper and nicely bound. To help pay for the production of the annual we charged a dollar a copy. Most seniors purchased a copy as did many of the juniors and sophomores. There were also some advertisements from drug stores and other merchants near Central and two or three business schools seeking particularly to attract girls who wanted to prepare for secretarial and other office work.

Once the CEHISEAN was available you were supposed to get your friends to sign it, and hopefully write something nice about you next to their signatures.

Some examples of notes written in my CEHISEAN: "To a swell guy who really knows his English." "Dear Caesar (Julius, get it?): I hope that you get into my classes next year. That is if you, er, I mean I, pass." "Hope you'll go far in journalism. I know you will." "Dearest Julius, Miss Allen's pet." "Best wishes to a swell kid." "To an up and coming journalist (so they tell me)". "Loads of luck to an English expert."

That is probably enough of high-school humor or pseudo-humor. The CEHISEAN had a sister annual called the World. It was a literary magazine, at least a magazine with literary pretensions. The World published poems, short stories and essays. It published an essay of mine, the subject of which I have unfortunately, or perhaps fortunately, forgotten.

But the Central High Times stood out as the star publication. It regularly won such student publication citations as the Columbian Medalist Award, All-Columbian Newspaper Award, both given by the School of Journalism at Columbia University, an International Rating for Excellence from the Quill and Scroll High School Journalism Society and the All-American newspaper rating from the National Student Press Association.

I must not end my discussion of the Central High Times and the CEHISEAN without mentioning Charles Schulz, the creator of Peanuts. He attended Central High School and sometime in the nineteen sixties or seventies I came across an interview with him in which he said that the editor of his high school annual turned down some cartoons he submitted because they were not considered good enough to be published.

My gosh! Could I have done that? Well, I searched around to find out when he graduated from Central and, to my relief, discovered that he was two years older than I and had got out of high school in 1940, two years before I was editor of the CEHISEAN and graduated. What a relief. I certainly did not want to go through the rest of my life knowing that I had failed to recognize Charles Schulz' genius.

In my senior year at Central I also was honored by being chosen as a member of the National Honor Society, and I still have the loving cup, a rather small one, I must admit, with my name and citation engraved on it. Membership in the Society is given to especially good high school students; so that made my parents as well as myself proud.

Senior year in high school also meant Friday or Saturday night dances generally sponsored by Hi-Y clubs, which were organized by the St. Paul YMCA. I was never much of a dancer, but I did go alone—stag, as they said—to some of the dances which were generally held in the St. Paul Hotel, one of only two first-class hotels in the city, the other being the Lowry.

I usually stood around with other stags watching the dancing and wishing I had the skill and gumption to dance myself. There was a lot of drinking of beer at these dances. No one was twenty-one, old enough to drink legally, but some of the boys always managed to sneak in beer. It was hardly in the spirit of the YMCA, but the dances weren't policed very carefully. I was afraid to drink any beer, and so far as I remember never did. But many boys and some girls did drink, some of the boys especially. I remember one who I really think became an alcoholic after imbibing much too much at the high school dances. He was a poor little rich boy who even had his own convertible, a real extravagance in those days.

My social life was decidedly limited by my work at the St. Clair theater. I almost always worked six days a week, sometimes getting a Friday or Saturday night off to attend a dance, but usually going to the dance late after finishing work at the theater.

One girl I knew—she was not a girl friend because I never asked her out for a movie or a soda—sometimes had Friday or Saturday night parties in the recreation room—rec room, as we called it—in the basement of her home on Wellesley Avenue. Six or eight of us would congregate there, drink a Coke, eat potato chips and try, at least in my case, to dance to records. But what I remember most about those parties was the presence of my friend's grandmother, who lived with the family. She was there much more as a participant than as a chaperone. She even danced with one of us boys. I guess she was the grandmother all of us wished we had.

The big social event of our last year in high school was the senior prom which was held at the St. Paul Hotel. As I have mentioned before, I was far from a social butterfly and had no date for the prom until I was told that the girl who was president of the senior class did not have a date for the prom. She was a brilliant girl but not very attractive. Julius, why not be a good sport and take Marilyn. Well, I knew Marilyn well, was a good sport and took her to the prom. I even danced some, and we had a good time. She looked quite nice in a long, colorful gown, and I thought I looked pretty spiffy in a white coat and black pants, a "summer tux" I had rented for the outrageous price of twenty-five dollars.

The biggest problem with the senior prom was the tradition that you had to stay out all night, absolutely all night until dawn. But what to do? The prom itself ended shortly before midnight. Then Marilyn and I and another couple piled into my car and started driving, first to a roadhouse north of St. Paul known for its jazzy piano players, but we were too young to be admitted. You couldn't even try to lie about your age, because the summer tuxes and the girls in long dresses were a dead giveaway that you were seventeen or eighteen-year-olds graduating from high school.

So then we drove to Minneapolis, up and down deserted Hennepin Avenue and other downtown streets, out to the fancy residential districts ringing Lake Harriet and Lake Nokomis, back to St. Paul and trips around its two lakes—Como and Phelan. Downtown St. Paul was another destination, and its Seventh Street, Cedar, Wabasha, wherever you went, deserted.

Finally, finally, we began to see streaks of light in the eastern sky and breathed a sigh of relief. Soon we could drop the girls off at their homes and head for our own beds. Our all-night adventure turned into a big bore. Our girls were as bored as we were. The night was neither romantic nor exciting. Just a big blah. A crazy idea and tradition. Good night!

Graduation ceremonies were held in the municipal auditorium in downtown St. Paul. I think the speaker was the city's superintendent of schools, but I remember nothing from what he said. I was one of the students on the Central High honor roll, and I was as proud as my parents were of that recognition. It was a nice send-off to college, or the "U" as we all called the University of Minnesota where most of the graduates who had followed the college preparatory course were headed.

I guess maybe a third of the Central High graduates went on to college. Another third or more took what was called the commercial course, most of them girls looking toward office jobs as secretaries or stenographers, as they said in those days. Then there was a group who had concentrated in such courses as machine shop, metal shop and carpentry and were hoping to find a job a job in the building trades or perhaps as automobile mechanics.

Although no one else on Stanford Avenue went on to college, I always seemed to know that I would go to the "U." My mother particularly always encouraged me to study; I was always a big reader and somehow knew from a very early age that college would be for me.

Was I adequately prepared for a big university like Minnesota with its thirty-thousand students? I guess so. Today it would be said that I had not been adequately challenged because school was so easy for me. I could spend—and did spend—an enormous amount of time working first on the Central High Times and then on the CEHISEAN yearbook, but they were certainly learning experiences. Both junior high and high school gave me a wonderful grounding in the fundamentals of writing, use of words and grammar. High school also gave me a good background and some understanding of both American and European history.

My days in Central High were also a maturing experience for me. I lost some of my shyness. I made new and different friends, from varying ethnic and social backgrounds whether, say, Jewish, Italian or even Mexican, or the sons and daughters of a the city's leading real estate broker or the most important clothier. In high school I became a much more confident boy who at times certainly thought he could conquer at least the journalistic world. I suppose, too, I began to drift away from the insular world of my parents and of Stanford Avenue where there were few college graduates and, let's face it, few success stories. Mr. Johnson, the insurance salesman, was one of the few success stories on our block.

On graduating from high school I looked upon myself as a success story, at least for a seventeen-year-old boy. I had done well at school making the honor roll and being elected to the National Honor Society, I had held editing jobs at the Central High Times and been THE editor of the CEHISEAN. I had done a good job as a carrier boy for the St. Paul Pioneer Press and Dispatch and now was working hard as an usher at the St. Clair theater where I would soon be promoted to assistant manager.

But would United States entry into World War II smash my little but expanding world? Would I be drafted into the Army and be sent to fight in Europe or on an island in the Pacific? I guess I didn't think much about that, and as it turned out I was classified as 4-F, unfit for military service because of my extreme nearsightedness. I didn't fight my classification, as some 4-Effers did, I suppose because I was scared of the Army.

Looking back, I think high school was even more of a maturing experience for me than college, but that is probably a subject for later discussion. At any rate, after graduating from high school I returned to Central High several times in the next two years to see favorite teachers like Miss Allen and to attend school plays and some social events. I guess it was simply hard for me to let go of a wonderful experience.

# 12

## *When the Birds Sing*

As my mind goes back to my boyhood and high school days, more side-bars pop up. Here they are:

Whenever my mother and my Aunt Emma wanted to talk about something that they deemed unfit for my ears, they lapsed into their father's native Polish. I have no idea how good their Polish was, but it was good enough to cut me out of the discussion. In later years I wished I had been taught at least some rudimentary Polish, but by the time I thought that it was too late.

One of the delights of a hot summer afternoon was the sound of the bell on the ice cream truck that slowly made its way up Stanford Avenue. This was not a small Good Humor truck, but a bus-like vehicle tall enough for the driver to walk to the back of the truck where he dished out wonderful cones. He didn't just put ice cream on top of the cones; he stuffed ice cream into the cones. I can still taste the vanilla.

There was a pretty good grocery store, as Garrison Keillor would say today, at the corner of St. Clair and Albert streets. It still had barrels of flour and sugar, and you placed your order with a clerk at the counter who gathered your purchases together for you. Self-service supermarkets were still in the future. But what I and other boys in the neighborhood liked most about the store, called Mashek and Vogel, was their delivery man who tooled around the neighborhood in a pick up truck and often let two or three of us boys ride with him—in the open-air back—and help him carry groceries to the homes of his customers. I never told my mother or father that I did that, of course, because they certainly would not have approved such dangerous behavior on my part.

The White family lived next door to us. Mr. White owned a coal and ice business and when he came home from his business he walked in the back door and plumped his small bag containing the day's receipts on the kitchen table where the bag sat until he took it with him back to work and presumably to the bank the next morning. The Whites never locked their doors and the money bag was never stolen. Most of us in fact never locked our doors then. Mrs. White was a volatile character who seemed to keep an eye on the neighborhood, night and day. When someone would come home late at night with a snootful of drink, as we used to say, she would tell my mother he was "all lickered up."

The importance of the radio in our lives cannot be exaggerated. I remember, for example, the Lindbergh kidnap case largely from radio reports about it. The young son of Charles Lindbergh, the first man to fly the Atlantic alone, from New York to Paris, was kidnapped in the early thirties and the trial of a man named Bruno Hauptmann who was convicted of the kidnapping and put to death for it was a sensation. I think it was the first trial to be broadcast, not live, of course, but detailed by announcers as they moved in and out of the courtroom in New Jersey. People stayed close to their radio sets so as not to miss a single word of the frequent reports from just outside the courtroom.

My father was a very gentle man. I never knew him to raise his voice to me, to my mother, to Emma or to anyone else. But like so many other men he loved boxing, which was big in the thirties and forties. The major boxing matches were broadcast on the radio. Joe Louis, a Negro called the Brown Bomber, was the most famous and best boxer. I still remember my father intently sitting by our radio listening to the storied boxing announcer Clem McCarthy describing the greatest fight of them all between Louis and the German Max Schmeling. Louis, and America, won. I don't think my father particularly liked blacks, even though he didn't know any, but he did like Joe Louis the boxing great.

As I have mentioned before my Aunt Emma never married because, I always thought, she was hard of hearing. In the late thirties, however, she did get a hearing aid—they were quite new then—and I still remember her saying that she could hear the birds singing now. It almost made me cry when she said that. Soon after she started wearing a hearing aid, she had a boy friend. At the time she was working part-time at a beauty shop downtown, the neighborhood shop where she had worked for so many years having closed down, another victim of the Depression. While waiting for the street car to take her downtown one morning, Emma was greeted by a man who had stopped his car and asked her if she would like a ride. The man was nicely dressed and somewhat older than Emma; so she decided that it would be safe to ride with him. That chance encounter blossomed into many Sunday drives and dinners for Emma and Andrew. He would call for her late on a Sunday morning and they would drive out into the country for a pleasant dinner and come back late in the afternoon. Andrew was married, apparently unhappily, but he brought some happiness to Emma's life. My mother was shocked that Emma would go out with a married man, but after awhile my mother got used to the idea, I think because she saw how happy Emma was as she looked forward to the Sunday outings. The drives and dinners, which I don't think you could call trysts, lasted several years until Andrew died. Emma found out about his death when she saw his obituary in the paper. I remember her weeping as she read the death notice.

Another of our neighbors who I still remember was Mr. Wildermuth. He was a small, bald-headed man but with quite a physique. What did he do? He was a masseur, my mother said. A what? A masseur, he rubbed men's backs, sometimes pounded them, at the St. Paul Athletic Club. I had walked by the club's rather forbidding building on Sixth street many times, and often wondered what went on there. Only rich men could get in the building, I was told. But I guess what I remember most about Mr. Wildermuth is that he was a vegetarian. What was that, I again asked my mother? It means he doesn't eat meat, my mother said. Why not? I couldn't understand not eating meat. Why, as hard-up as we were at times, we always had meat on the table. Mr. Wildermuth thinks meat is unhealthy for you, my mother explained. Is it? I asked. Oh, never mind, my mother said, go outside and play. Whenever I saw Mr. Wildermuth after that, I always looked at him kind of funny, wanting to ask him what he really had against meat. Just eating vegetables! Whew, that sounded awful.

Father Coughlin also made an impression on me. He was a Catholic priest who had a parish just outside Detroit and had a radio program every Sunday night with a large audience, perhaps not as big as that for Amos 'n Andy, but close. Father Coughlin was anti-Semitic, anti-Negro, anti-Roosevelt and probably anti—a lot of other things I didn't know about. He broadcast from what was called the Church of the Little Flower and at the end of his fifteen-minute broadcast always appealed for donations. And the money flowed in. Every now and then I would hear one of his broadcasts. I didn't understand much of what he talked about, but I knew I didn't like him. Some of my Catholic friends sold his weekly paper called Social Justice, where his radio harangues were reprinted, and I didn't care for the paper either. I later learned what an evil influence Father Coughlin was on the desperate Depression times.

From an early age, as I have noted before, I loved reading and treasured books. Perhaps the book I liked the most and went back to most often was a sixth-grade geography text. Books were not provided by schools then; you had to buy them each year as you progressed from grade to grade. Often you passed on or sold last yea's books, but I hung on to the large-size, green-covered geography text with its wonderful maps of North America, South America, Europe, Africa, Asia and on and on. As a boy I liked nothing better than to study the maps and dream about some day going to far away England, France, Japan or China.

Many jokes were made during the thirties about the WPA—Roosevelt's Works Progress Administration which provided jobs to the unemployed doing everything from raking leaves in public parks, as the cliché went, to building roads. WPA means We Poke Along, Roosevelt's enemies said, alluding to how slow men were said to work on WPA projects. There was also the PWA—the Public Works Administration—which let out contracts to constructions firms to build schools and other public facilities. In St. Paul these agencies were responsible for building a swimming pool in Highland Park, improving the park's golf course and other projects at the city's two lakes—Como and Phelan. Even as a boy I thought the WPA and the PWA were good for us Depression people.

Speaking of Lake Phelan, I should not forget the amusement park that was at the lake. The park had been built by the street car company, which was common in those days, and the best way to get to the park was on the street car line which ran right into the park. Everything you could want in an amusement park was there—a Ferris wheel, a merry-go-round, pony rides, bumper cars, floss candy. I didn't visit the amusement park very often, but it was always fun, and so was the street car ride.

The week before school opened every September was always a nice shopping time, particularly for school supplies. The neighborhood drug stores and the dime stores were the places to go. They stocked up with all manner of pencils, crayons, notebooks, lunch boxes and book bags. I loved to examine carefully all the supplies, drinking in the aromatic smells of the lead pencils and the crayons, fingering the notebooks and dreaming of having one of the Mickey Mouse or Lone Ranger lunch boxes or book bags, which unfortunately our family could not afford.

I learned early to be thrifty. Clean up your plate, Junior, remember those starving Armenians. A hole in your stockings? Mother will darn them and close up that hole tonight while she is listening to the radio. A rip in the knees of your knickers. Mother can fix that, too. Save the wrappers that the groceries came in. Even save the string. Shoes were routinely re-soled and re-heeled over and over. At least once a week you polished your shoes to try to keep them looking as good as new. When you out-grew your clothes, they were given to a relative or a neighbor with children who could use them. Waste not, want not.

# 13

## A Salute to St. Paul

Alvin Karpis, named Public Enemy No. 1 by FBI Director J. Edgar Hoover during the nineteen thirties, wrote in his autobiography that "if you were looking for a guy you hadn't seen for a few months, you usually thought of two places, prison or St. Paul."

Karpis was talking about my St. Paul, the city where I was born, grew up in the Depression years of the thirties, and lived until I was almost twenty-three years old when I moved to Washington, D.C., in 1947.

How dare Karpis call my St. Paul, so calm, orderly and peaceful, a hideout for gangsters, who found refuge there when the heat was on in Chicago? Alas, it was true. St. Paul, I learned before I was out of high school, was indeed a safe place for the gangsters of the thirties, thanks to a police department whose corrupt ways went all the way back to the early nineteen-hundreds. Not only did Karpis cool off in St. Paul, but so did Baby Face Nelson, Ma Barker and John Dillinger, himself, the most notorious of the Depression-era killers. In fact, as a boy I even walked by, quickly, the apartment house not far from where I lived where Dillinger once hid out over a weekend. I heaved a sigh of relief when I got by the building safely.

St. Paul, as I suppose everyone knows, is one half of Minnesota's Twin Cities, separated for the most part by the Mississippi River. St. Paul is the smaller city; its population was somewhat under 300,000 when I was growing up. St. Paul was, and still is, considered the lesser of the two cities, even though it is the capital of Minnesota. Minneapolis, with the University of Minnesota and a symphony orchestra, and a 1930's population of 500,000, has always been thought of as more sophisticated and wealthier. Perhaps, but St. Paul is still my city, and it had plenty of charms of its own.

Father Louis Hennepin of France was the first European explorer to reach Minnesota—in 1680—and named the falls he discovered on the Mississippi for his patron saint, Anthony of Padua. St. Anthony Falls later provided the power for the first flour mills in Minneapolis.

Nearly a century later France relinquished its claim what is now Minnesota and in 1803 the U.S. purchase of the Louisiana Territory from France placed all of the area of what are now the Twin Cities under American rule. Three years later Army Colonel Zebulon Pike signed a treaty with the Dakota Indians and established a military post at the confluence of the Minnesota and Mississippi rivers where St. Paul and Minneapolis now converge.

Later Captain Josiah Snelling founded a fort on the site and it was named Fort Snelling in his honor. As early as 1823 the first steamboat arrived at Fort Snelling from St. Louis. Fourteen years later, in 1837, a saloon keeper named Pierre "Pig's Eye" Parrant built a cabin a few miles downstream from Fort Snelling which became the first building in what is now St. Paul.

Pig's Eye? That's right, as I learned in grade school, that was the first name for my beloved St. Paul. Fortunately, Father Lucien Galtier arrived a few years later and built a chapel dedicated to Saint Paul, and the hamlet of Pig's Eye, thankfully, became St. Paul. By 1849 St. Paul became the capital of the Minnesota Territory, and six years later Minneapolis was founded. So, take that, Minneapolis.

Both cities grew and prospered, St. Paul becoming a center for railroads, eventually three of them—the Great Northern, Northern Pacific and the Burlington Route—and Minneapolis a center for flour mills—General Mills, Pillsbury and Washburn among them. By 1890 the population of Minneapolis surpassed that of St Paul, and the rivalry between the two cities that extends to this day was on.

As I was growing up, I slowly became aware of the Twin Cities rivalry, and of course always stuck up for St. Paul. In fact, I did not even set foot in Minneapolis until I was a senior in high school and had bought a car, enabling me to drive the rival city's Minnehaha Parkway and around its Lake Nokomis and Lake of the Isles.

St. Paul was certainly okay for me, with its Lake Como and the Como Park Zoo and Lake Phelan and the amusement park close by, which was easily accessible by a street car trundling through open spaces at perhaps thirty or even forty miles per hour.

Downtown St. Paul had plenty of attractions—the marble library with its commodious children's room full of books I just had to read, the art deco city hall reaching I don't know how many stories to the sky and containing a four-story onyx statute of an Indian filling its atrium.

And then there were the state capitol building dominating one hill above downtown and the Mississippi and the Catholic Cathedral on another hill, the two huge buildings facing each other and I suppose symbolizing the importance of both church and state. St. Paul, I was learning, had many Irish Catholic residents. The Irish had been recruited to build the railroads west and when their work was done drifted back to St. Paul.

I still have a picture somewhere showing me with a group of boys visiting the capitol, which is said to be with its dome and Minnesota marble the most beautiful of all the state capitol buildings in the United States. Its dome is a spectacular sight rising over the city, and inside the rotunda, I dare say, is as beautiful and breathtaking as the rotunda of the capitol building in Washington, D.C.

As a boy I even visited the cathedral, even though I was not sure that as a Lutheran I would be welcome, but I was greeted pleasantly by a priest who invited me to look around and take my time. The building is said to be modeled after St. Paul's cathedral in the Vatican.

The cathedral is at the foot of Summit Avenue, a boulevard that runs five miles to the bluffs above the Mississippi river and is one of the most beautiful thoroughfares in the country. The roadway is divided in the middle by flowers, grass, trees and shrubs, and many of the homes on either side are immaculate Victorians. The munificent Victorian built by the railroad magnate James J. Hill near the cathedral is a museum, and I still remember visiting it once and being awed by the size and luxury of the place. The house also has a magnificent view of downtown and the Mississippi.

Summit Avenue is also famous for the writers who lived there. F. Scott Fitzgerald finished his first novel "This Side of Paradise" while living in his parents' home on Summit Avenue. The novel makes fun of the rich people who lived on the street, and St. Paulites never forgave him. Sinclair Lewis, a native of Sauk Centre, Minn., whose first novel "Main Street" criticized his neighbors, lived briefly on Summit Avenue.

But back to downtown. The Kellogg Mall is a three-block esplanade built in the nineteen-thirties to provide vistas of the Mississippi River Valley, and the views down river are magnificent. The mall is named for Frank B. Kellogg, a St. Paul native who was Secretary of State in the nineteen-twenties and received the Nobel Peace Prize for his part in writing the Kellogg-Briand Treaty designed to help preserve the peace after the Great War. Alas, it did not do that, of course.

I liked to walk down the mall, and look out at the river and the Wabasha and Robert Street bridges over the river, and, yes, dream about the riverboats once so common the Mississippi. A steamboat still appeared in the summer months, offering daytime excursions and nighttime dances. I never went to a dance but did go on a couple of excursions.

I liked to stand on the rear deck, watching the giant paddle wheels that propelled the boat so easily. As I stood there, I dreamed of being the captain of such a ship and guiding it all the way down the Mississippi to New Orleans.

I also remember the First National Bank Building, an art deco structure completed in 1931 and with its "1st" neon sign atop its 31-story tower an instant landmark. The red and beige marble lobby and its escalator, a novelty in the thirties, were awe-inspiring to a boy.

But what I liked the most about downtown St. Paul was its Union Depot, once considered one of the nation's busiest railroad passenger stations. I never rode a train until after I started working as a reporter, but I loved watching trains steam in and out of the depot, and oh, how I envied the people lucky enough to be able to come and go in luxurious Pullman cars. In my boyhood there were at least three trains a day that went to Chicago, and just as many that left Union Depot for the Dakotas, Montana and the mysterious West Coast states of Washington and Oregon. In later years I was able to go by train to Chicago—on both the Zephyr and the Four Hundred, named that way because it took just four hundred minutes to go from St. Paul to the Windy City. But I never did take a train west.

While trains were only for watching as I was growing up, St. Paul's street cars were for riding. Called the Twin City Lines, the street cars that served St. Paul and Minneapolis moved over a total of 500 miles of tracks. It was one of the largest street car systems in the United States.

The cars were yellow behemoths that noisily trundled up and down St. Paul's hills and sped across the level right-of-ways. With their cane seats they provided a comfortable ride. You entered through front doors, deposited your dime in a fare box next to where the motorman stood and made your way to a seat. Some of the cars had a rear platform open to the elements where smoking was permitted. Summer or winter smokers were there, puffing away and talking about the day ahead or the day that they had just finished. The street cars were heated in the winter by a coal stove near the rear exit, and the fumes could become nearly unbearable. Coal for the stoves was stored in large wooden boxes at the end of the lines.

I rode the St. Clair line, two blocks from our house on Stanford Avenue, starting when I was ten years. Back and forth I went downtown to the dentist, the library or the five-and-ten-cent store. As I sat by a window in the street car I twiddled with a knob and pretended I was the motorman who stood up as he twirled his real knobs to power the car.

Today the street cars are gone. They began to be replaced by buses in the nine-teen-fifties. It is a shame. In today's crowded streets the buses go no faster than street cars, and the exhaust from the buses dirties the air. But such is "progress."

Speaking of fumes, I am reminded of the stockyards in South St. Paul. When I was growing up South St. Paul had one of the largest stockyards in the country. I visited the stockyards once with a school group and came away almost a vegetar-ian. But mostly the stockyards meant a rather foul smell over our neighborhood when the wind was blowing in the right way—or I should say the wrong way.

St. Paul also was the home of two large breweries—Schmidt's and Hamm's. I knew where they were, even went by them on Sunday walks with my father, but of course was never inside them. I also remember Yoerg's "cave-aged" beer. I saw the caves in the Mississippi bluffs where the beer actually was aged, but was never in one of the caves.

On top of some of the bluffs overlooking the Mississippi were mounds where Indians were buried. The city established Mounds Park to mark the Indian burial grounds. The park was a solemn and rather scary place to a boy like myself.

I have said little about Minneapolis because it really was not part of my boy-hood. Minneapolis came into my life when I started attending classes at the Uni-versity of Minnesota in 1942, but that is another story. As I was growing up, St. Paul was just fine, and just enough, for me. It had its own lakes and parks, beau-tiful old theaters downtown like the Paramount and the Orpheum, which still featured vaudeville acts and live performances by the Tommy Dorsey and Glenn Miller orchestras. And there were the Emporium and Golden Rule department stores with their array of goods our family could not afford. And then the dime stores where I loved to linger over displays of pencils, pens, scrapbooks and hard-ware supplies. What more could a boy want?

But was there something special about St. Paul? If there was I am not sure what it could have been. Of course, the place where you grow up always seems special to you because you do not know anything else. But as you develop and move away at a young age, as I did, the "specialness" if indeed there was any seems to disappear.

Minnesota has almost always been known as a clean, progressive state, and that is true. The old Farmer-Labor party was an important part of the progressive movement that swept through the plains states in the early years of the twentieth century. The Germans and Scandinavians who migrated to Minnesota brought with them church-going traditions of hard work, clean living and good educations for their children. The cold and snowy Minnesota winters also must have something to do with producing the sturdy, upright people who still seem to dominate the state.

I have always been proud to say that, yes, I am from Minnesota. But I still find it difficult to say what it was about Minnesota that made me what I am. The weather? My mother and father? My grade and high school teachers? Or something in the Minnesota air?

Who knows? Would I have preferred growing up in more prosperous times? Sure, but we are all dealt only one hand of cards when we are growing up, and I think I managed pretty well with what I found in my hands.

# 14

# *An Innocent Child of the Depression*

I tell everyone that I was a child of the Depression, the nation's worst economic decline, which began in 1929 with the stock market crash and did not end until 1942 after the United States entered World War II. The war had begun in 1939 with the German invasion of Poland. As I have noted elsewhere, my first memories date to 1928 when I was just four years old. Yet I have few memories of the Depression.

Why is that? I have often wondered. One of our neighbors was out of work for a long time. His wife found a secretarial job after a while and he tried to earn money by making rubber stamps in his basement. Rubber stamps have all but disappeared, but they were used everywhere in banks and all kinds of businesses in the nineteen thirties.

A man living across the street from us lost his job as a chauffeur and ended up in a much inferior job trying to sell Dad's Old-Fashioned Cookies to grocery stores. And as I have also noted elsewhere, earnings from paper routes helped keep some families afloat.

But the Depression was never a topic in our household. My father continued to work at the Emporium department store until 1937 when he was laid off, but even this terrible situation did not prompt my father or mother to talk with me about the Depression or about Franklin D. Roosevelt's New Deal efforts to turn around the reeling economy. I did know that things were tough for us when my father worked for a while with neighbor and friend Mr. Bour on construction projects. My father was so dejected and embarrassed at having to do such work that he walked up the alley in back of our house to meet Mr. Bour rather than expose himself and his overalls to the neighbors by using the front sidewalk.

I also knew we were in serious trouble when a man from Michaud's, the grocery store where we traded, came by one day, sat down with my mother at our dining room table and talked with her about how we could pay for the bills that had been piling up. Somehow, they were paid, but I have often wondered how my mother and father managed to do it.

Also, a few times my mother did not have the dime I wanted to see a Saturday matinee at the St. Clair theater, or a nickel for an ice cream cone at the St. Clair Sweet Shop.

Times were tough. Entertainment was confined to listening to the radio and going to an occasional movie. I ate lunch with my mother a few times at the Golden Rule department store's tea room, but otherwise we never went to a restaurant. I can remember going on a vacation only once—a few days fishing at one of Minnesota's ten thousand lakes. I also can remember visiting relatives in Sauk Rapids a few times.

It was not until I got to the University of Minnesota and began working as a reporter at the St. Paul Pioneer Press that I learned and realized how tough things really were in the nineteen thirties. For example, I was told that two of the editors at the Pioneer Press started working there in the early thirties without pay. Together with two other young men, they were taken on to "try out" for reporting jobs. The two who performed best were hired after a six-month trial and were then paid fifteen dollars a week.

My mother and father were conservative Republicans and never expressed much interest in politics. If they did talk about politics and the Depression, it must have been when I was in bed or otherwise out of sight. Still, I am puzzled why neither my mother or father ever sat me down to talk about the economic problems that faced them and their neighbors and friends—about "the facts of life," so to speak.

The only political comment I remember came when Floyd B. Olson, the governor of Minnesota, died in 1937. He was a member of the state's Farmer-Labor party—a sibling of Wisconsin's better-known Progressive party dominated by the LaFollette family. Olson died in his forties of cancer, and I still remember my mother gleefully announcing that she had heard on the radio that he had died.

She was happy to have heard the news, and felt that the state, the country and the world would be better off now that it was rid of Olson. He was sometimes called the "Huey Long of the North," a reference to the radical governor and then senator from Louisiana who also died young, from a bullet fired by an assassin. It was even said that Olson might have run for President had he lived.

The times were indeed tumultuous. But my mother and father seemed to want to shelter me from "the facts of life." Was it because I was an only child? Was it because I was thought to be too young to be told how bad the real world was? I don't know the answers, but I am still puzzled as I think back and realize how little I knew of so much of the world beyond Stanford Avenue, Randolph Heights school and Maria Sanford Junior High School, and Central High School and the St. Clair theater for that matter.

I did learn more about unemployment and other economic problems from my reading of the newspapers I was delivering and the newsreels—-Paramount News, "The Eyes and the Ears of the World" and Fox Movietone News with the sonorous and authoritative voice of Lowell Thomas, the Walter Cronkite of his day.

Nor, I should add, did I feel deprived or poor as I was growing up. Perhaps that is another reason why I did not realize or understand that a Depression had enveloped the country. Yes, we did not have a car, but many other people in our neighborhood did not have cars. Sure, we didn't go anywhere, but neither did anyone else. Yes, we ate simply, but good, and so did our neighbors. We did not have many clothes, or any fancy clothes, but we always looked decent and kept warm through those cold Minnesota winters.

Curiously, another important aspect of the nineteen thirties that I did know about at the time was the prevalence of gangsters. I knew about Al Capone, the legendary Chicago criminal; John Dillinger, another Chicago bad man who was killed outside a theater there when he was fingered by "the woman in red"; about Ma Barker; Bonnie and Clyde; and many others.

I also was quite aware of J. Edgar Hoover, the director of the Federal Bureau of Investigation, and his G-Men. I even had my own G-Man badge, and still have it. The badge came as a premium in a box of cereal, Wheaties, I think. Hoover and his G-Men were featured on a radio program, seen frequently in the news-reels and written about often in the newspapers. He and his G-Men were heroes to children and adults alike.

Also, St. Paul was sometimes a refuge for the gangsters based in Chicago. In the thirties St. Paul had a bad police department and was known as a safe place when "the heat was on" in Chicago. Once John Dillinger himself hid out in an apartment house not too far from Stanford Avenue, and I still remember scarily walking by the apartment house, almost on tip-toes and oh so quietly so as not to rouse anyone, after Dillinger had escaped.

The police department was later cleaned up and led by an honest, up-standing chief who lived in our neighborhood and was the father of a girl named Pat with whom I attended junior high school and high school. And I learned more about St. Paul's lurid, gangster-ridden past from reporters and editors at the Pioneer Press who had been there in the thirties.

It was not surprising that stories about gangsters and the G-Men were picked up much more easily by boys my age than were accounts of the Depression and the New Deal. Crime always has a genuine fascination. Economic matters are difficult for even adults to understand.

But what about what was going on in Europe in the thirties? Hitler? Mussolini? The Nazis? The Fascists? That is still another story, and for another chapter in the life of, I am afraid, this too innocent child of the thirties.

# 15

## A Boy—And Hitler

In 1933 I was eight years old—nine in November of that year—and aware of the world around me on Stanford Avenue, Randolph Heights grade school and some of downtown St. Paul. But I was not aware during most of the nineteen thirties of the Depression, as I have mentioned earlier, or of what was going on in Europe. In March of 1933 Franklin D. Roosevelt became president of the United States and just about at the same time Adolf Hitler became chancellor of Germany. In the Soviet Union Josef Stalin had been in power since the mid nineteen-twenties. These three men had more to do with the world I was living in as a boy and would live in for all of my adult life; yet I must confess that I was barely aware of Roosevelt, Hitler and Stalin as I was growing up. I have often wondered why this was so. Were my friends as ignorant as I was about the larger world and its increasing dangers? Did my parents know what was happening? Should my teachers have told me more? On and on the questions revolve in my head as I think back to the nineteen-thirties when I was growing up.

I began reading newspapers at any early age but tended to skip over articles from Washington or Europe. Early on I also read magazines, but mostly Boys' Life, Open Road for Boys and pulp fiction magazines about cowboys and Indians and detectives.

I also read Big Little Books and comic books. In grade school we received My Weekly Reader, a small, four-page publication which as I remember featured pleasant stories about "good" people doing useful things for their school or community. In junior high school and high school we graduated to Scholastic, a magazine of twelve or sixteen pages that again stressed good news.

My parents did not talk about what was going on in Europe any more than they discussed President Roosevelt and his New Deal efforts to lift the country out of the Depression. At least they did not talk about such things in my presence.

I have no memories of reading or hearing anything about communism, the Soviet Union and Stalin when I was growing up in the thirties. Yet these were the times of the terrible trials in the Soviet Union and of the killings of hundreds of thousands if not millions of Russians. My mother did say, "What are you, a Bolshevik?" sometimes when I misbehaved. But I didn't know until later that for her and many others the word "Bolshevik" was a synonym for Communist.

My first memory of Hitler came with his invasion of Czechoslovakia—or the Sudetenland—in 1937. I didn't really understand, though, whether Hitler had a right to this land. I also remember a year later when Hitler took over Austria. As German storm troopers marched into Vienna I knew that he was doing something wrong. I also remember crystal-nacht when Germans and Austrians smashed in the widows of shops owned by Jews in Vienna.

During those years in the late nineteen-thirties I did not connect Hitler's activities with war. I was vaguely aware of World War I—then still known as the Great War. My father had not been in the war, but I had heard about his brother who had died shortly after the war ended from the effects of being gassed during the conflict. Also, Great War veterans appeared at Randolph Heights assemblies marking Memorial Day—then often called Decoration Day because flowers were left on that day on the graves of men killed in the Great War—and on Armistice Day—now called Veterans Day—which on November 11 marked the end of the Great War.

I have thought, too, that my parents did not want to talk about Hitler and Germany because my father had been born in East Prussia when it was still part of Germany and my mother's father had served in the Prussian army before he immigrated to the United States. My mother and father could well remember the Great War and the anti-German feelings in the United States during the time of the war. Perhaps, I have since wondered, they did not want to talk about Hitler and Germany in the thirties for fear that such talk would stir up feelings that they were sympathetic to Germany because of their ancestry.

As I have noted elsewhere, too, my father was proud that he worked for the Emporium and not for the rival Golden Rule store, which he said was owned by Jews. Were my parents anti-Semites? I don't think so, but anti-Semitism was not uncommon in those days. As for myself, I did not know any Jews until I was in high school.

At any rate, war blew into the consciousness of most Americans when the Germans invaded Poland on September 1, 1939. I recall that day almost as well as I remember Pearl Harbor day—December 7, 1941. I heard the news of the invasion of Poland on the radio, and still remember a newsboy coming up Stanford Avenue that afternoon hawking an extra edition of the St. Paul Pioneer Press.

From 1939 on I was quite aware of what was happening in Europe. The German's easy victory in Poland. The German Panzer divisions. The French Maginot Line. Germans overrunning Belgium and the Netherlands and then bypassing the Maginot Line to arrive as conquerors in Paris. And finally the alliance between Hitler and Stalin.

Still, during all of these battles and other events related to the war I did not hear much about the conflict from my mother and father or from my teachers in either grade school or junior high school. Were they afraid to talk to children about these horrific events? Were these matters simply too awful for children to understand? Again, I don't know the reasons for my hearing so little about the events that led up to World War II and the beginnings of the war.

I have not yet mentioned Mussolini and the Fascists in Italy because I heard and knew even less about them. I do remember hearing that Mussolini made the trains run on time, right? Nor have I mentioned British Prime Minister Neville Chamberlain and his meeting with Hitler in Munich after which Chamberlain proclaimed "peace in our time" as its result because I was not aware of that historic encounter at the time.

Was it my fault that I grew up in the thirties so ignorant of the wider world around me? Or was it the fault of my parents? Or my teachers? I simply don't know. And would it have made any difference if I had been more aware of what was going on in the United States? Or Europe? Or Asia, for that matter?

All I knew about China was that it was a strange, kind of forbidding place where missionaries went to convert the heathen folk. I knew even less about Japan, except toward the end of the thirties when the Japanese were invading Manchuria—or Manchuko, as it was called then. As for India, I had heard of Mahatma Gandhi, a strange man who wore hardly any clothes and always sat cross-legged but in a prayerful position.

But I guess for now I should just rest my discussion about my woeful ignorance of the big and fractious world out there. I realize now that a lot of Americans in the nineteen-thirties were shutting the larger world out of their consciousness. In those Depression years there were too many things to worry about at home. And in those days before jet airplanes Europe and Asia were indeed far away and out of mind and out of sight.

# PART III

# A Reporter at the Age of 18

# 16

## *Watching Kelly's Spike*

My life-long love affair with newspapers began when I was ten years old and started reading more than the comic pages first of the soon to be gone St. Paul Daily News and then of the St. Paul Dispatch and Pioneer Press. At about that time I also sketched out small front pages of newspapers as I sat at my desk. The front pages included make-believe headlines.

Then as I graduated to junior high school and high school and worked on the school papers, I had paper routes that provided me with spending money and enhanced my growing interest in newspapers. From an early age I loved the smell of the printed paper and miss it now that new inks and printing processes that leave no discernible smell are used.

My first job in a newspaper office came in the fall of 1942 when I was entering the University of Minnesota as a freshman. (More about the "U", as we called the university, and my life there will come later, although my newspaper work and academic life quickly converged.)

My introduction to newspaper work came at a low level in the circulation department. At this distance I am a little vague as to how I got the job, but I think it was on the recommendation of the district circulation manager who liked how conscientious I was as a carrier.

However it happened, I found myself at a desk in the circulation department on the first floor of the Dispatch and Pioneer Press building at 55 East Fourth street in downtown St. Paul. Not only do I still remember the address but also the papers' telephone number, Cedar 5011.

I reported for work at 4 p.m. My job was to answer the telephone, which rang frequently. The callers were subscribers who had not received their paper and carriers who needed to adjust their "draw", the number of papers to be sent to them the next day. The complaints about non-delivery were immediately forwarded to the carrier involved with a telephone call to him. (No girls were carriers in those days.)

The only other person in the circulation department at that time of day was a young woman who also worked part-time in the afternoons as a secretary. She also took telephone calls and was what I guess you could call a flirt, wearing tight dresses and flashing heavily red-lipped smiles at me all too often. After all, I was only eighteen years old and by no means a man about town.

I worked about four hours each evening, leaving at around eight o'clock. Either I or my flirty friend would duck around the corner to a deli just before it closed at six o'clock and come back with sandwiches and Cokes. I also had to work Sunday mornings to take complaints from people who had not received their all-important Sunday papers.

After a couple of months on the circulation department job I made known my interest in becoming a copy boy in the city room. And before the year was out, to my amazement, I was a copy boy.

But before I move from the first floor circulation department to the third floor city room, I should mention a thin, harried man who always seemed to be working in the advertising department, which was adjacent to our circulation desks. He was generally hunched over what I guess was an IBM machine, shoving cards into the contraption and pulling them out once holes had been punched in them. I never did quite understand what he was doing, but later decided that the machine was some kind of an early computer that was being used to keep track of advertising accounts. Nor do I know whatever happened to this hapless man, who looked like he never slept and was never able to get on top of his job.

I was thrilled to be in a real city room, if only as a copy boy. I had been in the room only once before, when I was in high school and the editors of high school papers were invited for a tour of the paper one afternoon. Our visit was short and I hardly had a chance to take in the room. But now I could.

It was a long and fairly narrow room. From the elevator you walked down a hall to get to the city room. On the left were glassed-in offices for the society or women's department headed by Amy Birdsall, whose white hair was dyed a bluish color; an office for a man named Howard Kahn, the last editor of the St. Paul Daily News who wrote a chit-chat column, under the pseudonym of Paul Light (Get it? We were all St. Paulites as residents of the city.) Then came the photographers studio and finally the morgue, presided over by a quiet, scholarly-looking man and inhabited by older women who were forever cutting up newspapers and filing clippings in the drawers in the many cabinets that filled the morgue, or library.

To the right as you entered the city room were the offices of the editor, Herbert Lewis, a balding man who always played with a strain of what little hair he had left while he was writing, and his—and the city room's—secretary, an older woman who I was told was an old maid. She was important to all of us though because she handed out the weekly checks. I can't remember for sure' but I think my came to around fifteen dollars.

The telegraph editor sat not too far from the top editor's office. Dwight Jones, the telegraph editor known as "Jonesy" handled all the wire copy. The Associated Press and United Press machines were close to him and pounded out a steady typewriting sound. Occasionally bells on the machines rang, signaling the coming of an important story. Usually there were only three bells, but the occasional five bells meant a "flash" and a truly important news development.

Next to the telegraph editor—who retained that title from the old days when news did come over telegraph lines—was the U-shaped copy desk, presided over by Quintus Wilson, a quiet man who during the day was pursuing a doctorate in journalism at the "U". Around the rim, as it was called sat four or five copy readers. Quint, as everyone referred to him, passed the stories he got from the telegraph and city editors to the copy readers who edited them and wrote the headlines. Quint laid out the pages, deciding where stories would go. Later in the evening one of the copy readers, Ernie Larson, went down to the composing room to supervise the printers making up the pages.

The city editor was Bill Greer, a man whose striding walk and deep voice told you that he was a man of the West. He was from Montana and earlier in his life traveled the West searching out and photographing unusual outhouses. He gave them outlandish names like the castle or the apartment (two stories) and collected them in a little book, which I still have called Gems of American Architecture. The book was published by Brown & Bigelow, a company in St. Paul that specialized in calendars and small books suitable for distribution by companies as advertising. It was said that Bill made a fair amount of money from his gems.

The city editor sat at one of four desks pushed together to form what everyone called the city desk. One of the reporters who sat there was a rewrite man who took calls from the police reporter and other reporters who were out of the office covering a story on deadline. The rewrite man had to be fast in taking notes and in writing a story.

T. Roy Kelly, the night editor, sat at a desk close to both the desks of the telegraph editor and the city editor. The sports desk was on the other side of the room and divided from the city and copy desks by the stairs that led to the composing room on the floor below. There were always a few sports reporters and editors around in the evenings. One would be writing a column, others would be editing stories at a U-shaped desk similar to but smaller than the copy desk.

Just past the sports writers and editors was the Associated Press Wirephoto machine operated at night by a young woman. It was a fairly new innovation and I think was similar to today's fax machines. Pictures were transmitted from Associated Press headquarters in New York to the Pioneer Press and other newspapers throughout the country. The pictures came in rather slowly on a small device like a rolling pin that turned round and round. They were negatives that had to be developed in a small photo laboratory close to the machine. The woman who operated the machine and developed the pictures would rush them to Kelly or Quint Wilson who would then decide whether to publish them.

Across the room from the Wirephoto machine sat a rather sad looking man who was a telegrapher. I was told that during the day he worked for Western Union and then moonlighted at the Pioneer Press. He sat in a straight wooden chair before two strips of metal standing a foot or so apart which I soon learned transmitted the dots and dashes of the Morse code which as they came in were put into words by this little old man on a dilapidated typewriter that sat in front of him. Dispatches from the Pioneer Press Washington correspondent came in this way, as did St. Paul Saints stories when the baseball team was on the road. The paper did not send a reporter with the team when it was on the road, relying instead on local sportwriters in American Association cities to cover the games with stories running from three hundred to five hundred words at the most. I always felt sorry for the telegrapher, who was always so worn out and tired and often fell asleep when he was waiting for a story to dot-dash its way into the city room.

The rest of the city room was filled with desks, the tops of which were strewn with papers. Few of these desks were occupied in the evening because the paper had a small night staff. Beat reporters like those who covered city hall, the courts, schools and the state government for the Dispatch during the day also had to write for the Pioneer Press if something happened on their beat too late for the Dispatch's fairly early deadlines. Pioneer Press reporters were general assignment men.

The back of the city room was lined with offices for the editorial writers, the book and music critics, the artists who worked during the day and a Dispatch humor columnist named P.J. Hoffstrom whose daily offerings were headed Hawf and Hawf by Hoff. He was also a cartoonist and traveled widely in Minnesota giving chalk talks. Once a week he published a diary modeled after Pepys' diary including many old English phrases like betimes. Later he went on to the big time in Chicago, becoming an early television weatherman while still doing his cartoons.

Most of the editors wore green eyeshades I guess to protect their eyes from the fluorescent fixtures that lighted the city room. I always wanted an eyeshade and some years later one of my children gave me one as a birthday present.

My hours were four o'clock to midnight and I was thrilled to be shown around the city room on my first day, being introduced to some of the reporters and editors of the morning Pioneer Press. I was shown around by the copy boy I was succeeding. He was going on to a beginning reporter's job on the evening Dispatch.

My job consisted of running copy from desk to desk, going downstairs to the composing every 15 minutes or so to pick up proofs and sometimes going on errands outside the building to pick up sandwiches at the deli around the corner and even getting a bottle or two of whiskey from the liquor store up the street. Even though I was only 18 years old and three years shy of the 21-year age limit for purchasing beer or liquor, I had no trouble picking up the whiskey once I identified myself as being from the paper.

I also contributed a little to the paper. Before coming to work I stopped at the city hall a couple blocks away to gather the daily lists of births and marriages and, on Fridays, divorces, which were not so common then and were compiled only once a week. When I got to the office I pasted up the lists and gave them to the copy editor to be put in the paper. Later each evening I got a call from the police reporter—more about him later—with the day's fire runs and ambulance runs, which I took down and made ready for publication. It was then that I learned what DOA meant (dead on arrival). Every evening I also checked with the theaters to get the times they were showing movies and typed up that list. Finally, at nine o'clock when what we called the front desk closed, I went down to the first floor to pick up the death notices that were brought or phoned in to the woman on duty there. I took the death notices to the morgue—or the library—to check them against the clips. If I found any mention in the clips of a deceased person, I pulled the clips and showed then to the city editor to see if the person was worthy of an obit (obituary). I also gave all the death notices to the city editor so he could check them over for news-worthy names. I was always amazed at how many people he knew if only by name.

But my most important task, I was told right away, was to "watch Kelly's spike". T. Roy Kelly was the big, red-faced Irishman who was the editor of the Pioneer Press. The telegraph editor and city editor gave Kelly stories that were candidates for page one or otherwise of imporT. He read them over and noted on the stories what he wanted done with them and then put them on the spike on his desk. And I was told that he did not like to see stories lingering on his spike.

So when one appeared I was immediately to jump up and take it over to the copy editor for editing and to have a headline written for it. I sat a few feet across from Kelly and nervously kept my eyes on his spike all evening. Kelly cowed the editors and reporters but I never myself heard a cross word from him. Spikes, by the way, were all over the city room. They were six or so inches high and were used for all kinds of stories. The telegraph editor used several of them to sort out The Associated Press and United Press dispatches that were his responsibility.

Late in the evenings came the most interesting time for me when I went down to the composing room to pick up proofs of the front page and the section page where the most important local news stories were placed. The copy editor cut up the front page and the city editor cut up the section page. They distributed the stories to the copy editors and reporters to read to catch any errors or sometimes to make last-minute changes. Then I rushed the stories back down to the composing room where any changes were made and the pages were made ready for the presses. Finally before I went home I took the elevator down to the basement and dashed through a tunnel to the press room which was across the street to pick up a few copies of the early edition as they came off the press. The press room was noisy but the smell of the ink was pungent and wonderful and I loved the caps the pressmen made from a newspaper page to keep the dust and dirt out of their hair. After rushing the papers back to the editors in the city room it was time for me to go home and fall into bed exhausted but so happy to be at least an apprentice newspaperman.

The composing room was an exciting place, too, with its clattering linotype machines where skilled operators set type one line at a time and with the tables or stones where pages were made up. I did not, however, like my introduction to the composing room when I was asked if I had ever seen type lice. I of course had not seen or even heard of such creatures and was eager to actually see one. Well, said a printer, look very closing at this corner of a frame for a page, or a chase as it was more properly called. I bent over and looked closely as the printer pushed a line of type into the corner splashing dirty water into my eager and innocent face. The printer and his colleagues who had gathered around laughed and laughed as I smiled wanly and sulked back upstairs to the safety of my desk in the city room. I quickly was told by Bill Greer not to be offended as this was a rite every innocent copy boy and young reporter goes through.

Later I got to know some of the printers and liked most of them. I was intrigued by the history, lore and even adventure of the printing process, which now is sadly gone as computerized systems have taken over. They may be more efficient but they are not nearly as exciting and romantic as hot type with its noisy machines and delightful smells from printer's ink and smoldering lead for the linotype machines. I also wonder whatever happened to the jolly Pioneer Press printer who seemed to spend more time making book both in the composing room and the city room on baseball and football than he did sitting at a linotype.

# 17

## 'Oh, that's Just a Nigger Murder'

My days were long, but I was eighteen years old and excited that I was spending evenings and nights in a city room, even though I was just a lowly copy boy. But I was reminded more than once that many famous journalists had begun as copy boys. And I was never treated with condescension.

For me the day began at eight in the morning with classes at the "U". So I had to get up at six o'clock to get dressed and drive to the campus in Minneapolis. I often was tired, but I don't remember ever falling asleep in a classroom. By mid-afternoon I had to drive back to St. Paul and downtown to the Pioneer Press and Dispatch offices on Fourth street. Parking in those days was easy and I almost always could find a spot a block or so away from the offices. Dinner was usually from a deli around the corner and consisted of a sandwich and a Coke.

At that time the University of Minnesota was probably most famous for its football team, led by coach Bernie Bierman. The team was a power in the Big Ten Conference and its arch rivals included next-door-neighbor University of Wisconsin and further to the east University of Michigan. The winner of the annual Minnesota-Michigan game got possession of the Little Brown Jug for a year. The Minnesota Gophers became the Golden Gophers, and they deserved the accolade.

Academic life at the "U" did not seem too strenuous to me during my fresh-man year even though I was much more interested in my work at the Pioneer Press than I was in my studies.

In the fall of 1943 soon after I began my sophomore year I was called into edi-tor Herb Lewis' office and told that I had impressed everyone as a conscientious copy boy and was being promoted to a beginning reporter's job. I would start reporting as soon as I trained a successor for my copy boy work. I was walking on air. A real reporter! Wonderful! I could hardly wait to tell my mother and father. They were excited, too, even though my mother had wanted me to become a law-yer.

By 1943 the United States was deep into World War II and there was a man-power shortage. I was not drafted into the Army because of my poor eyesight. My near-sightedness had gotten worse since I started wearing glasses as a ten-year-old. I had decidedly mixed feelings about my being classified a 4-F, unfit for military service. My friends were going into the Army or the Navy and there was a certain stigma to be a 4-F, almost as if you were a draft dodger. On the other hand, I was scared of going into the military. Already I had heard of friends or neighbors who had been wounded or killed in the war. I still remember the sight of a neighbor-hood man coming into the corner drug store trying to hide his right arm. His hand had been shot off. He was despondent, and I have often wondered what happened to him in the rest of a life that had been shattered at so young an age.

And here I was a few weeks shy of my nineteenth birthday becoming—I am sure I thought—a big-shot reporter. I even sat at one of the three reporter desks that together with the city editor's desk made up the heart of the Pioneer Press city room. The man I replaced, Bob Eddy, went off to the war.

Also at the desk was Norm Katkov, who was in his early twenties, and had actually sold a short story to the Saturday Evening Post and would go on to write novels, a couple of which were made into movies. Norm was also famous for run-ning up a huge long-distance telephone bill talking to his girl friend in New York.

The third reporter at the desk was Walt Quigley, an older man who had been a law partner of Charles Lindbergh's father—the Lindberghs were Minneso-tans—but had been disbarred, for what infractions I never knew. Quig, as every-one called him, knew a lot of people and was a good reporter. He also chewed tobacco and spit frequently in the spittoon he kept at his feet. There were several spittoons in the Pioneer Press city room to accommodate the chewers of both tobacco and cigars. Quig was bothered by the Minnesota weather and always checked out the warm San Antonio, Texas, temperatures, repeating them and exclaiming, "God! What a climate!' I guess he visited San Antonio once and liked its dry climate. Quig also did some moonlighting, putting out the Minnesota edi-tion of the Townsend movement's monthly tabloid newspaper. The Townsend plan was a popular Depression-era movement seeking pensions for retired people. Townsend rallies began with the singing of "What a friend we have in Dr. Townsend..." to the tune of "What a friend we have in Jesus...All our fears and troubles to bear...." And when Quig had too much to drink or was just sitting around waiting for telephone calls he would start singing the Townsend song, and sometimes city editor Bill Greer would join in.

As the neophyte on the staff I got most of the obits—obituaries—that were generally called in by funeral directors who knew exactly what information we wanted and I am sure charged the mourners for the call. It was said that obits were good training because if you got something wrong in an obit a distraught relative would make sure the paper heard about it.

The obits were easy to write as they followed a formula—name, age, address, job or jobs held, church affiliation if any, survivors and so on. Today many newspapers are trying hard to make obits more interesting by including material about the deceased's hobbies and high points in his or her life. At the Pioneer Press we did check in the morgue for additional material on a person whose obit was called in by a funeral director. But most of the obits stuck to a formula. Obits were well-read then and still are today.

The hardest obits to take over the phone and to write were from a family reporting the death of a son in the war. Often the mother or father would be crying and I would be feeling remorse, thinking that there but for the grace a God—or actually bad eyesight—go I.

As a beginner I also took many police shorts—short pieces from the police reporter about minor crimes or accidents. St. Paul had just a central police station—no precinct stations—that also was the headquarters for the fire chief and his department. There were fire stations throughout the city, which then had a population of around 300,000.

Nate Bomberg was the police reporter. He had been on the job for a long time and knew many of the cops personally, and some of the criminals, too, I think. He remembered the early thirties when St. Paul was a favorite hideout for gangsters when the heat was on in Chicago.

Nate was a short man who dressed well, usually in a sport coat and matching pants. He always wore a neat white shirt and a colorful tie. But what I remember most about him is that he was the first man I ever saw who had polished finger nails. He obviously saw a manicurist every so often. He was single and came into the office before going to the police station where he was on duty from five-thirty in the evening until two the next morning. He would chat with reporters and editors and read the afternoon Dispatch.

Like so many other police reporters of that day and this, Nate never wrote a story. Instead, he dictated the information that would make a story. A rewrite man took it all down and did the actual writing. And that was one of my jobs as I was starting out. It was easy work because Nate almost wrote the story for you as he dictated the facts. One of the things I learned was whenever possible to include the name of the policeman involved in the story. Like everyone else, cops like to see their names in print, and the publishing of the names also might help in bringing particular police to the attention of their supervisors.

I also learned from taking dictation from Nate that certain things did not make it into the paper. If there had been an incident in a downtown store attracting police attention, the name of the store never appeared in the paper because the store was a good advertiser. I also discovered that the black residents—or the colored community, as it was then called—did not merit a mention. There were few blacks in St. Paul at that time, but there was some crime in the black sections of town.

But as Nate shuffled through the police reports in front of him as he was talking to me he would says things like "Oh, that's just a nigger murder." And move on to something else.

In my first months on the job I pretty much stayed in the office, taking obits, taking rewrite from Nate, rewriting press releases and covering stories by telephone. The Pioneer Press was thinly staffed and because of wartime restrictions on paper use the news hole was always pretty tight. And the war of course was the big news and took up a lot of space every night.

But what I did seemed to satisfy or even impress Bill Greer, the city editor. He was a man, I guess, in his mid-thirties, but of course he seemed old to me, a nineteen-year-old. He was always helpful, giving tips on how to handle stories ranging from obits to telephonic reports of meetings. With experience first as a reporter and then as an editor over a ten-year period he knew St. Paul well and usually could tell you whom to get in touch with to check out something.

Years later when Bill died and I was writing an occasional newspaper column I wrote a piece about him, titling it "My First Boss." It was published in the Pioneer Press, among other papers, and I received a note from Bill's son saying I had caught his father better than any other article written about him after his death. In the column I noted that inside his outwardly Montana gruffness was a sweet person always wanting to help bring along a young reporter.

Other reporters I remember were Ev Peterson, a beginner like myself, Walt Streitif, a veteran who had come over to St. Paul from one of the Minneapolis papers, and Fred Neumeyer, another old-timer who sat in as city editor on the weekends. He was a big man with a loud voice and I still remember his calling Governor Luther Youngdahl—you could reach a governor directly in those days even at home without going through a press secretary—and after apologizing for interrupting perhaps his dinner questioning him about a development in the news affecting the state. Usually Fred got a good answer from the governor which improved the story. I also remember Fred in his city editor role on Saturday when an excited Ev Peterson, who covered police on the weekends and would call in during the evening with what he considered a pretty good story for the big Sunday paper. "Yeah, Ev," Fred would say and listen attentively for a few minutes and then say, "It's a helluva good story, Ev—for Monday's paper." The Sunday paper was a huge production job, and only a truly big story justified a makeover which meant stopping the old and overburdened presses.

Then Fred would turn back to the cribbage game that he and two or three copy editors engaged in to while away Saturday nights. The stakes were low but sometimes the language got loud. A nice thing about Saturday nights is that Fred and two or three reporters would go out for dinner at about six-thirty or seven o'clock at a nice cafeteria down Fourth Street and around the corner on Robert Street. It was often the only decent dinner I had all week. I particularly remember the stories told around the dinner table about the good old days, and the luscious hot-fudge sundae served by the restaurant.

The four or five copy readers were a grizzled lot. A couple had worked on several other papers—the peripatetic copy reader being one of the romantic journalists of the time. One copy reader was a big drinker who kept his bottle in a large wire basket in the men's room where used paper towels were thrown. He tried to disguise his drinking by first buying a nickel bottle of Coke from a machine in the hall outside the men's room, pouring out half the Coke into a sink in the men' room and filling the Coke bottle with whiskey. I don't think he fooled anyone though, and he seemed to be able to edit copy and write headlines without too much trouble through the night.

Another copy reader also doubled as the art editor, which meant for the most part that he air brushed and otherwise retouched photos to highlight the principal people in the pictures or to make a building or bridge, say, stand out as the focus of the picture. Sometimes he would draw a small cartoon to drop into the text of a not-too-serious feature story. He had an extra-curricular activity, too. He liked to write letters to the editor. He had to do that under a pseudonym because the Pioneer Press had a rule that no employee of the paper could write a letter to the editor. But the copy reader's letters did get printed, and he delighted in taking issue with the paper's editorials.

Another reporter who I remember with a certain fondness was Norm Himle. I think he was Finnish. He was a bald fat man with a cherubic face and grin. When I first knew him he was fighting demon rum. The editor's secretary was given Norm's weekly paycheck and she cashed it for Norm and doled out money to him day by day or maybe three times a week so that he would never have enough money to go on a bender. He also was trying to give up smoking and when he arrived at work his desk became a veritable candy shop as he unloaded Baby Ruths, Milky Ways, Doublemint gum, Lifesavers and other candies from his bulging coat pockets. He felt that if he kept his mouth busy with sweets he would not be constantly craving cigarettes.

# 18

## *From City Room to Campus*

The constantly smoking and hard-drinking reporters is a city room cliché of the twenties, thirties and forties, and I guess there was some truth in it. I never smoked, but I was the only one in the Pioneer Press city room who did not smoke. I was not old enough to drink legally when I began as a reporter, but as I have noted we had at least one hard-drinking copy reader, a reporter trying to wean himself from the bottle, and then there was Kelly.

Kelly came to work at five-thirty in the evening and was supposed to be on duty until two in the morning, which was soon after the final edition went to press. But he would sometimes disappear to the Court Bar up the street at nine or ten o'clock and never return. Before leaving the city room he had laid out the front page, and in his absence the city, copy and telegraph editors put the paper to bed. I don't know if the top editor and the publisher knew of Kelly's drinking, but if they did they must have found other reasons to keep him on because he stayed on the job for several more years before going to an editing position on a larger paper in Florida.

I worked as a rewrite man and general assignment reporter through 1944 and into 1945 and even covered some political news for the 1944 elections which saw Franklin D. Roosevelt reelected to an unprecedented fourth term as president. In those days the Pioneer Press had a rule that said that space given to two candidates running for, say, mayor or Congress should be absolutely equal, and a ruler was used to measure the stories.

One candidate I remember well was Hubert Humphrey, later a Senator and Vice President under Lyndon Johnson. But as a Pioneer Press reporter I covered Humphrey when he was first running for mayor of Minneapolis. I still remember a speech of his given at the University of Minnesota. Even that early in his political career he was a powerful and engaging speaker. He did not win his first try for mayor, but he was victorious two years later and never again lost a race until he ran for president against Richard Nixon in 1968.

My interest in politics was piqued by early days at the Pioneer Press—even though city editor Bill Greer said the only way to look at a politician was down—as well as by my university friends Keith Peterson and Bob Gove. They were both law students and greatly interested in politics. The three of us frequently talked and argued about politics over coffee or lunch in the Coffman Memorial Union.

And Minnesota politics at that time was fascinating. There was the Farmer-Labor party in addition to the Democrats and Republicans. During the 1930's the Farmer-Labor party dominated the state with its governor, Floyd B. Olson, whose radicalism earned him the sobriquet, "the Huey Long of the North." Olson died in his early forties of cancer, and his party began to wither.

But then came the ascension of Harold Stassen, a charismatic Republican lawyer who became governor in 1938 at the age of 32. As early as 1944 he was being talked about as a presidential candidate and was one in 1948, losing the Republican nomination to New York governor Thomas E. Dewey who in turn was defeated in the general election by Harry Truman.

During the 1940's the Farmer-Labor party, which was infiltrated somewhat by the Communists, joined forces with the Democratic party to form what is still the Minnesota DFL. Humphrey was instrumental in bringing the two parties together. Elections for mayor in Minnesota are non-partisan, but Humphrey made no secret that he was a Democrat.

I covered bits and pieces of the 1944 local campaigns, but most of the coverage went to veteran reporters like Lu Parlin, who had even been a Washington correspondent, and Quig, who in his previous life had been involved in Farmer-Labor party machinations.

What I remember most about 1944 were the reports from Europe of the horrible World War II battles, particularly the winter Battle of the Bulge. My reporting remained for the most part the coverage of fairly routine stories—minor crime, obits about pretty ordinary people, accounts of civic dinners, evening chamber of commerce meetings and the like.

Meanwhile, I continued taking classes at the "U" but cut back to two rather than four each quarter. I joined a fraternity, Kappa Sigma, and also found time to write a column once or twice a week for the Minnesota Daily, the student newspaper. The column was labeled "Foot Prints," for what reason I have long forgotten, and consisted of sometimes rather inane comments on university life. I certainly wrote nothing for the ages.

As 1945 began the center of my life remained the Pioneer Press. The day I remember most from that year was the day Roosevelt died. I can still remember coming to work on a pleasant April afternoon and suddenly hearing the bells on the Associated Press and United Press machines clang five times, signalling a Flash! Editors and reporters ran to the machines and read the Flash! announcing Roosevelt's death. The instant reaction in the city room, as in most other places, was Oh My God! Now all we have is that terrible, incompetent Vice President Harry Truman, a product of the notorious Pendergast gang in Missouri. Well, we were all wrong. Truman became one of our better presidents.

That night I ended up writing a story recalling Roosevelt's visits to Minnesota, including an important speech about the economy that he made on a trip to St. Paul in 1932 during his first campaign for the presidency.

The war in Europe ended in May, a month after Roosevelt died, and the fighting with the Japanese in the Pacific was over in the summer. I wrote some stories about the end-of-the-war celebrations in St. Paul and elsewhere in Minnesota.

And then the soldiers began coming home, and reporters and editors who had been called to or enlisted in the services came back to the Pioneer Press. Advertising picked up, the news hole was increased, the staff expanded and I was given a new assignment.

And it turned out to be a great assignment. I was to report on the University of Minnesota, located mostly in Minneapolis, covering everything from the Board of Regents meetings and other "U" politics to the medical school and the Farm Campus. The Pioneer Press had a reporter covering the university before the war, but dropped the coverage during the war because of space and budget constraints. The "U" was considered a plum assignment because there was always so much going on.

I had no office of my own on the campus, but I was able to use a desk in the university public relations office on an upper floor of the building housing the Memorial Auditorium, where large lecture-classes for a thousand or more students were held and where the Minneapolis Symphony Orchestra practiced many afternoons and gave concerts three nights a week.

The university had three public relations men—an older fellow who was on the verge of retirement and did not seem to do much, a younger man who had just returned from the war and did the day-to-day press releases and a middle-aged man who was supposed to be a hot-shot hired to burnish the university's name. Later a young woman was hired to help write the press releases.

Except for covering obvious stories like Board of Regents meetings or press conferences by the university president or one of the deans, I pretty much could cover what I wanted. I had to cover spot news for both the evening Dispatch and the morning Pioneer Press, which meant that sometimes I had to dictate stories on deadline for the Dispatch. But that was good training and I soon learned how important speed was to a reporter's development.

I particularly liked the Farm Campus in St. Paul which had its own public relations office headed by an avuncular man who later went on to Chicago to become editor of the prestigious Prairie Farmer Magazine. The Farm Campus not only yielded news of developments in agriculture but also good feature stories on, say, why you should eat more vegetables, less meat but more chicken.

I also liked to go the Farm Campus because if I was not driving it meant two great street-car rides, one from the main campus on a special inter-campus line that ran through a wooded area and the other on a route from the Farm Campus to downtown St. Paul that traversed the city's Como Park which included a small lake.

# 19

## *A Blind Date—And Marriage*

I worked hard covering the University of Minnesota and some days my stories were in both the Pioneer Press and the Dispatch. I also did stories that were accompanied by pictures in the Sunday rotogravure section. Rotogravure was a printing process that produced brownish-tinted pictures much sharper than the quality of the pictures on ordinary newsprint. I did some of my writing in the university's public-relations office, but I also went back to the Pioneer Press city room most days to finish stories and to check in with the editors.

There was considerable competition on the university beat. The evening Minneapolis Star and the morning Minneapolis Tribune each had a reporter covering the university, and they were older and much more experienced than I was. And the Minnesota Daily, with its many student-reporters, was also competition, but I got my share of exclusive stories and I always thought I was ahead of the competition with bright feature stories.

One assignment I always liked was doing what was called a "color story" when the Minnesota football team played on Saturdays at home. These were stories about the mood of the crowd, high-school band day, the fathers of players, homecoming day and the like. The stories always ended up on the front page. Sometimes though I had to leave the game at half-time because of deadlines which were earlier than during the week because of the time it took to print the large Sunday paper.

I kept taking a couple of courses each university quarter—the academic year was divided into three periods or quarters of twelve weeks each with the fourth quarter of the year being summer session for make-up work and other special classes.

Soon after I started covering the university I moved into the Kappa Sigma fraternity house, which was located a few blocks from the campus near a collection of shops, restaurants and a movie theater called Dinkytown. Most of the businesses catered to students, and it was a lively area.

Fraternity life was different. Most of the Kappa Sigma members, fifty or so in all, were just back from the war. There was a lot of drinking, beer for the most part, but there were also some very serious fraternity brothers, one of whom became a political science professor. Because of my work as a reporter I could not participate as fully as I would have liked. I seldom, for example, was able to have dinner at the fraternity house and usually had lunch there only two or three times a week because of my busy schedule.

Three of my best high school friends—Fred Claasen, Bill Olson and Otto Meeker—were Kappa Sigs. Others I remember included a feisty, and funny Irishman, named Kelly, of course, and Billy Black, a handsome young man with an unfortunately large taste for beer and other alcoholic beverages which later led to a tragic end as an alcoholic.

One day Billy asked me if I wanted to risk a blind-date and go out with him and his girl friend the following Saturday night. I did not have a girl friend at the time; so I said why not. That Saturday we went a couple of blocks from the fraternity house to a rooming house to pick up his friend Barbara and her friend Priscilla McBride. It was a pleasant evening. After the movie, which was at one of the big downtown theaters in Minneapolis (part of Mr. Stiff's fiefdom), we stopped in a nearby bar for a beer. We were served even though only Billy was at the drinking age of twenty-one.

Thus began a whole new chapter in my life. I asked Priscilla McBride to go out with me the next Saturday night; we went to a movie by ourselves and talked a lot afterwards over a couple of beers. I learned that she was from Sioux City, Iowa, that her father was a pediatrician and that she was a junior at Minnesota, having gone for her first two years of college to a girl's school in Jacksonville, Illinois. She was majoring in psychology and Spanish and thinking about teaching in a South American country where Spanish was spoken. She had a sister Barbara and a brother Bill, both younger than her.

Priscilla was pretty. She had blond hair, a nice smile and a good figure. She was rather shy and I don't think she had dated much before we met. And she was almost the same age as I was, only a month younger. We met in February and soon were seeing each other two or three times a week. In a month or two I "pinned" her, which meant that I gave her my fraternity pin to wear and that we were "going steady". And I guess we were falling in love.

As the Minnesota snows melted and the trees began to bud, we were already thinking of marriage. Something clicks, and it did for us. We were together more and more. She was fascinated with my work as a reporter and sometimes accompanied me to the office when I had to finish up writing stories. All of my high-school and fraternity-brother friends liked her.

We decided we should get married that summer, at her home in Sioux City. I introduced Priscilla to my mother and father and Aunt Emma and they all seemed to like her. But later when I talked to my mother about our plans to get married, she asked: "Is she Catholic?" McBride could easily be a Catholic name. No, mother, she isn't Catholic; in fact, she is Methodist. Well, as far as my mother was concerned Methodist wasn't quite as good as being Lutheran, but it sure was better than being Catholic.

We were only twenty-one years old when we decided to get married, but in 1946, the first year after the end of World War II, all of my friends seemed to be getting married. Bill Olson and Otto Meeker had marriage plans as did Billy Black. There was a widespread feeling of making up for lost time, and even though I had not been in the Army, I was caught up in that idea of lost time.

Priscilla and her mother, who I later learned was domineering and wanted to run not only a wedding but also everything including Priscilla, set the wedding date for August the seventeenth.

In June I made my first trip to Sioux City which is in the northwestern tip of Iowa bordering on both Nebraska and South Dakota and about three hundreds miles southwest of St. Paul. I drove down to Sioux City one night after work and stayed only a couple of days before having to get back to work.

I don't guess there is anything much worse than being looked over for the first time by your future in-laws. Here I was a callow youth and a scruffy newspaper reporter being looked over by a thriving pediatrician and his society-climbing wife as well as Priscilla's sister and brother. I think I passed muster much easier with the sister and brother than with father and mother.

Priscilla's mother was no more happier than my mother was with our plans to be married. Too young! Do they know what they're doing? Will they have enough money to live well? Priscilla's mother and father were around thirty when they were married and of course my mother also was not married until she was in her thirties.

But we were determined and the wedding plans went ahead. I made another couple of trips to Sioux City, played golf with Priscilla's father (He was much better than I was), and got better acquainted with her family. I guess by August I was accepted if reluctantly.

The wedding was to be at the McBride home, a big, rambling place on a large corner lot in Sioux City. My mother and father came down to Sioux City for the ceremony, but they seemed to be kind of lost in it all. The night before the wedding there was a reception at the McBride home, and I think I met every doctor who practiced in Sioux City.

The next day the wedding itself was in the McBride living room. The best man was Bill Olson and Priscilla's sister Barbara was the maid of honor. The ceremony was performed by a Methodist minister.

Following the ceremony there was a reception in the backyard. Nothing too fancy, as I remember, and there were no alcoholic drinks. Priscilla's mother never drank and was opposed to anyone else drinking. We were never sure whether Dr. McBride took a drink, but years later when we favored a Manhattan as a before dinner cocktail we offered one to her father, who along with her mother was visiting us, and he enjoyed the drink and asked for another. But so far as I know Priscilla's mother never did have a drink.

The getaway after a marriage always seems to be a problem. To facilitate our getaway we enlisted the help of a Sioux City policeman who when he was in college had been a driver for Dr. McBride in the days when he had patients in the countryside. The morning of our wedding we had secreted our car at the policeman's home on the other side of Sioux City. He was one of the guests at the wedding and his car was parked on the street in front of the McBride's house. After spending a suitable amount of time at the reception, we sneaked out, ran to the policeman's car with him and we were off to his house, where we changed clothes, and then jumped into our car.

# PART IV
## On to Washington

# 20

# *A Raise on Friday—Fired on Monday*

Washington was still a segregated city when we arrived in 1947. Most blacks—or Negroes, niggers or colored, as they were commonly referred to then—lived in Northeast Washington. Our Washington was Northwest. Not all of the black population was poor. Blacks held many fairly well-paying jobs in the Post Office and a few other government agencies. But there were no black salesmen or saleswomen at Woodward & Lothrop or Hechts, which were the big downtown department stores. In those and other stores blacks could be seen in menial jobs such as mopping floors and taking out trash. In most restaurants they were limited to dish-washing and other kitchen jobs, although there were a few places with crews of all-black waiters.

Not only were blacks not admitted to the National theater, they also were not allowed in the downtown and Northwest Washington movie theaters like the Uptown or the Avalon. There were theaters catering to blacks on U Street Northwest, an area with shops and restaurants catering to blacks, and on H Street Northeast, another black commercial area. But blacks were admitted to Griffith Stadium, at Seventh and U Streets, where the Washington Senators baseball team and the Redskins football team played.

Public schools were segregated, too. But blacks had a high school, Dunbar, that was considered an elite black school, as was Central High School for whites. But there were two distinct school systems, one for whites and one for blacks. Howard University was in Washington and, then as now, was considered the best black college in the country. There were, however, two separate teachers colleges, one for whites and one for blacks.

Blacks could ride buses and street cars, but they were expected to move to the back when they boarded. There were quite a few black doctors, dentists, lawyers and other professionals, but their clientele was black. It was not a good life but there had not been a racial uprising—or riot, if you prefer—in Washington since the early nineteen twenties.

Perhaps we were insensitive to racial matters, but we did not pay much attention to the black-white situation and found that most people we talked with did not mention it much either. We were busy with our own lives getting settled in Washington and we seldom ventured into black neighborhoods. Washington was indeed a city divided, and I guess we thought that was all right. There were no blacks in important positions in the Federal government and only one in Congress, a largely unnoticed and ineffective members from Chicago, as I remember. Probably an Uncle Tom.

At Congressional Quarterly I seldom got involved in the big issues such as the Marshall Plan for the rebuilding of Europe or the coming 1948 presidential elections. I did write a bit about labor, but not specifically about the Taft-Hartley Act which restricted some union practices such as the secondary boycott.

Thinking back on the fall of 1947 and the winter and spring of 1948, I would say it was a hopeful time despite the growing disagreements between the United States and the Soviet Union and the fear of communism spreading in Western Europe. The U.S. economy was good and growing; our personal lives were just fine; I was learning my way around Washington; and Priscilla was pregnant.

But all was not well at Congressional Quarterly. The pay was not great, and the working conditions with Henrietta butting in all the time were not that wonderful. So what about the American Newspaper Guild? Could it help us? Pat Holt and I had both come from newspapers that had been organized by the Guild; in fact, the St. Paul-Minneapolis Guild was the second in the country, set up just after the first local unit was established in New York in large part through the efforts of the great columnist Heywood Broun.

I must confess that I probably was the first one to mention the Guild after we started talking over lunch or after-work beers about the problems at CQ. My colleagues were all interested, although a couple said that the Guild could not do anything about Henrietta. True, but we nevertheless decided to meet with an International Representative of the Guild, as the union's organizers were called.

The Guild's headquarters were in Washington and its officers were interested in organizing publications like CQ which though not a newspaper certainly was a respectable journalistic organization. So we signed cards petitioning for an election to make the Guild the bargaining unit for the CQ editorial staff.

When Nelson Poynter heard about our action he was outraged. After all he was considered to be a liberal. So how dare his employees want a union? Liberal employers took care of their own very nicely, thank you. At his newspaper in

Florida, it should be noted, there was no Newspaper Guild and he had recently broken a printers' strike by being one of the first publishers in the country to use cold type to produce a daily paper, thus bypassing the printers and their old and respected Typographical Union.

Well, a funny thing happened to me on our way to try to organize Congressional Quarterly. I got a raise in pay on Friday and was fired the next Monday. I was devastated. Here we were exercising our right under the laws of the land to become union members and organize our shop. But the great liberal Nelson Poynter couldn't stand that when it was his business that was the target of the organizing effort.

I was given two weeks severance pay, but when I ducked out of the office that Monday afternoon to use a pay phone around the corner to tell Priscilla what had happened I was in tears. It was May, we had only been in Washington for nine months or so, we were expecting our first child in just two weeks, and I was without a job.

Holt, Dick Dashiell and the others commiserated with me over beers that evening, and either Pat or Dick told me that he had heard Nelson Poynter had decided someone had to be fired to stop this union-organizing nonsense and that I was picked because I was the last to be hired and also did not have children.

I asked whether anyone had an idea where I could find another job. Dick suggested trying the Kiplinger News Letter and Pat said he had heard that the Democratic National Committee was looking for a writer with the election coming up and that I ought to see Sam Brightman, whom he knew, in the committee's publicity department.

I tried Kiplinger first, but did not get much response. They had no immediate openings; there were a lot of good applications already in their files......and so on. So then I went to the offices of the Democratic Committee. They were on the second floor of the Ring Building, the first post-war office building completed in Washington. It was gleaming white with big windows and nicely located just off Connecticut Avenue where M and Eighteenth Streets meet.

Sam Brightman was I guess about thirty years old then, a nice-looking, well-dressed man with black hair. He asked me about my experience in St. Paul and Washington and what my ambitions were. Sam was the assistant director of the publicity department—no fancy names then like public relations or outreach—and then took me into the next office to see his boss, Jack Redding, the director of publicity. Mr. Redding was somewhat older and much more gruff-speaking than Sam, but he was nice enough. After more discussion of my experience, whether I really was a Democrat, whether I had voted Democratic in the last election, and who back in St. Paul could attest to my Democratic credentials, both men said it was good to talk and they'd get back to me. I thought the interviews went well but I was concerned about the questions concerning my Democratic bonafides. I had never voted in St. Paul because of the two-year waiting period required after registration.

But a few days after my interviews Sam Brightman did call back and asked when I could start to work. Tomorrow? Fine, see you then. I was delighted. I still had another week of severance pay as a cushion and thus in effect would be paid double for my first week at the committee. So, take that, Nelson Poynter! The job, as I knew when I was interviewed, was guaranteed only through Election Day, in November, but it paid pretty good—something over one hundred dollars a week as I remember—and I would be involved, although at a low level, in a presidential campaign. And I was still only twenty-three years old.

For the most part the committee's offices were pretty fancy, but mine wasn't. I was put at a desk in an inside office that I shared with the secretary to the chairman of the committee, J. Howard McGrath, a Democratic senator from Rhode Island.

# 21

## *'Give 'Em Hell, Harry!'*

The Democratic National Committee maintained an office and staff year-round, but beefed up its staff during election years, particularly presidential years. In addition to Jack Redding and Sam Brightman, two former newspapermen who had met in London when both were in the Army during World War II, the publicity staff consisted of Fred Blumenthal, who later went on to work for columnist Drew Pearson, another ex-newspaperman from North Carolina and now me.

There was also a radio department staffed by a couple of broadcasters; television was in its infancy and little attention was paid to it. The committee also had a library headed by Mary Clines who had a staff of three. They spent a lot of their time clipping articles about politics from newspapers throughout the country to which the committee subscribed. The clippings were passed on to Jack Redding and Sam Brightman. Other offices at the committee were for an assistant to the chairman and fund raisers. There also were a couple of people who ran the then ubiquitous mimeograph machines that pumped out the many press releases and occasional speeches written by those of us in the publicity department.

A kind of an adjunct of the publicity department was housed in an old building on DuPont Circle. There five or six writers turned out very localized material about how much Franklin D. Roosevelt's New Deal programs had done for states, counties and communities. The material was used by President Harry Truman as he campaigned across the country during the summer and fall of 1948.

The presidential campaign itself was run out of the White House and was headed by Clark Clifford, the counsel to the president. Jack Redding and Sam Brightman went to the White House from time to time to confer with Clifford and the president, but I was never privy to such high-level meetings.

I turned out a press release from time to time; it was usually in the form of a statement by Chairman-Senator McGrath commenting on a news development or replying to a anti-Democratic charge made by the Republicans.

President Truman was not popular during that spring, and there was much talk that he would not be nominated at the Democratic National Convention soon to be held in July in Philadelphia. Efforts were under way to draft General Dwight D. Eisenhower as the Democratic nominee, even though no one knew whether he was a Democrat or a Republican. Another possible replacement for Truman was U.S. Supreme Court Justice William O. Douglas, a liberal Democrat who had been chairman of the Securities and Exchange Commission before Roosevelt appointed him to the Supreme Court. But at the Democratic committee no one seemed to have any doubt that Truman would be the nominee.

As the dates for the July National Convention approached, I was pleased to learn that I would be included in the group from the committee going to the convention, even though it would mean leaving Priscilla alone with our new son, Fred, who had been born just before I went to work for the committee. Priscilla told me not to worry and that she was delighted that I was able to have the experience of being at a national political convention.

And the convention was exciting, in many different ways. There was the continual undercurrent of dissatisfaction with Truman, the Draft Eisenhower movement, of which the general was not a part but about which he said nothing, and the rather small Douglas-for-President boomlet.

But one of the most memorable parts of the convention was the speech by mayor Hubert Humphrey of Minneapolis, then running for the Senate, urging the Democrats to support civil rights legislation. The convention heeded Humphrey. But Southern delegates walked out of the convention and then formed what became known as the Dixiecrat Party and nominated Strom Thurmond, then governor of South Carolina, as their candidate for president.

The other highlight of the convention was Truman's acceptance speech, delivered early in the morning when most listeners to the radio broadcasts of the convention were surely in bed. But it was a rousing speech in what later became the Give-'Em-Hell-Harry view of the president. The Congress was controlled by Republicans and Truman announced in rip-roaring terms that he would call that "Do-Nothing Eightieth Congress" into special session in August to try to get them to pass some of the Democratic legislation that Truman considered essential to the future of the country. Everyone knew, of course, that the legislation would not be passed, but Truman's call for action stirred the convention and gave the delegates a new view of the Man From Missouri as an aggressive, fighting candidate.

I was thrilled to be at Philadelphia to watch first hand Humphrey's performance and Truman's speech. I had a front-row seat in the press section just below the podium and knew that I was watching history being made.

Truman may have returned triumphantly from Philadelphia to Washington, but the general feeling in the country, buttressed by all of the pundits, was that he had already lost the election. The Republican presidential nominee was Thomas E. Dewey, the governor of New York who had first made a name as an aggressive New York City prosecutor in the late nineteen thirties and had run for president in 1944, losing to Roosevelt. Dewey's principal opponent in the Republican primaries and state conventions was Minnesota's Harold Stassen. The last showdown between the two was in the Oregon primary where they debated whether the Communist Party should be outlawed in the United States. Dewey said it should be; Stassen took the position that even the Communists should be able to exercise the right of free speech guaranteed by the First Amendment to the Constitution. Dewey won the primarily handily as Republicans and some Democrats continued to build up the Communists as a domestic menace.

Dewey was a small man who always dressed immaculately. His dark hair and smallish black moustache made him look something of a dandy. Truman was not a big man either, and he was dogged by charges that he was part of the corrupt Missouri Pendergast machine. And he certainly was not Franklin D. Roosevelt. Furthermore, in the spring he had taken a pre-convention "whistle-stop" tour on a train and had been met with less than overwhelming crowds. There was a devastating picture of him speaking in a one-third filled auditorium in Omaha, Nebraska. Also on that tour Truman made an off-hand comment when asked about the Soviet dictator Josef Stalin, saying "I like old Joe." Truman had met Stalin at the Potsdam peace conference in Germany following the end of World War II. Winston Churchill, the British prime minister who was also at that conference, had since then made his famous Iron Curtain speech in Truman's own state of Missouri, declaring that an Iron Curtain had descended across Europe dividing the Soviet Union and the Soviet-dominated countries in the East from the democracies of the West.

But when I got back to my little office at the Democratic National Committee after the Philadelphia convention I did not sense any feeling of doom from Jack Redding, Sam Brightman and the other staff members. I continued to write press releases and do research on topics aimed at likely Democratic voters who were labor union members, middle-class city and suburban dwellers and farmers.

Farmers became especially important when the Republican Congress refused to appropriate enough money for the storage of wheat, corn and other agricultural commodities. Storage space was vitally important under the New Deal farm programs. To try to get the best possible prices for their crops farmers generally stored them in grain elevators after first putting the crops under government price-support programs, using government loans to pay for the storage space while waiting for higher prices. So without an adequate loan program farmers were in trouble. In 1948 farmers still constituted very important constituencies in such important Midwestern states as Indiana, Illinois, Iowa, Minnesota, Nebraska and the Dakotas as well as such Western states as California, Colorado, Wyoming, Utah, Montana, Oregon and Washington.

The special session that Truman called for August did not produce any significant legislation, but it provided plenty of ammunition for the president's continually hammering at the Republican "Do-nothing Congress". But as September and Labor Day, then the traditional opening day for the fall presidential campaign, approached, the political stories in the newspapers and Time and Newsweek magazines continued the dirge—for Democrats at least—that Truman's campaign was a lost cause. There were not many pollsters in those days, but one, Roper, even announced that the campaign was really over before it actually started and that Roper would stop polling. Why waste money when the conclusions were foregone?

# 22

## *On the Sidewalks of New York*

Shortly after Labor Day I was told that the National Committee was moving most of the staff to New York City to finish out the campaign from offices in the Roosevelt Hotel, and that I would be among those going to New York. The Committee used to be in New York year-round, what with nominees Al Smith in 1928 and Franklin D. Roosevelt in 1932 coming to presidential races from the governorship of New York. So even though the Committee had relocated to Washington in the forties the tradition continued that during the last weeks of a presidential race New York was the place to be.

I was of two minds about going to New York. On the one hand I was sure it would be exciting to spend a few weeks there. But I did not like the idea of leaving Priscilla and Fred behind. We had recently moved from Jones Bridge Road in Chevy Chase to our first real apartment in Takoma Park, Maryland. It was on the ground floor, almost a basement unit, in a nice enough neighborhood of small apartment buildings, each with three to six units. And we were still getting settled, buying furniture, silver, dishes and decorations. But I realized that I had to go to New York or else be without a job again. So Priscilla and I agreed I should, and I was able to come back on weekends, which was a big help.

My six weeks in New York were mostly work. I did not have much time to sightsee or even to go to the theater. Late every Sunday afternoon Priscilla took me to Union Station in Washington where I boarded a train to New York. Usually I took the Pennsylvania railroad which brought me right into Grand Central Station, but a few times I went via the Baltimore and Ohio road which did not go into New York but ended its run in New Jersey. From there you caught a ferry into New York, and I loved that ferry ride with the great views of the Manhattan skyline.

In New York I had a room in a second or third-rate hotel on lower Madison Avenue which though lacking much was cheap. I walked up Madison Avenue each morning, stopping at a Chock Full of Nuts restaurant for a doughnut and orange juice, I was not yet a coffee drinker, arriving at my desk at the Roosevelt Hotel before nine o'clock. And except for lunch, again usually at a Chock Full of Nuts counter, I was at my desk often until seven or seven-thirty. For dinner I usually went to a Schrafft's restaurant, which served pretty good food at reasonable prices. And then back to a quiet evening in my hotel room with the afternoon papers. It was a lonely rather than an exciting time in New York and by the middle of the week I was looking forward to returning to Washington on Friday evening.

By mid-September when I went to New York the outlook for Truman in November seemed to be getting worse despite his aggressive and exhausting campaign. "Give-Em-Hell-Harry" was doing just that but seemingly to no avail. Not only was Strom Thurmond and the Dixiecrats threatening to take the once loyally Democratic South, but Henry Wallace had become the presidential nominee of a revived Progressive party that surely would drain votes from Truman in such liberal strongholds as New York and Massachusetts.

And Truman's running mate, Alben Barkley of Kentucky who was the Senate Democratic leader and was older than Truman, did not seem to be helping the ticket much. Barkley was kind of a grandfather figure, and I still remember the day he came by the Democratic Committee in Washington looking for material for the speech he planned to make at the convention. No speech writers for him. He did his own research and his own writing. I also still remember a wonderful line in the speech he gave to the convention. The Republicans were always denouncing Federal workers as "bureaucrats." "And what is a bureaucrat?" Barkley asked rhetorically. "A bureaucrat is a Democrat with a job a Republican wants." The delegates roared with laughter and cheered.

And what did I do while in my Roosevelt Hotel office in New York? I wrote some press releases and some material that could be used in speeches. But my biggest writing job was for what was called the Battle Page of the New York Daily News. As the campaign heated up in October the Daily News and quite a few other papers ran side by side material prepared by the Republicans as well as the Democrats setting out each party's position on major issues. The Daily News, a tabloid, devoted a single page to the "battle" arguments which after taking out space for pictures or other illustrations meant you had maybe five hundred words to make your case.

It was a challenging assignment and I was proud to have been selected to do it because the Daily News readership in those days was two or three million. As I remember the paper's circulation was well over a million, and each paper was read at least by two people and sometimes three or four. So one day I wrote about labor issues, another day about agriculture, then about housing, and so on. The assignment kept me quite busy because you had to work ahead and often had to do a lot of research on a topic.

I shared an office with a man whose name I have forgotten who came to help the Democrats from a job as public relations director for the Musicians Union whose president, Joseph Petrillo, was a dynamic and controversial figure fighting to make sure musicians always got a fair share of profits from recordings. My office mate was a friendly man and one day paid me a compliment I still remember. Somewhere along the way I had picked up the habit of sitting and thinking awhile before I began writing a newspaper story, and I carried that habit with me to press releases, speech material and other writing I was doing at the committee. "You will go far," my office mate and friend said to me one day, "because you think before you write, and not many reporters do that."

Also while in New York I got to shake Harry Truman's hand one day when he visited our offices. We didn't say anything to each other because he was in a hurry, but I was thrilled that I had shaken the hand of a real President. The only other time I saw Truman in New York was from my Roosevelt Hotel window on a rainy late afternoon shortly before election day when he ended the traditional Democratic open-car tour of New York. Despite the rain he got out of his limousine and shook hands with the fifty or so motorcycle policemen who had led the tour.

As I left New York for the last time on the Friday evening before the Tuesday election, there still was not much good news for Democrats. The latest Gallup Poll showed that Dewey and the Republicans would win handily. And of course I was off the payroll and would have to be looking for another job. Still, I reflected as the train carried me back to Washington, the experience was something I would never regret. I had enough of an inside look at politics to know that I wanted to be a close observer of politics if not a participant for the rest of my life.

Back in Washington, or rather the suburb of Takoma Park, Maryland, Priscilla had settled us into our first real apartment. We were in a congenial neighborhood full of other young couples starting their families. In fact, in Takoma Park we made lasting friendships with Betsy and Jack Snyder and Ed and Vivian Wetherby. Unfortunately, Ed died of a heart attack when he was only in his late thirties, but Vivian remains a friend to this day.

I remember another family. The man was in the Navy and later during the Kennedy Administration was an assistant naval attaché to the White House. But what I remember the most about them was the day his wife was talking to us and told us not to worry if Fred put a stone in his mouth from the gravel driveways in the area. "I think my boy has had every stone in his mouth," she said, "so they all should 'be clean."

Election night nineteen forty-eight will never be forgotten by me or by anyone else who stayed up until the results became final in the early morning hours of the following Wednesday. The early returns showed Truman running surprisingly strong. "But wait until the rural vote comes in," H.V. Kaltenborn, the radio oracle, and other pundits said, "Then we will see the Republican sweep that we all know is coming." The Chicago Tribune and other papers even gave Dewey a victory in their early editions so certain were the editors and political reporters that Truman was a sure loser. The Tribune's bold front-page headline proclaiming "Dewey Defeats Truman" is still famous and a valuable collectors' item.

But how wrong everyone was. By I think it was about four ayem it was clear that Truman was the victor. Priscilla and I were still up, having consumed I don't know how many beers and how much popcorn, and we were of course elated. We finally went to bed, but because of our excitement slept little.

Truman had done what everyone thought was impossible. How had he done it? Some political experts are still probably trying to answer that question.

My own feeling is that he won because he presented himself as a tough, aggressive president who genuinely convinced ordinary people that he was indeed on their side and would fight for their hopes and aspirations. And Dewey was, fairly or unfairly, the "little man on the wedding cake," as Alice Roosevelt Longworth, the daughter of President Theodore Roosevelt, derisively called Dewey. In the campaign Dewey came through as pompous, distant and removed from the concerns of the average man or woman. I think I realized Truman's strengths and Dewey's problems when I later learned that my father, a lifelong Republican, had voted for Truman, much to my mother's disgust, I might add. Also hurting Dewey was an off-hand remark he made during the campaign that was widely interpreted as being anti-labor and anti-working people in general. Dewey was giving a "whistle-stop" from the back platform of his train in a small Indiana town, when suddenly the train started moving, jerking Dewey who almost fell down. "What kind of an idiot is driving this train!" Dewey exclaimed into an open microphone. His remark was widely reported and repeated as often as possible in Democratic campaign material. The shortage of grain-storage facilities blamed on the Republicans by the Democrats also contributed significantly to Dewey's defeat.

The Thursday after the election I went downtown to the Democratic Committee's offices to talk with Sam Brightman and Jack Redding, and they had some good news for me. Because the Democrats had won they thought they could find me at least a temporary job in the government after the first of the year. And they did, in the Agriculture Department. I even was interviewed for the job by Secretary of Agriculture Charles Brannan.

But before going to work in January nineteen-forty-nine Priscilla, Fred and I went back to St. Paul and Sioux City for the Christmas and New Year's holidays. Again we drove first to Minnesota and then to Iowa. And Priscilla was pregnant again, with our second child due in July. The trip was not easy in the cold weather but both my parents and Priscilla's were happy to see their first grandchild. And there were no snow storms while we were traveling. But I don't think we particularly enjoyed the trip because we were anxious to get back to Washington and Takoma Park to see what the new job would bring.

Well, the job was not exactly exciting. I was made a writer in an information section of the department dealing largely with agriculture research projects. And there wasn't really much to do. I was the low man on the totem pole in an office of six or seven writers, most of them old newspapermen who had been attracted to the Agriculture Department when the farm crisis was big news in the nineteen thirties. Now they seemed to be mostly time-servers, often talking about their good-old newspaper days and the exciting New Deal days of the thirties.

I shared an office with a man named Forrest Hall who had come to the department from the U.S. News magazine and was now a disgruntled man seemingly counting the days to retirement. He worked slowly and never had much to say. Like Forrest Hall and the others in the office I wrote press releases about department projects and then waited while the proposed releases went through "channels" before they were made public. To show you how uninterested I was in the work, or probably how bored I was, I cannot remember a single topic about which I wrote a press release.

My salvation came in the spring when I got a telephone call from Dick Dashiell saying he wanted to get together with me. Over lunch a couple of says later he told me that he was leaving Congressional Quarterly to go to work for a new organization being setup up the American Federation of Labor. It was to be called Labor's League for Political Education and he was to edit a weekly newspaper to be sent to labor leaders around the country. And would I like to work with him?

# 23

## *Laboring for Labor*

Dick Dashiell didn't have to ask me twice whether I wanted to go with him to Labor's League for Political Education, or LLPE. I was bored at the Agriculture Department, and besides the job there would soon end, and I was looking to get back at least a little bit to politics. LLPE looked like a good move. It was set up by the AFL as one response to the Taft-Hartley Act of 1947 which restricted the rights of unions to organize employees. The Congress of Industrial Organizations, or CIO, was still separate from, and a rival to, the AFL, and the CIO had had its own Political Action Committee (PAC) since the early nineteen forties.

So, after giving a decent notice to my boss at Agriculture, I went to work for LLPE. There were changes in our domestic life, too. A two-bedroom apartment became vacant in the building next to where we were living and we moved into it at about the time I changed jobs. The two-bedroom unit was on the second floor of the building and because the move was such a short distance and seemed so easy we decided to move our furniture and other belongings all by ourselves. With the aid of neighbors who helped carry the bigger pieces of furniture we succeeded in making the move all on one Saturday. But we were so exhausted at the end of the day that we vowed never to move ourselves again, with or without a truck or the help of neighbors, and we never did.

The AFL, which was located in an old and crowded building at Ninth Street and New York Avenue in a crumbling neighborhood, rented a once magnificent house on H Street Northwest next to St. John's Episcopal Church on Sixteenth Street. It was called "The Church of the Presidents" because for many years Presidents had worshipped there on the mornings of their inaugurations. The house which became LLPE headquarters was owned by the church and was most famous for being the site of the signing of the treaty that ended the War of 1812.

It was nice to be working in an historic building, but the building, which was constructed as a magnificent residence, was not all that well suited for office space. LLPE occupied the first floor which was made up of four large rooms and a big hallway leading to them. Dick and I and a secretary occupied half of a room at the back of the house. In the other half were Al Clark, Paul Green and another secretary—Terry Honda—who was the first Japanese-American I had ever known. They constituted the radio department. Still no television of any consequence. Al and Paul, who became a life-long friend, spent their time recording interviews with government officials and others and then giving copies of the recordings to friendly senators and representatives who then could put the recordings together with their own questions to make it sound like they had personally talked to the officials. It was a good system—or trick?—that was being used by many other groups in Washington. As I remember the recordings were still taken down on wire. The tape recordings of today were still a few years away. Al was a nervous, wiry guy whose constant use of tablets to sweeten his breath did not disguise his heavy drinking habits.

One of the front rooms was the office for Joseph Keenan, the director of LLPE. He had come over from the International Brotherhood of Electrical Workers where he had been secretary-treasurer. He was a wonderful man. Like most labor leaders of the time, he had little education and had come up through the ranks during the tough nineteen-thirties, organizing shops and small businesses. Joe Keenan had no pretensions. He was always straight-forward, honest and a believer in hard work. Years after I left LLPE and I would run into Joe in Washington, he always remembered me—which is much more than I can say about Nelson Poynter!—and always took time to ask me how I was doing and how the family was.

And I always remember a piece of advice he gave Dick and me about the paper we put out. "Fellas (He always started conversations that way.)," he said, "don't bother with any jokes in your paper. The only jokes our fellas understand are dirty ones, and of course we can't have those."

In the other front room was Glen Slaughter, a young economist who was Joe Keenan's principal in-house adviser. A brilliant man who understood politics as well as economics and became a good friend, Glen was one of two economists hired by George Meany, who as secretary of the AFL was the Number Two man to the aging AFL president William Green. The other young economist who was hired was Lane Kirkland, who later succeeded Meany as AFL secretary and eventually became AFL president. Years later I would say to Glen that he might have become AFL president if Meany had kept him rather than Kirkland as his assistant. Glen would just smile when I would say that. The accidents of history! Speaking of history, Slaughter and Kirkland made history themselves. They were the first two men to be hired for important AFL jobs from outside the ranks of labor.

In the other back room was Tom Duncan, a sporty Irishman from Wisconsin who was Joe Keenan's principal political consultant. Tom was older than the rest of us—I suppose in his early fifties—and I am sure a lot wiser. He had been a confidant of and an adviser to the LaFollettes of Wisconsin and their Progressive party. I was told that he might have beome governor of Wisconsin himself if he had not been involved in a drunken driving accident that killed a man. I never saw him take a drink, and I was told he never did after that horrible accident. Tom lived alone in a small apartment up Sixteenth Street and I never knew whether he was once married or had a family. He spent a lot of time reading newspapers and magazines and talking on the telephone. Every day he also walked down H Street to a brokerage office on Fifteenth Street to check on the market.

Dick and I worked pretty much by ourselves on the paper, which was called the LLPE Reporter . It came out weekly, usually just four tabloid pages, and was filled with political news that we thought would be of interest to local officials of AFL unions. We were always looking for bad things to say about the Taft-Hartley Act and its Senate author, Robert Taft of Ohio, who would be up for reelection a year later, in 1950. For some reason we did not pay much attention to his co-author Rep. Fred Hartley of New Jersey. Both were Republicans, of course.

As editor Dick stayed in the office almost all the time, but I was able to get out of the office fairly often, usually to cover hearings on Capitol Hill. I was not eligible for a press pass because I was working for a special-interest paper, but there was usually room in the space in the hearing rooms set aside for the general public. I even got to cover some of the earliest hearings at which Republican Sen. Joseph McCarthy of Wisconsin testified about the Communist threat.

In 1950 McCarthy was already "discovering" hordes of Communists in the State department and other Federal offices. McCarthy was generally regarded as anti-labor, but the Communist issue was not an easy one of the AFL. Its foreign affairs operation, such as it was at that time, was led by a former Communist who I think, I guess I know, was sympathetic to McCarthy's anti-Communist crusade. In truth, the AFL was not all that liberal in the early nineteen-fifties. The Carpenters, the Teamsters and some other unions were more oriented toward the Republican party than to the Democrats, and there was a feeling running through many AFL unions that the rival CIO was a radical organization riddled with Communists. And there was some Communist influence in the CIO.

In addition to labor issues Dick and I covered such matters as housing and Social Security as well as a wide range of economic issues including the rising cost of living, unemployment reports and the beginnings of the movement of jobs overseas from the textile and other industries.

We also had a cartoonist, John Stampone, whose regular job was with the Army Times Publishing Company, which put out the Navy Times and the Air Force Times as well as the Army Times. The papers were weekly tabloids aimed at both enlisted men and officers. Stam, as everyone called him, did weekly pro-labor cartoons for us, and when he would come by the three of us would have long lunches over which we debated the issues of the day.

I stayed at LLPE for three years and for the most part enjoyed it. Dick and I got along well, I was able to get out and cover stories, and I even liked the large amount of rewriting we did of stories from the Washington Post, the New York Times and even the Wall Street Journal. Joe Keenan gave us a lot of freedom. The LLPE Reporter was unlike so many labor papers that devoted unconscionable amounts of space to stories glorifying their leaders. Joe Keenan never asked us to do that. We were looked upon with suspicion by Phil Pearl, the public relations man for the AFL itself, who considered our little paper a rival to the AFL News, which he supervised and which, frankly, I never thought was very good.

We had good working space and conditions and were located right across Lafayette Square with the White House and the classy Hay-Adams Hotel as our close neighbors. The exclusive Cosmos Club, which I would join many years later, was just kitty-corner from our offices.

How successful were we in getting local AFL leaders to become more concerned about politics? We probably did not do all that much. Senator Taft was reelected, as were many other conservatives. There was no chance of repealing the Taft-Hartley Act; in fact most of it is still on the books today. The Truman administration was best by scandals and Truman himself was unpopular and at a low-point in his career. The development of the hydrogen-bomb by both the United States and the Soviet Union set the world on edge.

But our own lives were okay. Our second son Steve was born in July of 1949 and early in 1950 we moved from Takoma Park to a small house we rented on Jones Bridge Court in Chevy Chase not too far from where we had lived a couple of years earlier on Jones Bridge Road. Our new home was in a kind of a pre-fab house. All of the eight or ten houses on the court were the same, a living-dining room, a small kitchen, a bath and two bedrooms. There was also a fireplace. Nothing fancy, but adequate for our needs. We were located close to Connecticut Avenue; so it was not difficult getting to work.

As 1952 and another presidential election year approached I got a call from Sam Brightman who was still at the Democratic National Committee. Would I like to come back to work for the committee? Well, let me think about it. Priscilla and I talked about the offer, and she said, well you enjoyed it the first time. So I told Sam I would come back.

# 24

## *Adlai and Ike*

The Democratic National Committee was still in the nice Ring Building. Jack Redding was gone, having been appointed an assistant postmaster general by Harry Truman as a reward for his work as the committee's publicity director in 1948. Sam Brightman had succeeded Jack, and although I was given no title I inherited Sam's old desk with its nice view looking toward Connecticut Avenue. There were two other assistants to Sam in the room, but it was a big enough room so that we all had a semblance of privacy.

I think it was February of 1952 when I rejoined the committee, and at that time everyone assumed that Truman would seek reelection despite his low standing in the public-opinion polls. We all remembered what a fighting candidate he could be and no one thought he would give up easily.

But to everyone's surprise he soon announced that he would not be a candidate for reelection. A lot of people thought he made this decision in the spirit of the constitutional amendment that the Republicans had pushed through Congress and the state legislatures restricting presidents to two terms. The amendment was an obvious Republican effort to get back at Franklin D. Roosevelt, who had been elected four times and was the first president ever to serve more than two terms. The two-term limit had been established by the first president, George Washington, and had been observed by all succeeding presidents except Roosevelt even though there was nothing in the Constitution limiting presidential terms.

Truman succeeded Roosevelt just three months into Roosevelt's fourth term and with Truman's election in 1948 he would serve seven years and three months as president by January 20, 1953 when the next presidential inauguration would occur, close enough to the two-term limit of eight years.

But whatever Truman's real reasons for not running again, it was time in late winter to think about a new Democratic nominee for 1952. And who would it be? It was now clear that Gen. Dwight D. Eisenhower, now president of Columbia University in New York, was a Republican. So the spotlight turned on Estes Kefauver, a Democratic senator from Tennessee who had become nationally and favorably known for a conducting a series of hearings exposing the Mafia and other criminals. They became known as the Kefauver hearings and were the first nationally televised congressional hearings. Kefauver's name was entered in the March New Hampshire primaries and he ran well.

But Truman and many other Democratic leaders did not like Kefauver and were looking for someone to be the Democratic presidential candidate. Vice President Alben Barkley was in his seventies and deemed too old for a presidential run even though he had become the country's favorite grandfather and was known affectionately as "The Veep," as in V.P. for vice president.

Gradually eyes turned toward Illinois where a man named Adlai Stevenson was attracting attention as governor. He was an attractive politician in his fifties with a gift for phrase-making and speaking. He was honest and had a good record as governor and was not part of the rather notorious Chicago Democratic political machine led by Mayor Daley.

Stevenson soon became Truman's choice for the presidential nomination and despite Kefauver's winning some other primaries and gaining more national recognition and popularity the political betting increasingly came to favor Stevenson, even though he seemed to be a rather reluctant candidate.

The political conventions in that summer of 1952 were in Chicago, the Republicans meeting first. I was sent out early to Chicago to supervise some printing for the Democrats and was lucky enough to wangle my way into the Republican convention to hear Republican Senator Everett Dirksen of Illinois make his famous speech excoriating Thomas Dewey for leading the party down what Dirksen thought was a disastrous road in the nineteen forties. Dewey was now leading the forces seeking the 1952 nomination for Eisenhower and Dirksen was a leader of the more conservative Republicans backing Ohio Senator Robert Taft. Eisenhower of course was nominated, and the Dewey wing of the party selected Richard Nixon, a young senator from California, as the general's running mate. Eisenhower was in his sixties and it was felt that he needed a much younger vice presidential candidate. Nixon, being just in his forties, qualified, and he also had made a national name as strong anti-Communist when he was in the House of Representatives and a member of its Un-American Activities Committee.

The idea that Communists had infiltrated the Federal government, trade unions, the motion-picture industry and colleges and universities was strong in the late forties and nineteen fifties. The most famous case that fueled this feeling involved Alger Hiss, a fairly prominent State Department official who was accused of being a Communist and was found guilty of perjuring himself in testimony before the Un-American Activities Committee and served time in prison.

At the Democratic convention Adlai Stevenson was easily nominated as the presidential candidate. His running mate was John Sparkman, a Democratic senator from Alabama. He was a pleasant enough man who was picked to run for vice president because he was from the South. There was no Dixiecrat ticket in 1952, but Democrats were understandably worried about the South after 1948 when Strom Thurmond carried four southern states.

Priscilla came to the Democratic convention. She had first gone to Sioux City to leave Fred and Steve with her parents and then had taken a train from Iowa to Chicago, a long overnight trip. I was able to get her a good seat for the convention, which was held in a huge arena in the Chicago Stockyards. Chicago was still "The Hog Butcher of the World," as poet and writer Carl Sandburg had called it years earlier.

My duties were fairly light at the convention—doing such things as supervising the printing of the party's platform—so Priscilla and I had time to have dinners together and see a bit of Chicago. After the convention ended it was back to Washington for me and back to Sioux City for Priscilla where she spent a few more weeks before returning home.

As in 1948, the prospects did not look good for the Democrats in that summer of 1952. Democrats had been in the White House for twenty years, and voters seemed to be getting tired of them. There were perceived scandals in the Truman Administration, some of them serious involving the collection, or noncollection, of taxes. And the there was the Korean war, which had broken out in 1950 and was still continuing in 1952. The Communist fear was pervasive with the Soviet Union seemingly becoming more and more menacing. There also were strikes by labor unions that often were blamed on Truman and the Democrats.

But most important of all there was General Eisenhower. He was indisputably the hero of World War II. He had led the Allied troops in the winning of the war in Europe. And he was a nice guy, not at all like the imperious General Douglas MacArthur in the Pacific during World War II and now leading the U.S. forces in Korea. Eisenhower's smile was infectious, and his nickname "Ike" led to the campaign slogan "I Like Ike."

He was not much of a speaker, but that did not matter. He was a war hero and seemed to be just the kind of leader Americans were longing for in 1952.

Adlai Stevenson, on the other hand, was a bald intellectual with a protruding stomach. He was in fact the first "egg head," as intellectuals were starting to be called. He insisted on writing his own speeches, and they were magnificent even though he was criticized for spending too much time on them rather than devoting more time to being out there on the road campaigning. As it turned out, there were not nearly enough "egg head" admirers out there and there were too many Democrats and other voters who did not understand what Stevenson was about but who almost worshipped the war hero General Eisenhower.

This time the Democratic National Committee did not move to New York in the fall for the final weeks of the campaign. I spent most of the fall writing for and editing a weekly tabloid newspaper put out by the committee and called "The Democrat." It was the first time I had been called upon to be an editor, and I enjoyed it, particularly going to the printer every Friday afternoon to supervise the make-up of the paper, moving stories around to make them fit, cutting a few lines out of some and then perusing the page proofs to catch any errors. The paper went to Democratic leaders around the country and articles from it were often used in local Democratic publications. It was always satisfying to see your work in print.

Of the other people working in the publicity department I remember Lee Miller most fondly. During the war he had worked for the Scripps Howard newspapers Washington bureau and had been columnist Ernie Pyle's editor. Pyle was famous in the nineteen thirties as a columnist who constantly traveled throughout the country writing human-interest stories about often obscure people and places. During World War II Pyle became first in Europe and then in the Pacific the spokesman for the ordinary soldier—the "dog face"—as he traveled in the front lines. Tragically, he was killed in the Pacific. After the war, Lee Miller edited a book of Pyle's best columns. By the time I met Lee he was drinking a little too much—the first man I knew who ordered scotch by the case—but he was still a first-class writer and editor as well as becoming a good friend. Also on the staff were an old Time-Life hand, and a man who became a golfing partner and later went to the St. Louis Post-Dispatch as an editorial writer. Both of them also had drinking problems, but they were still able to turn out good work.

In 1952 the committee also hired a New York advertising agency. The presidential campaign itself was run out of the capital of Illinois, Springfield, because Stevenson was still governor. Clayton Fritchie, who I later got to know quite well, handled the press relations in Springfield. He was a former New Orleans newspaperman and later became a Washington columnist. So the Democratic committee and the New York advertising agency functioned as something like adjuncts to the campaign headquarters in Springfield.

Stevenson campaigned doggedly both by train and plane. Eisenhower's campaigning was more leisurely. But I don't think any of the Democratic or Republican campaigning that fall made much difference. It seemed to me the election was over by Labor Day, when campaigns supposedly started in earnest. By then people had made up their minds. Eisenhower was no Thomas Dewey and Stevenson was certainly no Harry Truman.

So election night was no cliff-hanger this time. The returns came in fast and they all said Eisenhower! Eisenhower! I of course was disappointed but not surprised. The Korean war, the Truman scandals, twenty years of Democratic dominance and Eisenhower himself with his war record and pleasing personality and ways made it all but certain that he and the Republicans would win. And win they did—big—taking control of Congress, too.

So there Priscilla and I were on election night facing an uncertain future, with another child on the way. I did not know what I would do or what direction I should follow. Should I stay in Washington and look for another job with labor? Should I go back to the Pioneer Press in St. Paul where I was pretty sure I could get a job? Or should I go elsewhere? One thing I was interested in was becoming an editorial writer, and I thought about what possibilities that might hold. I was not pessimistic about my future, just not sure. After all, I was just 28 years old!

# PART V

## A Depression Boy Goes to Harvard

# 25

## *From Illinois to Harvard*

As 1955 began I started thinking again about the Nieman Fellowships at Harvard. Why not try again? I was older, 30 years old now, and had a lot of diverse experience. But would my work for the Democrats and for unions be held against me? On the other hand I had had a year of solid experience writing editorials and doing some editing, and that had to be in my favor. I also thought clips of my editorials in Decatur Illinois showed me to be thoughtful, even-handed and a good writer. And then there was my experience in St. Paul. So why not give the Nieman program a try again?

I wrote off to Harvard for information about making an application. After getting the material and looking it over carefully, I approached editor Ed Lindsay to see if the papers would grant me a leave of absence and guarantee me a job on completion of the fellowship as was required by Harvard, should I be lucky enough to be selected. Ed was enthusiastic about my applying and encouraged me to do so, saying he would grant me leave, guarantee a job on my return and write a letter to Harvard saying wonderful things about me.

I went ahead with the application, which was due by the end of February. I had to write a summary of my journalistic experience and evaluate it. That was fairly easy to do. Then I had to write another essay on what I would like to concentrate on during my nine months at Harvard, explaining why these studies would help my journalistic career. I decided that I should concentrate on European history and politics because I knew little about these subjects whereas I felt my knowledge of U.S. history and politics was pretty good. I spent a good deal of time on both the evaluation of my career up to now and what I would do at Harvard. I also spent a lot of time on selecting examples of my editorial and other writing to submit with my application. And David Felts, my immediate superior, wrote a nice letter supporting my application as did Ed Lindsay. Everything got off to Harvard in good time, and then I had to wait to see if I would make it to the interview stage. Late in April I received a letter informing me that I would indeed be interviewed, and in New York on a date in early May. I was overjoyed.

I took a train from Decatur to Chicago and then the Twentieth Century limited overnight to New York. I wasn't able to sleep much; I was too excited about the interview. What would the committee ask me? How I respond? Now, now, don't get too nervous.

The interview was in the Harvard Club on Forty-Fourth Street. The club itself was intimidating, and I was nervous as I sat in an ante-room waiting to be ushered into the room where the committee was doing the interviewing. The committee was running behind schedule, and when it was finally my turn it was time for lunch and I was asked if I would like to have lunch with the committee members and would mind if I was interviewed while everyone was eating. Of course not. In fact I thought I was lucky because I would get a little more time with the committee members than other applicants. But the longer I sat there picking at my food the more nervous I became and the more I wondered whether I was lucky to be their luncheon guest or not. The interview questions ranged all the way from whether I was committed to journalism given my political and labor soirees to what book I was currently reading. Luckily, I was actually reading a serious book—I've long since forgotten what it was—and I thought I made it clear that I wanted to stay with daily-newspaper work and not go back to working for a union or a political party.

Louis Lyons, the curator of the Nieman program, was still on the selection panel, as was the Harvard historian Arthur Schlesinger Sr. Another member I still remember was Josephus Daniels Jr., publisher of the Raleigh News & Observer whose father was a colleague of Franklin D. Roosevelt when he was assistant secretary of the Navy during World War I. It was a high-powered committee and I felt privileged just to be in its presence.

After the interview I just had time to get a standing-room ticket to a Broadway play. It was Agatha Christie's "Witness for the Prosecution," which later became a marvelous movie with Charles Laughton and Marlene Dietrich.

Then it was back by train to Chicago and Decatur and again to wait. But the wait was not so long this time. Within a week or so came a telegram informing me that I had been selected as a member of the Nieman class of 1955-56. I couldn't have been happier. The Decatur papers ran long stories about me and my selection. I was the first Nieman from Decatur and the first one in Illinois from outside Chicago. I was big stuff.

We immediately started making plans for our move to Cambridge. We would put practically all of our furniture in storage, although I must admit I was not planning to return to Decatur after the year at Harvard. Washington was in my sights again, perhaps even the Washington Post. We were renting the house we were living in and just had a month-to-month agreement; so we had no problem involving a lease.

In the middle of the summer I was asked if I wanted to come for a few days to Louisville, Kentucky, at the invitation of the Louisville Courier-Journal and Times. One of the Louisville Times reporters, Richard Harwood, had also been selected as a Nieman and the papers were going to have a dinner honoring him. And because Decatur was not too far from Louisville I was invited to attend the dinner. Of course I accepted the invitation and drove down to Louisville the day before the dinner was scheduled. It was an easy one day drive and I was invited to stay with a Courier-Journal editorial writer named Weldon James, who had been a Nieman fellow a few years earlier. He and his wife had a beautiful old house, and it was a pleasure to stay there.

The dinner was at an old Louisville men's club and was one of the nicest and fanciest evenings I had ever spent up to then. I met Barry Bingham, the owner of the Louisville papers and one of the saints among newspaper publishers. I also met Grady Clay, another Louisville Nieman who later became a nationally-known writer on urban design and other urban issues. Weldon James, I discovered, was not only an editorial writer in Louisville but a close friend of Barry Bingham. The two had met during wartime service in London. And of course I got to know Dick Harwood. The two days I spent in Louisville were wonderful and I began to feel like a big shot after meeting such important people and being treated so royally.

Back in Decatur I continued working, grinding out the editorials day after day but thinking more and more about Harvard. And sometimes wondering if it was all just a dream. Was it possible that Junior, as some of my aunts and uncles still called me, was actually going to Harvard?

Whether a dream or not, we did leave for Cambridge early in September in our car, towing a U-Haul trailer which contained our television set, a children's bed and a few other household items. We were told that the Louis Lyons and his wife helped Nieman fellows find housing and not to worry about it. The trip was difficult. I never did learn how to back up a trailer; so we had to find motels where we could drive straight in and park without having to back up. It was not easy, but we managed and made the trip in three days. Housing had been found for us in Watertown, about two miles from Harvard Square and we proceeded there. It was an apartment in a building with eight units. We were on the first floor and looked out on a courtyard and on Mount Auburn Street where streetcars ran to Harvard Square. There were two bedrooms and the apartment was sparsely but adequately furnished. So we settled in as best we could.

# 26

# *Crossing the Country on Hands and Knees*

The Nieman office was located on the top floor of an old building on Harvard Square. A subway station was in the middle of the Square, and the station was all but surrounded by a mostly outdoor newsstand which sold not only local papers but also papers from throughout the United States as well as any magazine you could possibly want. Also on the Square was the Coop—the Harvard Cooperative Society—which was a wonderful book store but sold many other things ranging from clothes to book bags. Next to the Coop was an old-fashioned cafeteria. There were other restaurants on the Square; the one I remember the best was a German place that featured real German beer.

Louis Lyons ran the Nieman program. He was a former Boston Globe reporter who had actually been in the village in Vermont when Calvin Coolidge took the oath as President after Warren Harding had died in San Francisco. Louis was also famous for an interview before World War II with Joseph Kennedy, the patriarch of the Kennedy family, in which Kennedy had some flattering things to say about Adolph Hitler. Kennedy was then the U.S. ambassador to the Court of St. James' in London and was furious when the interview was published, claiming that his remarks had been off the record. Louis said no, everything was on the record.

By the time I got to Cambridge Louis had long since left the Globe, but he was still an active journalist. He had a news program every evening on WGBH-TV, the educational television station in Boston. He was famous for his loquacious delivery, his long interviews and being able to continue the program beyond its stipulated half-hour length if there was important news or just things to talk about.

The Nieman fellowships began in 1937 a couple years after the widow of Lucius Nieman, the owner of the Milwaukee Journal, had bequeathed a million dollars to Harvard to improve the quality of journalism. James Conant, the president of Harvard, thought the establishment of a journalism school was not in the Harvard tradition; so he came up with the idea of mid-career fellowships for journalists. Editors and publishers did not take to the idea, saying that reporters would not want to take a year off from their jobs to go to Harvard. How wrong the editors and publishers were. By my time at Harvard the Nieman fellowships had become one of the most prestigious honors in journalism and were eagerly sought by reporters and editors. The year I won a fellowship there were more than one hundred applicants for the eleven positions available to American journalists working on newspapers.

In addition to the eleven Americans in the 1955-56 group of Niemans there were five foreign journalists, one each from Canada, Australia, New Zealand and, for the first time, Japan and India. The foreign journalists were supported by the Commonwealth Fund and, the Asia Foundation. The terms of the Nieman will restricted the use of the million-dollar grant to Americans working for newspapers. Magazine and radio journalists were excluded, and of course there was no television in the nineteen-thirties. Later funds were raised to extend the program to journalists from broadcasting and magazines as well as to established free-lancers.

My class was a varied group. I was the only one from a group of papers and the only editorial writer. There was of course Dick Harwood from Louisville, Bob Healey from the Boston Globe, Dick Mooney from the United Press Washington Bureau, John Dougherty from the Rochester, New York, Post-Bulletin and others from the Charleston, West Virginia Gazette, Portland, Oregonian, Denver Post, San Francisco Call-Bulletin and a small paper on the Florida Keys. The Canadian was from Ottawa; the Australian from Brisbane; the New Zealander from Christchurch; the Japanese from Ashai Shimbun in Tokyo; and the Indian from New Delhi.

Our ages ranged from twenty-nine to thirty-nine. I was just thirty at the time, and most of us were from thirty to thirty-two. Our years of experience in journalism ranged from five to about fifteen. Most of us were also married and had small children. With our three children we had the most in the group.

The year began with a meeting of the fellows in the crowded and cluttered Nieman offices. Louis Lyons presided. He seemed to be a casual, pipe-smoking kind of man who was disorganized. But that was kind of a pose. He had been running the Nieman program for more than ten years and it became clear after not too long a time that he knew exactly what he was doing. Arthur Schlesinger Sr. was also at our first meeting and was invaluable with information about Harvard, its classes and the comfortable way in which the place was run. He also had valuable advice on what courses to take.

Most of the fellows—it was an all-male group—were planning on concentrating on American studies—history, politics, social trends and the like. I was one of two or three who wanted to emphasize European studies, and I got some good advice from Louis and Professor Schlesinger on what courses to take. The history of Russia and the politics of the Soviet Union were of course high on my list.

One of the best things about the Nieman program was that you could do almost anything you wanted to at Harvard. The only requirement was that you stick with one class during the fall semester and take the final examination in that class. Otherwise you could drop in and out of classes if you wanted, could fully concentrate on one, two or three classes, or even just spend your time reading in one of the Harvard libraries. You were on your own and if you didn't get a lot out of your year at Harvard it was simply your fault, not Harvard's.

At first we were all awed at Harvard. I think all of the Niemans in my class had been to college and most had a degree. But in some previous classes there were reporters who had never been to college or even had not finished high school. Eddie Lahey, who I got to know later in Washington, was one of the most famous Niemans who went to Harvard without even a high-school education. He was a member of the first class and came from the Chicago Daily News. At Harvard he became a friend of Felix Frankfurter, an aristocratic professor of law who was born in Austria and later became a member of the U.S. Supreme Court. Frankfurter apparently was charmed by the tough Chicago reporter.

I guess during the first days of the Nieman year I did a lot of walking around Harvard Yard, as the campus was called, with my mouth open, staring at the dormitories, the massive Widener Library building, the Colonial church facing it across the Yard, the building where Harvard's president had his office. Harvard Yard is just off Harvard Square, but while the Square is bustling, busy and noisy, there seemed to be a serenity about the Yard even when classes were changing and it was full of students. Harvard was still an all-male school in 1955, but women who attended nearby Radcliffe, a sister school, could take some Harvard classes.

The favorite class of Niemans was taught by Professor Merke, a slight, bespectacled historian. It was called the Western Movement, but was known to Harvard students as "Crossing the United States on Hands and Knees" because of Professor Merke's detailed descriptions of the opening of the West and the pioneers who followed their dreams across the country to California, Oregon and Washington. I sat in on some of his classes and read one of his books. Professor Merke was hard to resist, particularly when one of my fellow Niemans would announce as we were having coffee some morning between classes that the lectures were really getting interesting and maybe even exciting.

During the fall semester my most interesting classes were one about British government and politics presided over by Professor Samuel Beer and another on the Soviet Union which was given by Professor Merle Fainsod. Professor Beer seemed always to dress in English tweeds and at times I thought was trying to be more English than the English. But his classes were most informative and often fascinating. Professor Fainsod, was soft-spoken and precise. His description of the Soviet system was, I thought, quite factual, and that was not easy to do in the mid-fifties when there was such hysteria about the Soviet Union.

Other classes I took in the fall were about European history in general and the economics systems of the Western European countries. I must confess that in later years I never did cover foreign-policy matters or report from Europe, but I always felt that my classes at Harvard on Europe helped me to understand better our own government and its antecedents. However practical my Harvard studies were, I certainly came out of the year more sophisticated and with more of a world view. I also managed to do a lot of reading both in European and American history. The Harvard libraries were indeed inviting.

Our apartment turned out to be not too badly located. The streetcar ride to Harvard took about twenty minutes, and the car went past the famous Mount Auburn Cemetery where many Harvard and other notables were buried and took me right into Harvard Square. Most mornings I had a nine o'clock class and if I did not have another class until eleven I would drop by the cafeteria in Harvard Square for coffee and a doughnut and would usually meet up there with one or two other Niemans. We would talk about our classes, the world and whatever was in the news that day.

Nieman fellows were not supposed to do any journalistic writing during their Harvard year, and I think all but perhaps one or two in our group lived up to that restriction. I know I did. It was frustrating at times not being able to be out there reporting and writing, but I was so busy with classes and reading that I often forgot about covering stories and writing about them.

I and some of the other fellows did take a class in writing. It was given by English Professor Theodore Morrison, who had written a couple of well-received novels and taught at the summer Bread Loaf writing school in New Hampshire. He was also a close friend of the poet Robert Frost, and many years later I read that Professor Morrison's wife was Frost's mistress.

Under Professor Morrison's guidance I wrote a couple of short stories, but without much success. I discovered I was not very good at describing characters and situations; nor was I particularly good at developing a story. The message seemed to be: Stick to journalism. Later in life as I wrote for magazines as well as newspapers I did find that I could develop a story-like approach with a beginning, a middle and an end to my pieces.

# PART VI

## To the Big Nation's Capital

# 27

## *To the "Big Time"*

After returning to Decatur and a couple of days of looking we found a brand new house, never before occupied. It was on Riverview Avenue, a new street where several houses had just been built. The street was on the outskirts of Decatur and near the Sangamon River. We joked that we were below sea, or water, level, and we were. In back of our house and the other houses on the street was a large mound of earth concealing water and sewer lines that were level with if not above the houses on the street.

But the house was nice. There was a large living-dining room as well as a good-sized kitchen. We had three bedrooms, two fairly large and one on the small side. There was also a full basement, and more about that later. One contractor had built all the houses on this block of Riverview Avenue and had hope to sell them. He did sell a few, but then the market slumped and he rented the rest.

Soon we got our furniture out of storage and settled into the house and back into the routine of Decatur and the Lindsay-Schaub Newspapers. The house was close to a bus line and to the elementary school where Fred and Steve were in the third and fourth grades. They could walk to school and I could take the bus to work, leaving Priscilla with the car.

I was welcomed back to the job, and for the first week or so asked many questions about the Nieman year. My colleagues were envious of my experiences, but I think they also looked on me at times as being rather stuck-up now that I couldn't claim to be a Harvard alumnus and would forever be known as a Nieman fellow. I didn't care much what they thought. I was so proud of the honor Harvard had bestowed on me and still so full of memories of a wonderful year. And I still felt that writing editorials in Illinois would not be my lot for the rest of my life.

I had not been back in Decatur long when I received a telephone call from Sam Brightman at the Democratic National Committee asking if I would like to come back once more for the 1956 campaign. I was tempted, but I knew I should say no, and I did.

I was able to go to the Democratic Convention in Chicago that summer though. Lindsay-Schaub editor Ed Lindsay asked me if I'd like to cover the convention for the papers, and of course I said yes without a moment's hesitation. The convention was in Chicago, and I took the train up there. This would be the third Democratic convention I had attended.

Once I got to Chicago I ran into Dick Harwood, who was covering the convention for his paper, the Louisville Times. We covered some press conferences and other events together, had a drink or two together, and a couple of dinners. He was happy to be back in Louisville, but thought that he would soon be sent to Washington by his paper, and I told him of my high hopes of landing a job with the Washington Post.

The Democrats nominated Adlai Stevenson for president again, but this time chose Senator Estes Kefauver of Tennessee as their vice presidential nominee. President Eisenhower and Richard Nixon were looked upon as being unbeatable though in their quest for a second term. The country seemed to be in good shape, the world was relatively quiet and Eisenhower had pretty much left alone the New Deal reforms of the Democrats. So to no one's surprise he was easily reelected in November.

During the fall campaign Priscilla and I drove up to Bloomington, Illinois, which is about an hour north of Decatur and incidentally was Stevenson's home, to hear Eisenhower speak at an evening rally in a large arena. Eisenhower was not much of a speaker, but the crowd loved him, and with his smile and pleasant demeanor it was easy to understand his popularity.

Back at Decatur the routine in the two rooms where the editorial writers had their desks was much the same as before. Coffee klatches twice a day, grinding out three or four editorials a day, occasionally writing a longer piece for the Sunday editorial section and sometimes a trip to Chicago or the nearby state capital of Springfield to work on an in-depth piece. I liked the work and felt I was keeping up with the world as best I could from central Illinois, but I was certainly restless and impatient for a break that would get me back to Washington.

Early in 1957 I began sending examples of my work to Bob Estabrook at the Washington Post. I would carefully select two or three editorials and send them on with a note. Estabrook would usually reply with an encouraging note, and my hopes of getting to the Post remained high.

David Felts, my immediate editor, knew of my ambitions and although he said he would hate to lose me I think he understood why I did not see my future in Illinois. I always felt that Dave had wished he had tried for more than Decatur, Illinois. He had grown up in southern Illinois and had graduated from the University of Illinois about the year I was born. He was now fifty-seven years old and at that age obviously had nowhere to go.

Dave was a nice enough fellow, a good enough writer and a great reader, despite his eyesight difficulties. He obviously had a literary bent, and he was hard-working, turning out six columns of five hundred or more words six days a week as well as an editorial or two a day of three hundred or so words. But he was unsung, and his position made me think of how many other editors and reporters there were laboring on smaller papers, unsure if anyone was reading them and dreaming of the big-time that unfortunately would forever elude them.

On the other hand, Otto Kyle, the editor of the afternoon paper's editorial page, was a rather small-bore guy, nice enough but without much talent in my opinion, who had gone about as far as he could go, and besides was a year or so from retirement.

My two editorial-writing colleagues were young like myself and hoping to do more in life than just pound out editorials day after day. One did go on to a public-relations job in Cleveland and another went on to a similar job in Chicago.

I wondered at times in Decatur who we were writing for and who indeed read our editorials and even more what did the editorials represent. We seldom met with editor-in-chief Ed Lindsay, but we had a general idea of his views on the world, which were I would say mildly liberal on domestic matters and internationalist on world affairs. But as often as not an editorial reflected mostly the personal views of the writer although they were presented to the reader as the views of the paper in which they were published, whatever that really meant. We received few letters to the editor commenting on our editorials; letters quoting the Bible were far more frequent. And seldom was there a telephone call from an irate reader or one with a compliment.

I plodded through 1957, sending editorials to Bob Estabrook every couple of months and soon, but not too soon, 1958 was upon us. The big story I remember from 1957 was the school desegregation crisis in Little Rock, Arkansas, and I wrote many editorials supporting desegregation and criticizing Arkansas Governor Orval Faubus. I thought the editorials were particularly good and I sent some to Bob Estabrook, who told me in a replying note that he too thought they were good. But still no job at the Washington Post.

But 1958 was different. Late that spring I finally got the letter I had been waiting for since the end of the Nieman year. Bob Estabrook offered me a job! He said that Alan Barth, one of the Post's editorial writers had accepted a fellowship at the University of California at Berkeley and would be on leave for the 1958-59 academic year. Would I be interested in sitting in as an editorial writer while Barth was gone? Estabrook said he could make no promises beyond June of 1959, but something else might open up.

Priscilla and I talked about the temporary nature of the job offer, but quickly agreed that this was a chance I should take. Something was bound to develop that would lead to a permanent job at the Washington Post. So I wrote back to Estabrook saying I accepted the job. It was agreed that I should be in Washington early in August to start work because Alan Barth would be taking some vacation time before going to Berkeley.

I was flattered to be hired by the Washington Post but even more flattered to be sitting in for Alan Barth, one of the great journalists of our time. He was a beautiful writer and an ardent defender of civil liberties and civil rights who in the early nineteen-fifties had written a book, "The Liberty of Free Men," that had become a classic. I never told anyone I was sitting in for Alan Barth or replacing him for a year, because he was irreplaceable and I was just a comparative youngster using his office while he was gone. Later we did become good friends.

# 28

## *"Rule Britannia—Down With Chiang Kai-Shek!"*

So once again we drove east, arriving in Washington in a couple of days. Again we landed in a motel and immediately began searching for a house to rent. It was much easier to find a place than the first time we went to Washington in 1947. We decided we wanted to live in Chevy Chase, Maryland, and after a day or two we found a satisfactory house on Turner Lane just off Brookville Road and were ready to move in just as our furniture arrived from Illinois. The house had both a living and a dining room, a fairly large kitchen, two bedrooms on the second floor and a large third floor finished room that had been an attic, which turned out to be a nice place for Fred and Steve, with both enough space and some privacy. The entrance to the attic room was through the bedroom Priscilla and I took for ourselves, but that turned out not to be a problem. The other bedroom on the second floor was small, but big enough for Suzie.

Once we were settled in our new home it was time for me to be off for work—at the Washington Post! At that time the Post was still consolidating its operations following the purchase of the Washington Times-Herald three years earlier. The Post still ran the Times-Herald masthead below its own on page one and the paper was referred to as the Washington Post and Times-Herald.

By acquiring the Times-Herald the Post had almost doubled its circulation, to around 400,000. But the Evening Star was still the Number One paper in Washington in terms of advertising although its circulation was somewhat over 300,000. The third paper, the Washington Daily News, was an afternoon tabloid with a circulation of less than 200,000. The Post had the morning field all to itself but was still struggling to try to get more classified and retail advertising than the long-dominant Star.

The Washington area was growing as the suburbs reached further and further out. The population of the District of Columbia was stagnant and becoming

heavily black. As the number of blacks increased; so did white flight to the suburbs. And even some blacks were leaving the District for Prince Georges County
to the northeast in Maryland.

My introduction to the Post was through Bob Estabrook's office and the cubicles for the editorial writers that ran along the windows overlooking L Street and
the rear entrance to the Hilton hotel. The Post was located on L Street between
Fifteenth and Sixteenth streets in a building constructed for the paper and first
occupied by it in 1950. Previously it had been for many years on E street between
Thirteenth and Fourteenth streets just off Pennsylvania Avenue.

The editorial-writing staff seemed huge to me after my years in Decatur where
three or four of us ground out eight editorials a day. In addition to Bob
Estabrook, there were Merlo Pusey, a conservative who had won a Pulitzer prize
for his biography of Chief Supreme Court Justice Charles Evans Hughes; Malvina Lindsay, who also wrote a weekly column plus an advice column, ala Ann
Landers; Joseph Lalley, a crusty Baltimorean who still commuted daily from his
city and had been a close friend of H.L. Mencken; Robert Albrook, who was a
few years older than I was and who had worked on Capitol Hill before coming to
the Post; and Karl Meyer, who was about my age but was no relation to Eugene
Meyer, an investment banker who had served in the Wilson and Hoover admin-
istrations and had bought the bankrupt Post at auction in 1933 and was still
actively involved in the operation of the paper.

I soon learned how the editorial writers operated. Every morning at eleven
o'clock we met in Estabrook's book-lined office, everyone that is except Joe Lalley
who I quickly found out was a law or writer unto himself and would confer only
privately with Estabrook. Lalley was a good writer though and was famous for his
baseball editorials during the World Series. He also was an expert on the Catholic
church and in addition wrote beautiful editorials on such subjects as Christmas,
the Fourth of July and other holidays.

At our morning meetings we discussed the day's news and Estabrook parceled
out the writing assignments. James Russell Wiggins, the editor of the Post and
the man to whom Estabrook reported, often sat in on the meetings, but I don't
remember Phillip Graham, the publisher who was married to Eugene Meyer's
daughter Katherine ever sitting in on one of the meetings. But both Wiggins and
Graham as well as Estabrook saw copies of the editorials before they appeared in
print.

Estabrook, who had a tremendous capacity for work, tended to take the big
issues for himself while, as I used to say, the rest of us were left with water and
sewer problems in Fairfax county. That's a bit of an exaggeration. Merlo Pusey

was the expert on courts and the law. Malvina Lindsay, like Joe Lalley, pretty much picked her own subjects. Bob Albrook concentrated on District of Columbia problems. Karl Meyer was concerned with cultural matters among other subjects. And I was assigned labor issues and miscellany of other issues.

After the morning meetings we all returned to our cubicles to research our subjects and start thinking about writing. Often lunch was with someone involved in a subject you were going to write about. The afternoons were for writing, and the deadline was at five o'clock. You would write one or two editorials a day, each one running from 300 to 400 words. But you didn't grind them out the way we did in Decatur. A great premium was put on good writing, and of course your facts had to be facts, not just conjectures.

The work was not easy, but I enjoyed it. Sure, there was some pressure to produce, but there was never a shortage of editorials. In fact, there was always a surplus, even though five or six editorials were run each day spread over two fat columns. Every Monday we would get proofs of the editorials in overset and there usually were thirty or so. We were to look over the ones we had written, decide whether they were still timely and make any changes updating them. As I soon learned one out of every three editorials you wrote was not likely to see the light of day. But that was a small price to pay for being able to write editorials for as important and influential paper as the Washington Post.

Once a week one of the editorial writers stayed into the evening and went down to the composing room to supervise the make-up of the page and to read oh so carefully a page proof to catch any errors that might have crept in. Bob Estabrook of course decided what editorials would be run each day and in what order they would be on the page.

And then there was Herblock, the celebrated editorial cartoonist who had been drawing cartoons since the late nineteen-twenties and doing them for the Washington Post since the end of World War II. Herbert Block, or Herb as everyone called him, was responsible for much of the Post's reputation for liberalism. Herb's office was separate from the editorial writers' cubicles and was at the other end of the fifth-floor newsroom. It was indeed a most private sanctorum. He never invited anyone in his office, and the few times I caught a glimpse of it through an open door about all I could see were piles of newspapers, magazines and books. Herb did not participate in the morning meetings of the editorial writers in Estabrook's office. Herb was a loner. He often ate lunch by himself at the counter in the basement coffee shop of the Hilton hotel across the street from the Post building. During the day, as far as I could figure out, he read the papers and the magazines and the in the afternoon sketched out on ordinary copy paper several ideas for a cartoon. He showed these to Estabrook, and sometimes to a reporter or editorial writer who was covering the issue he wanted to comment on. Then Estabrook and Herb would decide which idea seemed to be the best and late in the afternoon Herb would draw the cartoon on a large sheet of paper. He almost always worked right up to his deadline—I think it was six or seven o'clock—and often could be seen rushing the cartoon down to the engraving department on the third floor. I said Herb was a loner, but he was a friendly man. A bachelor, he lived in a small apartment on Massachusetts Avenue not far from the Post. His only recreation that I knew of was playing golf on the Haines Point public course down near the Waterfront.

Bob Estabrook was certainly a workaholic. He was in the office no later than nine in the morning and often didn't leave until seven or so, and then several times a week to attend a dinner or other social function tied to his job as editorial page editor. He also wrote two or sometimes three editorials a day in addition to editing the pieces written by the rest of and having lunches with important people. He was not a great writer, but he was good enough. When I went to the Post Bob was in his early forties and had comes to the paper from the Cedar Rapids, Iowa, Gazette. Bob had worked for several years as an editorial writer before succeeding Herbert Elliston as editor of the page a few years before I came to the paper. Elliston had been picked as editorial page editor by Eugene Meyer shortly after he bought the paper in 1933 and was known as a thoughtful, learned person, perhaps even something of a philosopher.

The Post's reputation as a liberal newspaper was not quite right. It certainly took a liberal position on civil liberties and civil rights. But on economic issues it was middle-of-the-road if not quite conservative sometimes. I guess this reflected Eugene Meyer's banking and Wall Street background. On foreign-policy issues the paper certainly took an internationalist stand, supporting America's expanding role in the world and backing the United Nations. Joe Lalley used to say that he could not figure out where the Post stood except for "Rule Britannia! And down with Chiang Kai-Shek!" Well, maybe.

The views of the editorial staff ranged from the conservatism of Merlo Pusey and Joe Lalley to the liberalism of relative youngsters like myself and Karl Meyer. At our morning editorial conferences the mix of views expressed some times diluted ideas and even took the fire out of our bellies but I suspect more often than not led to more reasoned and thoughtful editorials. But there is a school of thought among many editorial writers and editors that it is better to write from shall we say the gut than to risk being namby-pamby or on-the-other-hand-ism.

I wondered how Merlo Pusey, who was not only apolitical conservative but also a Mormon, could be comfortable at the Post with its liberal reputation, but as I got to know him I realized that he was a very sensible person who could see all sides of an issue and understand viewpoints that he did not agree with. We in fact became good friends and would often have lunch together to discuss the pressing issues of the day. And how those issues have changed. I remember how concerned everyone was in 1958 about Quemoy and Matsu. Quemoy and Matsu? Well, they were islands off the coast of China and there was concern that Chiang Kai-Shek, who was still alive and ensconced on Formosa, now Taiwan of course, was planning to mount an invasion of China from the two tiny islands. The United States was Chiang's most powerful friend, and… The invasion never came, but the possibility of it claimed a lot of newsprint.

After a few months I got to know the newsroom and the other editors. Under Russ Wiggins, Alfred Friendly managed the news room, or city room as it was still called. Al was the managing editor. He came from a good family in Salt Lake City and was very social. He had a big old house in Georgetown and frequently held dinners for important people. As an editorial writer, I didn't have much to do with him, but he seemed nice.

Then there was Ben Gilbert, the city editor. He was the scourge of the city room, feared by most of the city-side reporters, hated by some. He was a big man with a New York accent who always seemed to be at his desk or roaming the city room doling out assignments, checking on how a project was going, cajoling and criticizing. He had been with the Post since about 1940 and knew Washington well. I am sure he hoped to be editor-in-chief some day but his prickly personality stood in his way.

The staff was divided between what was called the city-side and the national staff. The city-side consisted of 30 to 40 reporters who covered the local news ranging from the District of Columbia government, police and courts to the suburban counties in Virginia and Maryland. The national staff, which consisted of only ten or eleven reporters covered the White House, Congress, the State and Defense departments and all the other aspects of the Federal government including of course the Supreme Court. Many of the city-side reporters aspired to be on the national staff, but the openings were few and far between.

Among the veteran reporters I got to know were Eddie Folliard, who had covered the White House since Calvin Coolidge was president in the early nineteen-twenties, and Bob Albright, who had covered the Senate since the New Deal days of the nineteen-thirties. Bob wore crepe-soled shoes and it was said that the soles got thicker each year as the marble floors of the Capitol and the Senate Office Building seemed to get harder and harder.

And Shirley Povich should not be forgotten. He was the Post's premier sports columnist who came to work for the paper when he was only in his teens after he worked as a caddy on a golf course in his native state of Maine where a previous publisher of the Post played during summer vacations. That too was in the nineteen-twenties. Shirley was an unassuming man always ready to talk about sports, particularly baseball, when he sat down for coffee at a table with you in the second-floor cafeteria.

I met Phillip Graham only once, lunching with him and Bob Estabrook in the executive dining room on the seventh and top floor of the Post building. He was a very nervous man, but I could see why he was always described as charming. Our luncheon consisted mostly of small talk about my background and a few issues of the moment. Later, of course, he was diagnosed as a schizophrenic and committed suicide in 1963.

# 29

## *Sparrows Point, Alabama—and Groceries*

As time went on and I became more comfortable in my job at the Post, Priscilla and I and the children settled into life in our house in Chevy Chase. Fred and Steve walked to the Chevy Chase Elementary School, known as Rosemary School because that was the street on which it was located. We had congenial neighbors, one of whom was a correspondent for a newspaper in Madrid who worked out of his house, which was right next door to us. The family on the other side of us was very southern and the woman called everybody "Honey." Her husband worked for a company that serviced and maintained elevators. Fred made friends with a boy his age who lived down the street and whose father worked for the Civil Aeronautics Board.

On weekends we would often drive to historic places outside Washington like George Washington's home at Mount Vernon, Fredericksburg, Virginia, and Frederick, Maryland. A few times we drove up to Baltimore to have lunch at Hausner's German restaurant famous for its kitschy paintings and statutes as well as its generous portions of tasty but fattening German food. It also had creamy pies that seemed to be a foot high.

One weekend we took a train to Harper's Ferry in West Virginia to watch a reenactment of John Brown's raid on the arsenal there which was one of the events that led to the Civil War. The reenactment marked the one hundredth anniversary of the raid in 1959. I remember it was a great train ride and a stimulating afternoon.

I think it was in 1959 too that Fred and Steve got a paper route, a Washington Post route of course. It meant they had to get up early every morning, but the route was in the neighborhood and it provided them with spending money. Suzie even helped them deliver papers on some mornings. So we were truly a Washington Post family.

153

We also renewed friendships with Pat and Laverne Holt, Betsy and Jack Snyder and some other old friends, and made a few new friends from the Post. Everything seemed to be going well even though the time was approaching when Alan Barth would be returning to his cubicle which I had been occupying and I was not sure about my future.

In May I talked with Estabrook, Wiggins and Friendly and also with Ben Gilbert. It was clear that there was no chance of my staying on as an editorial writer; the editorial-page was fully and adequately staffed, if not over-staffed.

The national staff certainly could use more reporters but there did not seem to be money in the news budget for more reporters covering national news. But after talking with Ben Gilbert, he said he could probably use me on the city-side staff. He was not sure about me though, saying at one point that he could hire two reporters right out of journalism school for what he would have to pay me, which was around ten thousand dollars a year, not exactly a princely sum but a good wage for those times and for the Post's circumstances. The paper was still not making much money despite its acquisition of the Times-Herald and continued growth in circulation and advertising revenue.

Nevertheless, Ben Gilbert decided to take a chance on me and although I was not exactly thrilled about covering just local Washington news I was more than happy to be able to stay on at the Post. And it turned out that I would not be confined only to local news.

After covering several important local stories to Gilbert's satisfaction I was sent to North Carolina to cover a long-simmering strike at a textile plant. I spent a few days talking to both the union and management sides in the dispute and even getting an interview with the governor who had tried to mediate the dispute which concerned the familiar issues of wages and working conditions. The textile industry was a low-wage business, particularly in the South, and many plants, as was the one closed by the strike, were in small towns where the few jobs available were at the local plant. So if you needed a job there was only one place to go. After getting back to Washington I wrote a fairly long story about the strike; it was given good play in the Post; and I seemed to be on my way as a reporter. The workers gained a small pay increase.

Another story that helped my career at the Post involved another strike, this one in the steel industry. A major steel plant was located at Sparrows Point in Baltimore. It was part of the Bethlehem Steel Corporation which was headquartered in Bethlehem, Pennsylvania. Its Sparrows Point plant was said to be the largest integrated steel plant in the United States if not in the world. At an integrated plant everything was done from the processing of raw iron to the manufacturing of finished products ready to be shipped to automobile plants or other industrial consumers of steel.

The strike had been going on for several months when early in 1960 I was sent up to Baltimore to interview strikers and management representatives. I still remember the dinghy bars near the plant where I caught up with workers and union representatives. And I still remember that covering this story made me realize for the first time the importance of the increasing number of married women who were now working. Many of the strikers were surviving because their wives were still working, maybe just as secretaries or office clerks, but they were working and money was coming in besides the rather slim strike benefits the workers were receiving. In fact, I discovered that some strikers even had been to Florida for a week when their wives got some time off.

I went back to Sparrows Point a couple of more times, and all of my stories again received good play and I got compliments from both editors and reporters on the good job I had done. The strike ended with a minor union victory. I guess by then I thought I had really arrived at the Post.

But my next big assignment helped me even more. One day in February I was suddenly sent to Montgomery, Alabama, where Martin Luther King Jr. was making news again by trying to desegregate more lunchrooms and buses. The lunch counter sit-ins had begin in 1959 in Tennessee and the bus boycott in Alabama a year earlier.

I have forgotten a lot of the details of the issues in Montgomery in that long ago winter of 1960, but I remember that not only was I there representing the Post, Claude Sitton, the southern correspondent of the New York Times, was also covering the story as were Harry Reasoner of CBS, Sandy Vanocour of NBC and someone whose name I've forgotten from ABC. I also met Ray Jenkins of the Montgomery Advertiser, and we are still good friends.

I remember, too, press conferences with Governor George Wallace, a smarmy guy who didn't like me any better than I liked him. He said something like this to me: "Why are you running down here and bothering us good people when you've got plenty of nigger problems up there in Washington?" I didn't get into an argument with him about why I or the New York Times or the networks were in Alabama; he knew the real reasons as well as I did.

I also will never forget Martin Luther King Jr. and the meetings he led in Montgomery's black churches. He was indeed a charismatic figure and a spellbinding speaker. His speaking, the music and the singing of the grand old hymns at the church meetings were enough to make me and the other reporters stand up and march with the civil-rights demonstrators. Those were powerful meetings and unforgettable times.

I spent a week in Montgomery and also a little time in Birmingham. It was my first exposure to the civil rights movement and I was impressed. I sent back daily stories to the Post and wrote a column, my first one, about the week for the Post editorial page. These were heady times and I was making an impression on editors, as I would soon learn.

Another big story that I covered in 1960 was a strike that closed all the big supermarkets in the Washington area—from Safeway and Giant to Acme and A & P. The strike lasted for well over a week and my story on it led the paper every morning. As the dispute dragged on I often worked until two or three o'clock in the morning, mostly waiting for the negotiators to come out of the room they were occupying in the Hay-Adams hotel, which is located just across Lafayette Park from the White House. There were of course other reporters there, from the Evening Star, the Daily News, Associated Press, United Press International and radio and television stations. The Hay-Adams was not a bad place to be holed up in. It was, and still is, one of the best hotels in Washington, and the hotel even provided all of us weary and hungry reporters with sandwiches when the labor negotiations went into the night and the wee hours of the morning. During the strike I was never pressured by an editor at the Post to slant my coverage. The stories I wrote got into the paper just the way I wrote them, even when they had a pessimistic tone. And the paper of course was losing valuable advertising throughout the strike. I learned during the strike just how fair the Post tried to be even when an issue hit directly at its economic interests.

I also earned a lot of overtime covering the strike, and the money was surely welcome. But Ben Gilbert said to me afterwards not to expect overtime on any regular basis. The Post was still penurious, and I wasn't really expecting even a raise, although it would have been nice. Later, in fact, my pay was raised to put me just above the overtime cutoff figure. Reporters above that figure did get compensatory time off, a day for every day worked beyond the five-day week.

The year 1960 was of course an election year, but so far I had not been involved in any election coverage. I had, however, spent an evening with a group of reporters at a private dinner in the National Press Club with John F. Kennedy. The group was made up of Nieman fellows-I learned that once a Nieman fellow always a Nieman fellow, the word "former" never being used. Several of the reporters at the dinner—there were about fifteen of us in all—had covered Kennedy and some knew him quite well.

I don't remember any of the details of our discussion that evening, but I do remember that I was quite impressed with Kennedy. He indeed did have that charm everyone talked about; he was obviously intelligent; and although he was just in his early forties, he seemed ready for the presidency.

# 30

# *A Post Political Reporter!*

In 1960 I didn't get to go to either the Democratic or Republican national conventions—after having been at Democratic conventions since 1948—so I had to watch the 1960 meetings on television. I was sure Kennedy would be the Democratic nominee, and he was. Everyone was surprised that he picked Lyndon B. Johnson of Texas, the Senate Democratic leader, as his running mate, a choice that I later learned Phillip Graham was involved in. The Republicans nominated Vice President Richard M. Nixon as their presidential candidate, which was hardly a surprise, and he picked former Massachusetts Senator Henry Cabot Lodge as his running mate. Lodge also was a former U.S. Ambassador to the United Nations. Everyone said the Republicans had a formidable ticket and that Kennedy and Johnson had a difficult, if not impossible task ahead of them if they were to win.

After the political conventions that summer I received a wonderful promotion—to the Post's national staff. I was an addition to the staff becoming the twelfth national reporter, as I remember. A national reporter, as the age of just thirty-five. I am sure my promotion did not go down well with a lot of the other city-side reporters who were hoping to move to the national staff. Some of them had been working on the city staff ten years or more, and here was I a national reporter after only two years on the city staff.

But if there was grousing over my selection, I didn't hear any of it. I had done a good job on the city staff, working hard, producing, as they say, and demonstrating that I could also right well. Years later I heard from a colleague that Russ Wiggins had said of me, "the best damn reporter that ever walked through these doors." That was high praise, indeed.

My initial assignments as a national reporter were rather miscellaneous. The Agriculture and Interior departments were my principal beats, but I was also supposed to keep an eye on some of the regulatory agencies like the Securities and Exchange Commission and the Federal Trade Commission. As I have noted, the

Post was thinly staffed and all of the national staff reporters had to do a lot of things.

But 1960 being a presidential election year I was soon helping out with political coverage. One of the editors, I think it was Al Friendly, thought it would be a good idea to see who were the real advisers to Nixon and Kennedy and to write a series of stories about the advisers. Three other Post reporters and I were assigned to the project. We all spent a good deal of time tracking down the advisers, talking to them at length and writing in-depth piece about them. I talked to experts on agricultural and Interior department issues like water, the West and oil and coal. Others worked on foreign-policy, defense, economic and civil right issues. The series was well received and won the Sigma Delta Chi award for distinguished Washington coverage that year. A genuine honor indeed.

In September I was assigned to cover Kennedy's campaign, and how excited I was. I stayed with Kennedy for more than two weeks, starting out in Tennessee, moving on to Illinois, Iowa and South Dakota. Kennedy spent a night in Sioux City—where I had a little time to see Priscilla's mother and father. In South Dakota Kennedy spent a rainy, muddy day at the National Plowing Contest, a ritual stop then for presidential candidates. In South Dakota he also spoke in the town of Mitchell, at its Corn Palace, a building decorated on the outside entirely with cobs of corn. The corn was of different colors and the Palace is really quite an impressive sight, corny as that may sound!

From South Dakota we went on to Denver and then to Salt Lake City, the headquarters of the Mormon church. I still remember the forty-two-year-old and Catholic Kennedy meeting with the ninety-two-year-old patriarch of the Mormon church. It was considered rather daring of the Catholic Kennedy to visit the Mormon leader, but the short meeting between the two seemed to go off well. That evening Kennedy spoke at a meeting that filled the magnificent Mormon Tabernacle in Salt Lake. To me, the meeting was a memorable because of the opportunity to see the Tabernacle and hear the stirring Mormon choir. As for Kennedy, he not only spoke but answered questions from what was thought to be a hostile audience. Some questions were hostile, but most of them were friendly enough, as was the audience.

After what we all thought was a rather triumphant tour of the West, Kennedy went back east to the family compound near Hyannis Port on Cape Cod to prepare for the first of three debates to which he and Nixon had agreed. For the press following Kennedy Hyannis Port gave us time to get laundry and cleaning done and to rest up from some strenuous campaigning. Kennedy usually started his campaign days with a breakfast or hand-shaking outside a plant sometimes at six in the morning but never later than seven. And the days often did not end until close to midnight. It was not unusual for him to be in six or seven cities in a single day.

While Kennedy studied and practiced for the debate, we reporters caught up on our sleep and speculated about how you prepared for a debate and how the debate would go. We agreed that both candidates were taking a big chance by agreeing to a debate, something that had never been done before in a presidential campaign.

The first debate was to be held in Chicago and after a few days on Cape Cod we were off to the Windy City. We arrived in Chicago the day before the debate, and spent that day talking to the aides traveling with both candidates, trying to pick their brains about how Nixon and Kennedy had prepared themselves for the unprecedented event and what subjects were likely to be discussed.

The debate was held in a television studio. In the studio with the candidates were four reporters who would ask questions of Nixon and Kennedy and a fifth journalist who was the moderator. The debate would last an hour and be televised live. Like all the other presidential campaign debates since then, this was not a confrontation as was the case with the Lincoln-Douglas debate; rather it was a question-and-answer format. But it was called a debate then, and the word has stuck.

The reporters covering Nixon and Kennedy made up the studio audience but they were not allowed to ask questions. Nixon looked uncomfortable throughout the debate, and beads of sweat appeared on his face. Kennedy was calm and exuded a picture of confidence. All of us who were there—and most of the nationwide television audience—thought Kennedy was the easy winner of the debate.

But it was said the next day that if you heard the debate on the radio and did not see Nixon and Kennedy, Nixon seemed to be the winner. His voice came through strong and his answers to the questions, which concerned domestic issues in this first go-around, appeared to be better thought-out than Kennedy's.

However the debate seemed to radio listeners, there was jubilation in the Kennedy camp as we flew out of Chicago that night to Cleveland. After landing in Cleveland we took buses to a motel in a small town nearby where Kennedy would begin the next day's campaigning. That next morning we knew Kennedy had won when we saw Governor Lausche of Ohio waiting for him at the motel. Lausche was a conservative Democrat, some said a Democrat in name only, and had not yet endorsed Kennedy. But the governor gave him a ringing endorsement that morning, a sure sign, everyone felt, that Kennedy had come out on top in the debate and that perhaps he was no longer the underdog in the presidential contest. The day after the debate was surely one of the most exciting days so far of the presidential campaign, and I felt privileged to have witnessed it as well as the first debate itself. I never tired of telling people about the debate and its immediate aftermath.

But then it was back to Washington and to turn over coverage of Kennedy to another Post reporter. The editors had decided to rotate coverage of both candidates. As much as I enjoyed covering Kennedy, I think the decision of rotating reporters was a good one. Campaign coverage was exhausting physically, and mentally. Also, there was always the possibility that a reporter would get too close to a candidate if he covered him too long. You can get to have a vested interest in a candidate, hoping that he will win so that you as a reporter who know him well will be picked to cover him in the White House.

And what did I learn from my first foray covering a presidential campaign. Well, I certainly learned that it was hard work, and that you had to work fast, writing a story on a portable typewriter precariously perched on your lap during an often bumpy plane ride, and being prepared with new ledes to the story or inserts late at night as the candidate moved from one city to another. But it all was exciting and fun.

# 31

## *"What Has Richard Nixon Done for Culpeper?"*

During the next few weeks I stayed in Washington, writing some political stories and checking into the Agriculture and Interior departments which were still part of my regular beat, but in presidential election years departments like those two seldom make much news as their political leaders wait out the election. When back in the office I got a good deal of praise from colleagues about my coverage of Kennedy, as well as some kidding. It seems that in describing the large crowds that turned out for Kennedy's motorcades and speeches I mentioned two or three times that nuns standing in the crowds cheered Kennedy mightily and sometimes jumped up and down as he passed in an open car. "So, Julius, how are your leaping nuns today," I was asked more than once, and I would reply, "Enthusiastic!"

Toward the end of October I received another political assignment, this time to cover Richard Nixon through Election day. By that time, according to the polls, Kennedy was catching up to Nixon, though the Vice President was still favored to win. There had been two more debates, and Kennedy had done well in them. It was turning into an exciting campaign, probably the most interesting since Roosevelt won his first term by beating Hoover in 1932, almost thirty years earlier.

Because the campaign and the polls indicated that Kennedy might win or at least that it would be a close election, the Post editors decided to double-team the candidates in those last days of October and the first days of November. I was assigned to cover Nixon along with Eddie Folliard, the Post's veteran reporter who had been covering the White House since the nineteen-twenties and the days of Coolidge normalcy. Eddie was to write an interpretive or analysis story every day and I was to provide the news story, the what, when and where of the day. Covering Kennedy were Carroll Kilpatrick, another veteran reporter who would do analysis stories, and Dick Lyons, who would write the news stories.

Dick, incidentally, was the son of the Nieman's Louis Lyons and had become a good friend.

So one morning off went Eddie Folliard and I and a lot of other reporters with Nixon. The reporters traveled in the same plane, a then quite new and big Boeing 707, as Nixon and his aides. Kennedy traveled in a private, fairly small family plane while the reporters covering him were in a separate plane. By the way, newspapers, magazines and television and radio companies paid for all the travel expenses, which were considerable. The airplane costs were pro-rated.

The Nixon trip began in New York City where Nixon had a couple of joint appearances with his running mate, Henry Cabot Lodge. The Republican candidates never drew as large crowds as Kennedy did, but the Nixon-Lodge crowds were respectable enough in New York. I remember, too, that the New York press room for the Nixon visit was in the Waldorf-Astoria hotel and the press corps even spent a night in the Waldorf, quite a treat for a depression-era boy from Minnesota.

After the New York campaigning Nixon flew to Columbia, South Carolina. It was thought he would do well in the South because of Kennedy being a Catholic and the feeling that many southerners were anti-Catholic and did not think a Catholic should sit in the White House. Early in the campaign Kennedy had confronted the issue of his Catholicism by speaking to a Methodist group in Texas, and the general feeling was that his Texas speech had just about neutralized the issue. But I still remembered how my mother had reacted to our neighbor supporting Al Smith, a Catholic, in 1928 and the stories that I later learned were repeated at that time that if a Catholic were ever elected President the Pope would have easy access to the White House, perhaps even having his "evil" forces dig a tunnel from Rome to Washington!

And then of course there was Lyndon Johnson, a Texan, who had early in the campaign made a well-received tour through the South, stopping at many places like Culpeper, Virginia, and asking in his booming Texas voice: "What has Richard Nixon ever done for Culpeper?" Carroll Kilpatrick had covered that trip for the Post and had told me that it seemed to have been a great success and that Johnson was probably doing a lot to help Kennedy in the South, once a Democratic stronghold but now a part of the country that during the Eisenhower years the Republicans had begun to wrest away from the Democrats.

In Columbia, the capital of South Carolina where the 1948 Dixiecrat candidate Strom Thurmond was now a senator and nominally a Democrat (but not for too long), Nixon drew a huge crowd at a meeting in front of the state house. What is more, the Reverend Billy Graham, an evangelist with a large following throughout the country and himself a North Carolinian, was on the platform and got as big a reception when he gave the invocation to start the proceedings as Nixon did later with his speech. The Reverend Graham did not endorse Nixon in so many words, but his mere presence at this South Carolina event surely told people where he stood politically.

Once the meeting was over we flew to Texas, landing in San Antonio where Nixon made a speech at the Alamo, naturally. Again, the crowd was large and speculation continued among the reporters about Nixon's good chances in the South, perhaps even in Texas despite Johnson being on the ticket. Seeing the Alamo—where Davey Crockett had fought!—was almost as big a thrill for me as sleeping in the Waldorf.

The next morning we took off on a beautiful fall day for Laramie, Wyoming, but we soon ran into stormy weather and by the time we got close to Laramie it was snowing heavily. Nixon had promised after he received the Republican nomination that he would campaign in every single state and he had not yet been in Wyoming. I don't know whether our pilot was a Democrat or a Republican, but it seemed incumbent on his part to land at the Laramie airport. The snow kept falling—heavier and heavier, it seemed to me—and the pilot came down for a landing but at the last minute he aborted his approach and up, up we went. After circling the field a few times he made another try and landed, actually fairly easily. There had been a lot of heavy breathing on that plane, and I suspect some praying, but we made it and Nixon could cross Wyoming off his list. He made the usual speech and soon we were in the air again.

There were a lot of unhappy campers on that plane as we flew out of the snowstorm even though we were soon under blue skies as we headed for Spokane, Washington. The pilot came back to try to reassure us that he would not have landed if he did not think it were safe, and that he like most of the rest of us had a wife and children at home. Well, we were still all alive, somewhat reassured but I suspect Nixon lost some votes on that trip. Some political figures have died in plane crashes, but the planes have always been small. But every time I have thought of that trip from Texas to Wyoming I have said to myself that it could happen to a large plane loaded with reporters or even with a candidate or the President and his staff on board. I hope it never does, of course, but it could.

It was another fine fall day in Spokane and nothing much happened there—same speech, same bunch of flowers for Mrs. Nixon to hold on her lap, same bus trip from the airport to an auditorium. Covering a campaign is exciting, but at times it also can be boring. The candidates tend to give the same speech everywhere and reporters get to learn some of the better phrases by heart. Nevertheless, I wouldn't trade my experiences covering campaigns for anything. In fact, I consider it a distinct privilege to have covered campaigns.

From Spokane we headed for California, first to San Jose and then to Los Angeles. The weekend before the election was approaching, and Nixon apparently felt he had to try to shore up his support in his own state of California. By the time we got to Los Angeles we were all exhausted. In the last few days Nixon had been campaigning with a pace almost as fast and furious as that Kennedy had been maintaining throughout the campaign. So we welcomed the selection by the campaign of the stately Ambassador hotel on Wilshire drive as our headquarters. Eddie Folliard and I both had rooms in what the hotel called bungalows, very nice small buildings each with four rooms. Attractive gardens surrounded the cottages, which were set back from the main hotel building.

Both Eddie and I had been so busy that we had not had time to talk much until we got to the Ambassador. Eddie was a wonderful man, with an easy writing style. It was at the Ambassador that I learned from Eddie about how to handle "seepage" on an expense account. "And what is seepage?" he asked somewhat rhetorically. "It is this drink we are having here. The money has to be accounted for somehow, but of course you can't put a drink on an expense account. So perhaps you have bought extra papers or magazines, or your dinner did not cost quite as much as you put down."

Eddie was full of wisdom like that. He was usually in good spirits, as befits the proverbial Irish temperament, but I later learned that he had a troublesome problem that was on his mind much of the time. He had a son who was mentally retarded, but not bad enough to be in an institution. But Eddie was already in his sixties, and what would happen to his son when Eddie and his wife were both gone? I don't know what did happen to his son after both Eddie and his wife died, but I often wondered.

On the Sunday before the election Nixon went to church—obligatory for candidates; he was a Quaker—and then appeared on Meet the Press—a good place to be just before the election—and then we were off to Alaska, Wisconsin and Michigan before returning to Los Angeles on Monday night. Yes, that was the schedule. Whew!

We left Los Angeles late on Sunday afternoon, but because of the time difference we would get to Juneau, Alaska, in time for an evening meeting. It was a long flight north, made longer I guess by the fact that we were all tired and generally feeling ragged. I boast that I have been in every state—and I have—but several of the visits have been like the trip to Alaska. I suppose we were there all of three hours, landing at the airport, taking a bus to a high school auditorium, listening to a speech we had already heard too many times, going back to the airport and quickly taking off. But it was Alaska even though it was dark when we got there and I saw little of the state except for the airport and the high-school auditorium. But I was there! Honest!

From Alaska we took what seemed to be an even longer flight, across Canada and back into the United States, finally touching down in Milwaukee, Wisconsin. By the time we got there, once again because of the time differences, it was Monday morning. I don't remember getting much sleep, but here it was another day—the last day of the campaign—and it would be another long day. After speaking in Milwaukee Nixon and the rest of us flew over Lake Michigan to Detroit. By then it was afternoon and Nixon had agreed to a telethon, which meant that he would appear on a local television station and take questions for two or maybe it was three hours. This was considered a rather daring thing for a presidential candidate to do at that time, particularly since Nixon had not seemed to be doing too well on television; all the reporters assembled in the studio to watch and listen carefully. To the surprise of some of us, Nixon appeared to do quite well, expertly fielding questions about everything from the economy and civil rights to foreign and defense policies. Some of us thought it would have done Nixon a lot of good if this had been televised nationally.

And then it was back to Los Angeles for Election Day and Election Night. Happily, we went back to the Ambassador where Eddie and I had the same bungalow rooms where in fact we had left most of our belongings because of course on the long trip to Alaska and then more than half-way across the country and back we had hardly time to brush our teeth and shave, let along change a shirt.

Nixon had made good on his promise to campaign in every state. The stop in Alaska had made it the fiftieth state in which he had campaigned. The stops in Wisconsin and Michigan were considered good ways to shore up support in the Midwest. But some did think that he could have better spent time in Illinois than in Wisconsin, and they turned out to be right. But now it was over and the voters would decide on Tuesday.

Campaigns are exciting, but wearing, for the candidates, their staffs and surely for the press. But even in the early television age of 1960 they were certainly necessary. Voters want to see the candidates in person, and a visit to a state does say that a candidate considers that state important. And in 1960 people did still turn out for motorcades and meetings. That has changed a good deal since then. There is still no question though that a candidate's presence in a state creates local excitement—and local news.

# 32

## *The End of Nixon?*

The stories I wrote while covering the last days of the Nixon campaign were mostly what we called "color" pieces, about the crowds, their reaction to the candidate and about whether Nixon seemed charged up or whether he felt the election was slipping away from him. Eddie's stories emphasized the political importance of the states we visited and the likelihood of Nixon carrying those states. There was some overlapping in the stories, but not too much and the idea of double-teaming had made sense, I thought. And it was wonderful traveling with such a wise and nice man.

None of our stories mentioned much about what Nixon was saying because he had long since perfected what politicians call "the speech," a compilation of the lines that get the most applause and the ideas to which people react. So there was little "news" in what Nixon was saying. He had said it all many times before. It was new of course to people who had not heard him speak before, and his words often made the local papers and local television and radio broadcasts.

There is a strong belief about some political consultants that people turn out for political events not so much to hear what the candidate says but just to get a look at him. And I think there is some truth in that idea. For one thing, it is sometimes hard to hear a candidate when the crowd is large and noisy. Also, candidates often tend to use platitudes because they don't want to offend anyone. As a campaign progresses, candidates move to the center on issues, again to try to please as many voters as possible. Anyway, the whole process remains fascinating to me, and I have never lost my interest in politics.

So after the mad and exhausting trip to Alaska, Wisconsin and Michigan it was a pleasure to get to bed at the Ambassador and to know that the action on Tuesday would not come until the evening. I did not go to watch Nixon cast his ballot at the Los Angeles suburb of Yorba Linda where he grew up and still maintained a voting residence. Nor did many of the other reporters. Instead I stayed around the Ambassador and tried to clear my mind for covering Nixon on Election Night. Eddie Folliard, meantime, had flown back to Washington where he would cover the election results and write the lead election story for the Post.

It was a quiet but long day. Most of the reporters who had been covering Nixon stayed at the Ambassador to which Nixon returned after voting. His Election Night headquarters would be at the hotel and presumably he would appear before the press once the returns indicated who would be the winner.

By early in the evening we were all in a ballroom at the Ambassador where the Nixon people were getting the returns. By seven o'clock California time it was already ten o'clock in the East and we were expecting some definitive returns. But we didn't get them. The election was too close to call. Television did not yet have sophisticated polling that could predict results state-by-state, and even if they had the polling that was developed later they probably would not dared to use it because the results were so close in many states.

Soon it was eleven o'clock then twelve, and still no one knew who had been elected. It looked though like it was going to be Kennedy. Then suddenly Nixon appeared and kind of made a concession. What he said was enough for me to write a quick piece about how disappointed he was and how his wife appeared with him with tears in her eyes. They were on the platform in the ballroom only a short time and Nixon refused to answer any questions. The night was over, but it was hard to get to bed as returns kept coming in, mostly indicating that Kennedy had probably won but that the election was so close that it was possible that Nixon still could win.

Finally, totally exhausted, I did get to bed. The next morning Kennedy looked like the winner, and we were told that Nixon had decided to go back to Washington. So all of us hurriedly packed and piled on the B-707 for what was a quiet trip home. Nixon did not talk to any reporters; nor did Herb Klein, his press secretary, or any other members of his staff.

It was good to get home and Priscilla and the children were happy to see me. That fall we had bought our first house, a two-story, three-bedroom white Dutch Colonial on Stanford Street in Chevy Chase between Connecticut and Wisconsin Avenues. It is hard to believe now, but the house cost $19,500 and was the only house in Chevy Chase listed at less than $20,000. Today the house probably costs half a million dollars or more. The house also had a fireplace, a screened-in porch across the back and a side porch that had been closed-in and served as a den or office for us. There was also a good-sized dining room and a fair-sized kitchen. The house was close to the Rosemary elementary school as well as a junior high school and the Bethesda-Chevy Chase high school. And the monthly payments were only $115 or so including real estate taxes. Nevertheless, I used to think some months how are we ever going to meet that payment. At the Washington Post I think I was making about $12,000 a year, not much in today's world but not bad for a Washington reporter in those days. We managed and even had money for dinners out, theater and summer vacations. We weren't rich, but we were comfortable.

I had a lot of what we called "comp time" coming, which meant because of my "high" salary level under the terms of the contract between the American Newspaper Guild and the Post I got time off in lieu of overtime. The money would have been better, but I did enjoy the days at home. I think I had accumulated about two weeks of "comp time." I used the time to catch up on magazines and other reading and to help Priscilla get the house a little better organized.

There was one day I did not particularly enjoy, however. It was a Saturday and Priscilla and Suzie had gone to a camp for the weekend. I think it was a Brownie's outing, as Suzie was still too young for Girl Scouts. Late that Saturday afternoon a huge moving truck pulled up in front of our house. The driver got out and came up the steps to inform me that he had some furniture for us. Furniture? Yes, from Sioux City, Iowa. Oh, yes, Priscilla's mother and father were moving into a smaller house and had said they would ship to us some bedroom and other furniture they no longer needed. Well, bring it in, I told the driver. Well, sir, he said, I can't do it all by myself and you know how hard it is to get some "niggers" to help on a Saturday afternoon—they're all off getting drunk—so would you mind helping me, sir? The stuff isn't too heavy so it shouldn't take long.

Fred and Steve were home and offered to help, too, but they were only eleven and twelve years old and hardly big enough for heavy lifting. So I helped the driver as much as I could, sweating and lifting a heavy old bed, an even heavier chest of drawers, some chairs and a few other items. Finally, the driver said he thought we had got it all out. Oh, no, wait a minute, here's something else. And he handed me a mop handle. Thrifty, that was Priscilla's mother. The mop handle, after all, was still good, and, you know, waste not, want not. So forever after that load of furniture became known as the mop-handle cargo. But I should say the bedroom furniture was very nice and we used it for many years.

# 33

## *"Ask Not What Your Country Can Do For You"*

After my "comp time" ended I returned to work and was soon sent to Miami in December, 1960 to do a story on the Cuban refugees who were fleeing Castro's takeover of Cuba and coming into Florida. It was another nice assignment and I spent some time in Miami with several people trying to help the refugees. I remember in particular a priest who was very helpful. I even had dinner with him and some others at his rectory. However, I did not become aware of the plans then being made for the ill-fated invasion of Cuba that was attempted by refugees with CIA backing the next March.

The New York Times broke the Cuban invasion story much to the dismay of Kennedy, who was then President, and the CIA, but I don't think the Post would have run the story even if I had stumbled on it because by revealing the invasion plans the Times did put the lives of the people involved in jeopardy.

Kennedy had won the election by the slimmest of results, and Nixon, to his credit, had not challenged the outcome. Kennedy took Illinois and Texas by a very few votes, giving him the requisite number of electoral votes he needed to win, and there were reports of illegalities in the voting in both states.

As Kennedy began organizing for the presidency, reporters at the Post were trying to find out whom he would appoint to important positions. Phillip Graham proved to have the best pipeline into the people around Kennedy and provided the Post with "beats" on some important appointments including Robert McNamara at the Defense department and Dean Rusk at the State department.

I had a small part in this coverage, dropping by from time to time at offices headed up by Sargent Schriver, Kennedy's brother-in-law, where a small group was searching for what later came to be called "the best and the brightest." I knew one of Schriver's colleagues, Ralph Dungan, quite well (He had also worked at

Labor's League for Political Education) but I never did get any "scoops" from Ralph or anyone else in Schriver's operation.

I do remember calling Governor Orville Freeman of Minnesota after reports surfaced that he was being considered as Kennedy's secretary of agriculture. It was being said around Washington that Freeman, a protégé of Hubert Humphrey's, might be a good politician and governor but really didn't know much about agriculture. When I asked Freeman about that, he paused a moment and then said, "Well, I do know the difference between horse shit and bull shit." End of conversation.

Soon after becoming an editorial writer at the Post I started writing pieces twice-a-month for the New Leader, a liberal and fiercely anti-Communist magazine. It had a small circulation but was read in influential circles. The pieces were what we called "thumb suckers" about the mood in Washington and likely developments involving major issues. The pay was small, actually tiny, something like twenty-five or fifty dollars per piece, but I enjoyed the writing and the exposure. However, as I got more deeply involved in reporting, I had to drop the assignment because I no longer had time to do it well.

Soon it was Christmas time and then 1961 and January the twentieth, Inauguration Day, was fast approaching. The night before the inauguration a heavy snow storm struck Washington, and I was not sure I could get to work, but I knew I had to be there. I would have a small role in covering the inauguration, and I certainly did not want to miss it. And I didn't. I walked through the snow to Chevy Chase Circle and managed to get one of the few buses that were running. After checking into the office, I walked to Capitol Hill where I had a front-row seat for the ceremonies. The snow was so bad that the Army had been called out to clear the area on the East Front of the Capitol where the inauguration was held. Soldiers also were put to work clearing Pennsylvania Avenue for the Inaugural Parade.

It was a cold day, but the skies were clear and so blue. Poor Robert Frost was blinded by the sun and glare, but he recited his Inaugural poem from memory. And Kennedy gave his famous "Ask-not-what-your-country-can-do-for-you" speech. It was the dawn of a new era and it was hard not to be excited, particularly being right there in a front-row seat. It was another one of those times in my life that I felt privileged to be where I was and that I have never forgotten.

I don't suppose there was as much excitement about a new president and a new administration since Franklin D. Roosevelt entered office for his first term in March of 1933. Then the country was in its worst Depression and everyone wondered whether Roosevelt could bring back the good economic times of the nineteen twenties. In 1961 the country was in pretty good shape and people were wondering what this young president—only Theodore Roosevelt had been younger on taking office—would do once he was in office. There were high hopes certainly among Democrats and probably even among some Republicans.

One of Kennedy's early programs that I covered was the food-stamp plan to help poor people get more to eat and to eat better. The program was a revival of a New Deal effort to help the hungry. People with low incomes were issued stamps—actually coupons this time around—that were as good as money for the purchase of food. I covered the beginnings of the program from the bureaucratic Washington standpoint, and also talked with people getting food stamps and did some stories on what the recipients actually purchase. The program was set up in the Agriculture department and is still in operation some forty years later. It is sometimes abused but it is generally helpful to the poor.

# 34

## *A Mason Jar of Moonshine*

Another Kennedy initiative that I covered early in 1961 was called the Depressed Areas Program. It was a program long championed by Democratic Senator Paul Douglas of Illinois to try to help areas where unemployment was high and chronic. Coal-mining areas were often cited as examples of places where redevelopment of some kind was badly needed. In 1960 I had toured the Appalachian mountain areas of Kentucky, West Virginia, Virginia and Maryland and had written a series of stories about unemployed coal miners and dying towns and cities. At that time the cliché was retraining mine workers to become automobile mechanics. There was a surplus of miners and a shortage of auto mechanics. Easier said than done, however. It turned out that many ex-miners were unable even to read and write; so retraining had to start with in effect putting the miners back into grade school. And it also turned out that many of the miners were so embarrassed that they were unable to read or write that they did not want to admit their problems, let alone go back to school to read and write. I remember well going to a small class of miners in Kentucky struggling with reading and writing and being most sympathetic with them. In the end, not many out-of-work miners became auto mechanics—another example of the difficulties of dealing with chronic unemployment.

I also remember spending a day in the terribly depressed eastern Kentucky town of Hazard, particularly a dinner I had with the mayor of Hazard who also owned the only dry goods store in town. He was Armenian and his father had come to eastern Kentucky as a peddler, later opening the store now run by the son. We talked first in the store and then over dinner in what was probably the only real restaurant in Hazard. After pretty much covering all the economic problems of Eastern Kentucky and possible solutions, the conversation got around to moonshine. The making of moonshine—Illegal whiskey—was one of the very few thriving businesses remaining in Eastern Kentucky, and the mayor asked me if I had ever drunk moonshine. I kind of made a face and said no, I hadn't. He said, well, it's something a worldly reporter like you ought to try at least once; so why don't you come home with me and I'll give you a taste.

I could hardly say no; so we went to the mayor's modest home and down into the basement where there was an astonishing display of bottles of moonshine. It seemed that the county sheriff gave him a bottle of confiscated moonshine every now and then. I tasted a spoonful and reluctantly swallowed it, shaking my head and saying, my, that is strong stuff. Like some more? Oh, no thank you!

The mayor pressed a Mason jar of moonshine on me, and I felt that I could not very well refuse him. So I flew back to Washington with a jar of moonshine between my feet, not wanting to risk putting it in my suitcase for fear it would burst. We kept the jar for years afterwards, always putting it out at parties. A few hardy souls tried a sip, but not many. I myself never tried moonshine again.

Later in 1961 I went to Arkansas and Detroit to do some stories on how the Depressed Areas and Food Stamp programs were working. In Arkansas I headed for the small town of Mountain Home where a shirt factory had been established as part of the Depressed Areas program. I toured the factory, talked to workers and the manager, who offered me a couple of shirts, which I shouldn't have taken, but I did. He of course wanted to show off the workmanship on the shirts, which actually were of rather low quality and were made to sell cheaply, in J.C. Penny stores.

Mountain Home was a rather pretty place with a man-made lake formed fairly recently by the building of a dam on a nearby river. At Mountain Home I met Tom Dearmore, who with his cousin owned the town's weekly paper. Tom had been a Nieman fellow a year or so earlier and we got along fine reminiscing about our Nieman years. He was also most helpful in filling me in on the economic problems of this area of central Arkansas. He was a native of Mountain Home, his father having been one of the founders of the paper. Tom became a lifelong friend and later moved to Washington to take a job as an editorial writer for the Evening Star. As for Mountain Home it developed into a retirement area, with its fishing and other outdoor activities drawing Midwesterners, particularly from the Chicago area.

From Arkansas I flew to Detroit where I talked with the administrators and recipients of the Food Stamp program. It appeared to be starting out quite well. Detroit itself was continuing to decline and I was appalled how bad the downtown area looked with its many old, vacant and deteriorating office buildings and even hotels. During my stay in Detroit I was able to find time to spend an evening with Priscilla's sister Barbara and her family who lived in nearby Ann Arbor.

So it was back to Washington and covering a miscellany of stories as the Kennedy administration recovered from the ill-fated effort to invade Cuba. Now and then I got to the White House when something was going on there concerning the Agriculture or Interior departments. I also tried to get to Kennedy's press conferences, and often did.

The press conferences were held in a large auditorium in the State Department building in the Foggy Bottom section of Washington near the Potomac River. The auditorium was large enough to accommodate reporters like myself who did not regularly get to the White House. Kennedy usually held press conferences every two weeks and although like most presidents he said he did not particularly enjoy the sessions most reporters thought he did well fielding the questions. Kennedy had a keen wit, and it was often displayed as he answered questions. Most reporters liked Kennedy, but that did not prevent the asking of tough or unfriendly questions. I was able to get in a few questions about subjects I was covering, but for the most part I sat quietly through the sessions while Washington Post White House regulars Eddie Folliard and Carroll Kilpatrick represented the Post at the press conferences and regularly asked questions. Sometimes some of the Post reporters would get together before a press conference to decide what questions should be asked.

One press conference I will never forget, particularly in light of what later happened to Kennedy in Dallas, was when a reporter, a woman, incidentally, asked why more families could not join their husbands and fathers who were serving in the military in Germany. Isn't it unfair to keep families apart like that? Kennedy looked at the reporter, thought a moment, noted how expensive it was to send military families abroad and then said, "You know, life itself is unfair."

A big story I did cover was the General Walker affair. It involved an Army general who had had an important command in Germany. His political views were pretty far to the right and he was accused of trying to indoctrinate his troops in his political ideas. General Walker was relieved of his command and returned to Washington where the Senate Armed Services Committee held hearings on the charges against him.

It was the first big hearing I ever covered in the Caucus Room of the original Senate Office Building. The room is quite large with a high ceiling, marble walls and a marble floor, and has been the scene of Senate hearings going back at least to the Teapot Dome oil scandals of the Harding years during the early nineteen-twenties. There is indeed the feel and smell of history in the cavernous room. The senators sit at a long podium at one end of the room looking down at the witness who is at a rather small desk. Photographers sit on the floor below the senators and in front of the witness desk. Reporters are at long tables behind the witness and behind the reporters are chairs for the general public. When there is a big, sensational hearing the room almost seems to crackle as if it were filled with electricity.

General Walker clearly was a strange and perhaps even a dangerous character. He was a bellicose Texan who seemed to be opposed to whatever was happening around him. But the most electric moment in the long days of the hearings was not anything that happened during his testimony. Rather, it was one morning when Secretary of Defense McNamara himself sat down at the witness table and waited for the members of the Senate Armed Services committee to file into the Caucus Room. The afternoon before questions had arisen as to whom General Walker directly reported and who was responsible for putting him into an important position in Germany. Rather than send the responsible subordinate, McNamara himself decided to appear and take all responsibility—or blame—for the General Walker problem. As I remember, McNamara was brilliant in his testimony and succeeded to dampen down the Walker controversy. Walker soon retired from the Army and went home to Texas where he lived in a house in Dallas that looked like a fortress.

# 35

## *Billie Sol Enters My Life*

The year 1962 led to my first book. It all started with a Texan with the nice southern name of Billie Sol Estes. He lived way out in West Texas in a town called Pecos. It seemed that Billie Sol was able to get money out of the U.S. Department of Agriculture by using mobile fertilizer tanks to bamboozle the bureaucrats. He had only a couple of the fertilizer tanks but by constantly moving them around he fooled the Agriculture Department into thinking that he had a lot of tanks and was thus eligible for government loans on many tanks. Soon it was learned that the tanks were nonexistent, phantoms, and a scandal erupted.

The scandal sent me to Texas twice, on the initial trip first to Austin where a state prosecutor was looking into the scandal and welcomed reporters and then on to Pecos in dreary West Texas where Billie Sol lived in a magnificent mansion. On the second trip I went to cover the opening of his trial in an East Texas city. That was the only time I saw Billie Sol, and I never did speak to him. He was convicted of swindling the government and spent several years in prison. He may still be living, but I have no idea.

In between trips to Texas I covered Senate and House hearings about the case. Billie Sol never appeared at the hearings, but several Agriculture Department employees did. The story had legs, and it received prominent play for weeks. It was complicated, but I think lots of people followed it. I find the name Billie Sol Estes still rings a bell with people.

It was thought in the beginning that Lyndon Johnson, who was then vice president, might be implicated in the scandal, but it never happened and I don't think Johnson was involved. Billie Sol did not appear to be a Johnson supporter; he was closer to Texas Senator Ralph Yarborough who was part of the liberal branch of the Texas Democrats.

But Johnson was concerned about the Billie Sol story as I learned one day from Washington Post editor Russ Wiggins, who while wandering through the city room one afternoon stopped at my desk and said, good-naturedly, "God damn you, Duscha, I had dinner with Johnson last night at his house and all I seemed to hear was Johnson denouncing your coverage of the Billie Sol Estes story."

That fall after the Billie Sol story appeared to have run its course Carroll Kilpatrick, who covered the White House and had the desk next to mine in the Post city room, said he had been talking with Julian Bach, a former Life magazine reporter who had become a New York literary agent, and that Bach was looking for books with a Washington background. What about the Billie Sol story? The idea of writing a book intrigued me, and at Carroll's suggestion I sent a kind of an outline to Julian Bach.

In my outline I said that I thought the book would be more interesting if the Billie Sol story were tied to an account of the development since Roosevelt's New Deal days of the programs designed to prop up the income of farmers. Without any immediate further thought about a book I was off to other things.

It was the fall of 1962, which meant another election, an off-year election. The big story was the House of Representatives, where the Democrats held only a slim majority and where Kennedy's legislative program was in constant peril. The big question was whether the Democrats could increase their House majority enough to be able to move bills through the House. In the Senate the Democratic majority was large enough to be fairly comfortable and to move the Kennedy programs along.

Editors at the Post decided that the paper should concentrate its House election coverage on a dozen or so districts where the elections would be close enough to determine the outcome for Democratic control of the House. Such coverage seemed to be a good idea to me and the two or three other Post reporters who were assigned to go to the districts, survey the local situations and write stories about the campaigns and their likely outcome.

The first district I was assigned to cover was in far western Kansas. I remember flying to Kansas City and then to a town in the center of Kansas where I caught up with a lawyer who was active in state Democratic politics. It seemed that I had arrived at a propitious time. With its declining population as documented in the 1960 census Kansas had lost a congressional seat and the contest I was to cover involved two members of the House who had been thrown together in a single district that covered much of western Kansas. One member was a Democrat and the other a Republican, who happened to be named Bob Dole. I have forgotten the name of the Democrat, but I do remember that he was a kind of an old-shoe guy who had the weathered face of a rancher. The important thing was that the two candidates were to be debating the next day at a town way out there almost in Colorado.

My new-found Democratic lawyer friend had a half interest in a small airplane and was going to fly out to the debate. Would I like to fly with him? Well, sure, why not. Had I flown a lot? Well, yes, quite a bit. Good, said the lawyer. To help pay for the plane, he explained, he checked on rural-electrification lines and would be doing that on our flight west.

So for two hundred or so miles we flew just above the electric lines and as he flew the plane glancing out at the power lines frequently, he talked about Kansas politics, the close race he expected in the congressional district we were visiting and the likely outcome. I must admit I was a little nervous, but we got to our destination without a mishap.

I have long since forgotten what subjects were debated, but I am sure farm policies were a big part of the discussion. It was a pleasant, gentlemanly encounter, and I guess Dole must have been considered the winner. He won that election, went on to become a Senator from Kansas, ran for vice president on the ticket with President Gerald Ford in 1976 when Jimmy Carter won and unsuccessfully ran for president in 1996 against Bill Clinton. I got to know Dole somewhat and found him to be an engaging and witty man. Now he is retired from the Senate but his wife Elizabeth Dole is a Republican senator from her native North Carolina. So there are obviously some good political genes there.

The other congressional district I remember going to in 1962 was in Arizona. I don't recall who the candidates were, but I will never forget the trip because it was during the last days of October and coincided with the Cuban missile crisis. After following the two candidates around and attending a western chuck-wagon barbecue on what looked to me to be a dude ranch, I was told by my editor that Kennedy was going to make a very serious speech about the missile crisis and that he wanted a reaction story from me. So, how to do it? I decided to find a crowded bar where everyone would surely be listening to the speech and I could get comments afterward. I easily found the bar and was able to get some good quotes after Kennedy finished his scary speech warning the Soviet Union to remove its missiles from Cuba. I filed the story and the next day headed back to Washington. I guess I did not fully realize the seriousness of the situation until I got back to the Post city room. As we all learned later, the Cuban missile crisis was the closest we had ever been to a nuclear war. Fortunately in the end a peaceful solution was found to the crisis. I still think about those ten days of crisis and how lucky we were to avoid war. Those were certainly Kennedy's finest hours.

As for the election, the Democrats did gain a few seats in the House but not nearly enough to ease significantly Kennedy's difficulties in moving legislation on Capitol Hill. Kennedy was a cautious president and he once told my colleague Carroll Kilpatrick that he would not engage in any legislative struggles that he did not think he could win.

# 36

## *Bathtubs in the Capitol*

When I got back from Arizona I learned that Julian Bach had been trying to get in touch with me and that he thought he had found a publisher for my book on Billie Sol Estes and the farm problem. It was a prestigious publisher, too, Little Brown, now part of the Time Warner AOL conglomerate but then an independent publishing house in Boston. After a quick trip to New York to meet a Little Brown editor stationed there and some negotiations I had a book contract. Now all I had to do was write the book!

Looking back on those days, I am amazed at how much work I was able to do. I continued to work full-time at the Washington Post while working nights and weekends on the book. But as Winston Churchill once was reported to have said, writing a book is like building a brick wall, brick by brick, page by page and soon you have a wall and a book.

Somehow the book got written during the first six or seven months of 1963 while I continued to cover the Agriculture and Interior departments among many other things for the Post. I wrote one or two stories almost every day. I am sure I must have been tired much of the time, but I certainly didn't feel oppressed. And Priscilla and the children put up with my seemingly constant pounding at the typewriter at the desk in the converted porch off our living room that we had turned into an office or study.

As I remember I spent a lot of that year on Capitol Hill, a place that I liked. If things were dull on my beats, an editor would say to me, Why don't you go up to the Hill and nose around, meaning see if you can find another Teapot Dome scandal. I never did find such a story but every now and then I would run across a congressional hearing that no one else was covering and that produced a good story, sometimes good enough to make page one.

In those days the Post ran two fairly short stories at the bottom of page one called "readers." They were stories that you would read and say, Did that really happen? Jim Cutlip, an editor who was in charge of putting together page one, would himself get excited when he saw a particularly good story for one of those slots and mutter, "Jesus Christ, Jesus Christ," as he read it over.

I guess what I particularly liked about Capitol Hill was, for a reporter at least, its comfortable atmosphere. Both the Senate and House had press galleries behind the seats overlooking the Senate and House floors that were reserved for reporters. Each press gallery was run by a superintendent, and each superintendent had a couple of assistants. They took telephone calls, saw to it that press releases were available to the reporters and even collected printed testimony from committee hearings. The press galleries had communal desks and typewriters but the big papers like the Post had their own private desks, typewriters and telephones. There were also were some nice comfortable leather chairs where older reporters would take their afternoon naps. And there seemed to be continuous card games in both galleries.

Sometimes senators or representatives would come into the galleries to hold informal press conferences. I remember Republican Senator Everett Dirksen of Illinois in particular doing that. He would appear after the weekly luncheon meeting of the Republican Senate leadership, sit on a table, his legs dangling, and take questions from the dozen or so reporters who were usually around the Senate gallery. Some of the reporters were close enough to him to call him "Ev" and he always had a good quote or two. It was at one of those informal press conferences that I heard his famous remark about government spending: "You take a billion here and a billion there and pretty soon you're talking about real money."

Most congressional offices welcomed reporters. The coin of the realm for politicians is talk, and so it is too for reporters. It seemed then that senators and representatives were always good for some talk, serious at times but gossipy at other time. Democratic Senator Paul Douglas of Illinois, a big, shaggy-haired man, would sit down to lunch with two or three reporters once every week or two—and I was invited to the lunches every so often—and talk about what the Senate was doing and his particular legislative interests. These sessions were held in his office, the food was brought in by waiters from the Senate restaurant, and the conversation was always good. Douglas had been an economics professor at the University of Chicago and at the age of fifty had enlisted in the Marine Corps in World War II. During the war his left arm had been struck by a bullet and he had no use of it. He was a tough combination of a scholar and a fighter. As they say, once a Marine always a Marine, and he certainly was that. He was a favorite of mine, and of many other reporters, so different from Dirksen, who was called the "wizard of ooze."

On quiet days when I was on Capitol Hill I also found time to explore the nooks and crannies of the Capitol building itself. My guide was usually Arnie Sawislak, who covered the House for United Press International. Arnie and I had gone to Central High School together back in St. Paul. I remember particularly one afternoon in the Capitol when we saw everything from the catafalque on which Lincoln's body lay in a casket in the Capitol rotunda before it was taken back to Springfield, Illinois, for burial. On that afternoon we also went far below the Senate side of the Capitol to see the long-abandoned bath tubs placed there after the Civil War at a time when few homes or rooming houses in Washington had private baths. The tubs were only for the use of senators. We explored the original Senate chamber, later used by the Supreme Court as its meeting place. We saw a much smaller room where the Court met until it moved to the old Senate chamber. In addition, we ducked into a few of the rooms now used by senators as hide-away offices. The Capitol has so many tucked-away spaces that you could spend days wandering around and never go to the same place twice. Despite its huge size, the Capitol is a comfortable place with its many smaller meeting rooms and offices. It's too bad tourists cannot see these places.

Speaking of tourists I also picked up a lot of the lore about the Senate and House chambers. I was in fact on the floor of the Senate a few times. It was the custom in the Senate for the majority and minority leaders to have conferences at their desks with reporters before the beginning of a Senate session. I participated in a few of those conferences, which were mostly about the Senate business planned for the day. "Dugout chatter," it was irreverently called by a press secretary to Republican Hugh Scott of Pennsylvania when he was Senate leader for his party.

I also remember a Saturday when Suzie and I went up to the Capitol to pick up a document I needed for something I was writing. I was showing her around the Senate side when we ran into Democratic Senator John Sparkman of Alabama. He spoke to us and I introduced myself. He remembered me from my Post byline and stories and asked, "Have you ever been on the Senate floor?" I said I had, and then he said, "What about your daughter? Come on, I'll show you around."

So Senator Sparkman took us onto the floor, the Senate not being in session on a Saturday, and showed us where he sat, where the leaders sat, and such historic desks as the one used by Daniel Webster and John Kennedy. He also pointed out the spittoons and snuff boxes that are still there.

One other Saturday I remember was when we were taking some visitors on a tour of the Capitol. We were in the House gallery when a tour group came in and sat down near us. As the tour guide went through his canned spiel I was going through my much more detailed description of the House chamber, and soon I discovered that the tour group was listening to me, not to its guide. The guide of course did not like my upstaging him, but I just smiled and continued my discourse because I knew my knowledge of the Capitol was much greater than his.

As you can see, I really enjoyed being on Capitol Hill whether I was covering a hearing, big or small, or just wandering around picking up the fascinating lore of the place. Unfortunately now, because of security concerns, I don't think even a reporter can wander around the Hill the way I did in my days there.

# 37

## *A Warm Bucket of What?*

I was doing so many interesting things that it is hard to remember everything. But one event I will never forget was a long, and I do mean long, day spent with Lyndon Johnson in Texas when he was Vice President. The purpose of the trip was to dedicate the Padre Island National Seashore and to open a saline-water plant. The seashore stretches from Galveston west and the water plant was not too far from Galveston. There was room for only three reporters on the trip. In addition to myself, there was Russ Baker of the New York Times and Roy McGhee of United Press International. Russ, who later became a columnist, was covering the Senate for the Times, and Roy was a Texan who was also covering the Senate and had covered Johnson for many years.

We all met before dawn at Andrews Air Force Base and flew direct to Houston. From there we went in cars to the seashore dedication, the saline-water plant and a couple of other places. The weather was hot and it was an exhausting day. But what I remember best was the trip back to Washington.

Johnson's plane was not Air Force One, but it was nice enough. On the way back Johnson sat in a seat with a small table that opened up in front of him. Russ Baker and I sat opposite Johnson and Roy McGhee sat next to him. We all had drinks and chips and peanuts. As reporters knew, Johnson drank scotch but for obvious political reasons said he was a bourbon man.

The conversation ranged from the day's events and Texas politics to the outlook for the 1964 presidential election. We also talked about legislation before Congress, and I remember Johnson saying that a particular difficult bill could be passed once he sat down with "Ev," Ev being Senator Dirksen who was then the Republican Senate leader. "I think I know what Ev will take on this," said Johnson, who was justly famous for being able to negotiate compromises that would ease a bill through the Senate.

Then we started talking about the vice presidency. "A difficult job, Mr. Vice President?" Russ Baker asked. Johnson admitted that it was not an easy job, particularly under someone like Kennedy who wanted to be, and was, a strong president. "Knowing all this, why did you take the job?" Russ went on to ask Johnson.

Johnson never really answered the question, but he did go on to say that when he was offered the vice presidency by Kennedy, he called up "Mr. Garner" to seek his advice. Mr. Garner was John Nance Garner, a Texan who was vice president during Franklin D. Roosevelt's first two terms in the nineteen thirties. Before that Garner had been Speaker of the House. He had been out of politics for twenty-some years but still was revered in Texas, if not elsewhere. The United Mine Workers president John L. Lewis had once called Garner "an evil, whiskey-smelling old man." As vice president, Garner had seldom seen Roosevelt and had been nothing more than a fifth wheel during the New Deal years. Garner was William Randolph Hearst's choice for president in 1932 when Roosevelt was first elected, and Roosevelt chose Garner as his running mate in large part to placate Hearst and gain the support of his newspapers, which he succeeded in doing. But Hearst soon turned on Roosevelt and became one of his worst enemies.

But back to Lyndon Johnson and Mr. Garner. In our conversation on that late night flight back to Washington, Johnson said that when he told Garner he was offered the vice presidency, Garner replied, "Well Lyndon you do what you think is best for you, but let me tell you the vice presidency isn't worth a warm bucket of piss!" I think that was the first time Johnson had ever told that story, which has been sanitized as "a warm bucket of spit," certainly not as graphic or interesting as in its original telling but still a great story.

We arrived back at Andrews Air Force Base in the early morning hours, all three of us reporters thoroughly exhausted while Johnson seemed ready to talk the rest of the night, or morning, through. He could be irascible and unlikable but he could also be charming and ingratiating. A fascinating man.

Another trip that I took in 1963 and will never forget was with President Kennedy. It was billed as a conservation trip. The word "environment" was not yet part of the political vocabulary. Kennedy was to tour some conservation projects or areas ranging from Pennsylvania to Wyoming and end up speaking to a meeting in Las Vegas before going on to spend a weekend in Palm Springs. This was a full-blown presidential trip with a large press contingent in its own airplane. Kennedy of course traveled in Air Force One.

We first went to a park in Pennsylvania named after Gifford Pinchot, the founder of the conservation movement in the early nineteen-twenties. From there we went on to an area comprising both northern Minnesota and northern Wisconsin. The area was being considered for designation as a national park or wilderness area. We were to fly over the areas in helicopters so that we could get a good look at things. But instead we flew into a thunderstorm that had come up suddenly and unexpectedly. It was scary, so scary that we had to make an emergency landing in a hay field. We made the landing successfully and waited out the storm. But I think the pilots of the helicopters were as scared as the reporters and the rest of the presidential party including Kennedy himself.

From Minnesota we went to Montana and then Wyoming. The primary purpose of the stop in Montana was the dedication by Kennedy of the modest home where Montana Senator Mike Mansfield was born as an historic landmark. Mansfield was then the Democratic leader in the Senate, a gentle man loved by all and a great admirer of Kennedy's.

That night and the next morning were memorable. We spent the night at the magnificent lodge in the Grand Teton Mountains. The rooms were wonderful, the dinner even better and the company of the reporters was good, as always. There is a great camaraderie among reporters, particularly when you are traveling in a group covering the president or a campaign.

I will never forget the next morning when we gathered in the dining room of the lodge for breakfast. One wall of the dining room consisted of huge windows looking out to the Grand Tetons, some of the most beautiful mountains anywhere in the world. We could see elk, deer and moose grazing in the distance. Senator Mansfield sat down at the table where I was eating with a couple of other reporters, and we talked mostly about the spectacular setting outside the windows and the other beauties of the West that Mansfield so loved. And whenever I saw Mansfield after that he always recalled our breakfast. I always said politics needed more people like him, unassuming, down-to-earth and so genuine. He was one of a kind.

The next day Kennedy went to Salt Lake City where that evening he made a speech defending the signing of a treaty with the Soviet Union banning underground nuclear testing. It was thought that the treaty was unpopular with Americans because of the continued fear of communism and the feeling that the Communist Soviet Union could not be trusted. But the response to the speech, delivered in the Mormon Tabernacle, was quite good and Kennedy and his entourage were delighted.

From Salt Lake we were off to Las Vegas where Kennedy gave a speech to a conservation group, a speech unlike the Mormon Tabernacle address, long since forgotten. It was my first trip to Las Vegas, but we were there only a short time and I did not see much besides the airport, a meeting hall and the outsides of the hotels and casinos. The Las Vegas reputation was still not very good, and a president would not dare stay in the city overnight; so after his speech Kennedy was on his way to Palm Springs for the weekend.

It had been a good trip. Kennedy had done a lot to show his interest in the conservation movement and his speech on the nuclear treaty had helped to clear the air on feelings about U.S.-Soviet cooperation on such an important issue as nuclear testing.

# 38

## *San Francisco Here I Come*

Before I left Washington the editors at the Post had decided that rather than returning to Washington with Kennedy I should stay in California and look into the political situation there, particularly the Republican movement supporting Senator Barry Goldwater of Arizona for the GOP presidential nomination in 1964.

From Palm Springs I flew to San Francisco where I decided to stay at the St. Francis Hotel. When I arrived at the airline terminal in downtown San Francisco, I was approached by what I later learned was called a "walking porter." He asked me where I was going and I told him the St. Francis. He said, Oh, that's only a couple of blocks away. I'll take you there. He grabbed my bags and off we went. Within five or ten minutes we were in the St. Francis lobby and I was registering for a room, which I believe was fifteen dollars a night. Amazing! Today that room probably costs four hundred dollars.

I arrived in San Francisco in the early evening, saw the cable cars going past the St. Francis on Powell street and was eager to see some of the city. But I was tired after the trip with Kennedy; so I stayed in the hotel, had a light dinner and got to bed early.

The next morning was gorgeous. This was late September, the summer fog was gone and the sky was as blue as blue can be. I walked around a few blocks but then got back to the hotel to begin my work. One of the first persons I saw was former Republican Senator William Knowland who was in Oakland and invited me to come right over. I took a bus across the Bay Bridge and found my way to his office.

Knowland had left the Senate in 1958 to run for governor, a ploy negotiated by Nixon. But Knowland lost the governorship race to Pat Brown and was now back at the family newspaper, the Oakland Tribune. Knowland was a big man, but he had an awfully small office in the Tribune tower. The office provided a nice view, but it was so small and he looked so uncomfortable.

But we had a good conversation. He obviously was happy to talk with someone from Washington, even though the reporter was from the Washington Post, a paper that never liked him and that he turn never liked. We gossiped a bit about Washington and the Senate in particular and then got on to Goldwater and his chances of getting the Republican presidential nomination, of carrying California and of being elected president in 1964. Knowland was a Goldwater supporter and thought he would do well. Knowland never again ran for public office and came to a tragic end when he committed suicide some years later. The family also lost the Oakland Tribune after owning the paper, once a powerhouse in California Republican politics, for decades.

Another important California Republican I interviewed was Casper Weinberger, who was then practicing law in San Francisco and later became Ronald Reagan's Secretary of Defense. In 1963 Weinberger was more of a centrist or even a bit liberal in Republican terms; so he was not so sure about a Goldwater candidacy. He was I think leaning toward Nelson Rockefeller, then governor of New York and viewed as a likely presidential candidate in 1964.

I talked with several other Republicans and some Democrats including Roger Kent, a lawyer very active in the California Democratic party. In Kent's office I ran into Dick Kaplan, an old friend from University of Minnesota days who had gone on to law school at the University of Michigan and was now practicing law in San Francisco. Dick's office was right off the reception room to the Kent firm's suite and when he heard me announcing myself to the receptionist he came bounding out to greet me. He did not know I was working for the Post but had seen articles of mine in the Reporter magazine.

I also saw Lionel Horwitz, another old friend from Minnesota days. Lionel was living at the foot of Columbus Street near Fishermen's Wharf and was working at the Stockton Record. Stockton is an hour or so west of San Francisco. Lionel had bought a weekly paper in Livermore, which is also west of San Francisco, in the early nineteen-fifties but had recently sold it.

One night he took me on his special tour of San Francisco, which included North Beach and the Old Spaghetti Factory restaurant; Broadway, not yet topless, but with an Italian restaurant featuring aspiring opera singers; Chinatown with its many restaurants and exotic shops; and the Top of the Mark, in the Mark Hopkins hotel on Nob Hill.

From this first visit I knew that San Francisco was now my favorite city, even more so than Washington. Everything seemed just right, from the views of the Bay, the cool air, neighborhoods like Chinatown and North Beach, and the cable cars.

But all too soon it was back to Washington and the Post. It was now October and then November. Congress was still in session, but I don't remember covering any significant stories until that fateful day in November.

# 39

## *November 22, 1963*

Everyone of my generation knows where he was shortly after noon on November 22, 1963. I was in the Senate press gallery, having just finished lunch at the press table in the Senate restaurant when someone shouted, "Kennedy's been shot!" I immediately went into the Senate chamber where a desultory debate had been going on. Only a few senators had been on the floor, but suddenly more began to appear. The debate ceased and senators talked with one another, or rather seemed to whisper.

All too soon the horrible news came that Kennedy was dead. I called my editor and asked what I could do. He said he didn't know, but that I better get back to the office as quickly as I could. So I left the Senate gallery, was able to get a cab and soon was back at the Post.

At first no one was quite sure what to do, but after putting out an "Extra," most unusual in those days, the editors began to sort things out. Eddie Folliard had been covering Kennedy's Texas trip and would be coming back with Lyndon Johnson, who also had been in Texas and was sworn in as President on Air Force One. Kennedy's body had been placed on the plane. Eddie of course would write the main story. Larry Stern, a national reporter, was immediately sent to Texas to cover the story there. There was an immediate feeling that Kennedy's assassination was part of a right-wing conspiracy, and I was told to put together a story on the right-wing movement in the United States and particularly Texas. Of course it turned out not to have been a right-wing conspiracy at all.

The story I wrote during those terrible days that I was most proud of was an account of the kings and princes and presidents and prime ministers who gathered at the White House on the day of Kennedy's funeral and walked behind his casket up Seventeenth Street and Connecticut Avenue to the Catholic church on Rhode Island Avenue where the funeral services were held. Charles DeGaulle was there as was Prince Phillip and so many other world leaders. After watching them leave the White House I too made my way to the church on Rhode Island Avenue and I still remember watching John Kennedy Jr., then just two years old, saluting his father's casket as it was brought out of the church on its way to burial in Arlington Cemetery. I did not go to the cemetery; other reporters were assigned to that party of the day's tragic story. My piece on the kings and princes and presidents and prime ministers walking the streets of Washington was prominently displayed on page one of the *Post* the next day. And I am still proud of that story.

I encouraged Fred and Steve to go downtown to see the Kennedy cortege move down Connecticut Avenue, and they did come with me when I went to work and were able to get a spot where they could see everything.

Those were terrible times and I still think about them. And then of course Lee Harvey Oswald, who had shot Kennedy, was himself shot a few days later by a Dallas night-club owner. It was a bizarre situation. I have always felt that Oswald did it himself and was not part of some conspiracy. But for years the stories of conspiracies continued to be printed and books were written about the supposed conspiracy. The conspiracy theories have not been heard much in recent years, but I am sure we will hear about them again.

But life goes on, as it must. In Washington the spotlight immediately shifted to Lyndon Johnson. What sort of a president would he be? What would be his priorities? Would he keep the Kennedy Cabinet and the Kennedy White House staff.?

Johnson was so different from Kennedy. Kennedy was suave, sophisticated; Johnson was a dyed-in-the-wool Texan, with all that implies. He was rough and tough, and, as it turned out, could not get over the many negative comparisons made between him and Kennedy. I think, no, I know, that harmed Johnson's presidency. But as Johnson used to say, "I'm the only President you got."

I covered the White House a little bit during Johnson's first days in office, and I still have a picture showing me and other reporters gathered around Johnson in the Oval Office as he conducted an informal press conference. Johnson tried many places for press conferences from the East Room of the White House to a field stacked with bales of hay on his ranch in Texas, but never seemed to be comfortable with the press. I think he liked to see the press in his office, because that's the way his hero Franklin D. Roosevelt always did it.

It's hard to believe today, but what Johnson considered the biggest immediate issue facing him was how to hold the federal budget below one hundred billion dollars. A hundred billion! Why that's small change in today's budget world of trillions of dollars. But Johnson did manage to keep his first budget just under one hundred billion dollars.

After reining in the budget, Johnson looked to his State of the Union address. What should be his program? How could he, a Texan, deal with the burgeoning civil rights issues? What about the economy? And it would soon be 1964 and a presidential election year. He surely would run for election in his own right, but could he win.

The year 1963 was important to me for other reasons in addition to those I have recounted above. That summer Priscilla became pregnant again. We had thought our family had been complete with three children, but then we discovered that another child was on the way, and we were both thirty-eight years old, almost forty! Too old to have a child. Well, my father was forty-eight when I was born, and we were ten years younger. Priscilla's doctor father reminded us that children born of older mothers often could have problems, but Priscilla's health was excellent and after taking a while to getting used to the idea of having another child at our age we settled back and looked forward to an addition to the family.

Meantime, at the Washington Post tragedy struck. Late in August Publisher Phillip Graham committed suicide. He was only in his early forties but had been suffering from mental illness for some time. He was in and out of private mental institutions and killed himself with a shotgun while on leave from an institution to spend a weekend at the Graham's house in the Virginia hunt country. It was a beautiful day, as I remember. I was not working that Saturday but I still vividly remember how shocking the news was when I heard it on the television news that evening.

When I returned to the Post the next Monday it was a sad place. I did not really know Graham. As I mentioned earlier I had lunch with him and Bob Estabrook shortly after going to the paper. And I chatted with him a couple of times during his infrequent visits to the news room. The editors and older reporters who knew Graham said that he was a brilliant man, quick-witted and a wonderful conversationalist. He was credited with the purchase of the Washington Times-Herald in the mid-fifties, which as Eugene Meyer said, made the Post "safe for Donny," the Graham's then young son and now the publisher of the Post.

But on that fateful August day in 1963 everyone was asking what would happen to the Post. Katharine Graham, Phillip's wife and Eugene Meyer's daughter, now owned the paper in her own right, but had never been active in the management of the Post. Would she sell the paper? If she did sell the Post, would it be bought by some conglomerate like Hearst or Gannett? Or would she become publisher herself and try to run the paper and continue the present management?

Or would she fire the current executives and start over with people she personally selected?

Those first months after Graham's death were trying times, even for a reporter like me who was far down the pecking order, had no editing position and wanted none. Before his death Graham had taken up with a secretary who worked for Newsweek, a magazine Graham had bought only in 1962. He had purchased Newsweek against the advice of many who pointed out that the magazine had never much money and seemed to be consigned forever as a second-rate news weekly to Time magazine.

It seems that many of the editors and executives at the Post had known of Graham's affair with the secretary but had not told Mrs. Graham about it. She later learned about this secrecy, was very angry about it and it was said that she was determined to get rid of the people who had failed to inform her about what was going on. There was obviously a good deal of truth in this because in 1964 as she took over the paper several executives were let go.

In 1963 I also spent a week in Salt Lake City, Utah, and Boise, Idaho investigating some right-wing groups that were becoming prominent in the Republican politics in those two conservative states. I have long since forgotten the details of the stories I wrote about these groups, but I still remember a couple of long evenings I spent with a political scientists in Salt Lake who not only filled me in on the right-wing movement but also described to me in some detail how the Mormon church dominated and ran Utah and much of Idaho.

One other political event from 1963 that sticks in my memory is a Republican meeting held in Hershey, Pennsylvania, the chocolate town. And it is indeed just that, with the wonderful smell of chocolate permeating the air everywhere in Hershey, which is a couple of hours from Washington and near the Pennsylvania capital of Harrisburg.

The meeting was held in the baroque Hershey Hotel, built by Mr. Hershey himself, the founder of the chocolate company. He was a benevolent businessman who also started a home in Hershey for orphans. The hotel itself is on a hill and surrounded by beautiful rose gardens. The meeting I covered was in June and the roses were in bloom and were a wonderful sight.

The Republican leaders gathered in Hershey to try to patch over the major differences between the middle-of-the-road to liberal eastern wing of the party and the conservative Goldwater wing that was becoming dominant in the South and Midwest as well as the West itself.

But the big story coming out of the meeting came to be something quite different. Governor Nelson Rockefeller of New York, who everyone was sure would be a Republican candidate for the party's presidential nomination in 1964, had shocked the political world by announcing a few weeks before the meeting that he was going to divorce his wife of many years and marry a much younger woman!

So the issue that really dominated the meeting was whether a divorced man could ever be elected president. How times have changed! Adlai Stevenson was divorced, but single, when he ran against General Dwight Eisenhower in 1952 and 1956, but divorce never became an issue in those elections, perhaps because no one thought Stevenson ever had a chance of defeating Eisenhower. Or it may have been because Stevenson had not remarried, and never did, although it was said that he was quite the womanizer.

At any rate, the Republicans agreed at their meeting that Rockefeller's divorce had all but killed his presidential aspirations. Rockefeller of course did not think so and ended up seeking the Republican nomination in 1964.

Today divorce is no longer an issue in politics. Divorce has become as accepted a part of life as marriage itself. But forty years ago it was different and I think if Rockefeller had got the Republican presidential nomination in 1964 the issue of his divorce would have hurt him badly. But in 1980 Ronald Reagan, a divorced man, was elected president and I don't recall any mention of his divorce in that campaign.

Speaking of divorce, I am drawn to the somewhat related issue of Kennedy's sexual adventures. I am frequently asked why the press did not write about Kennedy's women friends. Well, I did not know anything about his sexual proclivities. I of course did not cover the White House much, so was not in a position to know any intimate details of Kennedy's life. But I never heard a whisper of his sexual activities from Carroll Kilpatrick, the Post reporter who covered Kennedy the most.

Would the Post and other major papers have printed stories about Kennedy's sexual adventures if they had known about them? I'm not sure they would have. A lot has changed in the last forty years. When I started working as a reporter, newspapers never even used the word rape. A woman was attacked, not raped. So I doubt very much that the Kennedy stories which later emerged would ever have been printed in the nineteen-sixties.

So 1963 was quite a year for me, for politics, for the Post and for the country. It certainly was a year none of us would ever forget. And in addition to my work for the Post and the Bille Sol Estes book I also found time beginning to free-lance for magazines. My articles were appearing in the Reporter magazine, which had a fairly large circulation, and the Progressive magazine, with a smaller but influential readership.

The Reporter had been started in the early fifties by Max Ascoli, an Italian-born intellectual who had married well into the family of a Sears, Roebuck heir. So he had plenty of money to start a magazine. The Reporter came out every other week and was a serious publication on the liberal side of the political spectrum. The Progressive was started by Robert LaFollete of Wisconsin, who later became a senator and ran for president in 1924, the year of my birth, on the Progressive party ticket. The LaFolletes and the Progressive party were long since gone by the nineteen-sixties but the magazine survived, but barely. Its editor, who I got to know quite well, had to raise money every year to keep the magazine, which had a circulation of only around forty thousand, going, but he managed to keep it alive. Later Erwin Knoll, a Washington Post colleague, became editor of the Progressive but died prematurely in his fifties. The Progressive is still being published monthly but Ascoli closed down the Reporter in 1968. Both magazines had a devoted readership at the time I was writing for them. The pieces I did were based on reporting that I had done for the Post. The Post editors did not mind reporters writing for magazines as long as the reporters gave their all to the paper first, and I certainly did that. And people still remember that I wrote for the Reporter and the Progressive.

The free-lance writing brought in a little extra money, but not that much. I remember the Reporter paying three hundred dollars or so for an article, but you were lucky to get a hundred dollars from the always broke Progressive. But there was a certain prestige in being in magazines like that. Also, the Post has never had the national circulation of the New York Times or the Wall Street Journal; so even if a lot of what you had written for the Post appeared in your free-lance magazine articles you could be sure that few of the readers of the magazines had read your Post articles.

Anyway, I liked to write and I will brag and say I was a pretty good writer. Strangely, many reporters are not good writers and in fact do not like to write. These reporters often like the excitement of the chase, talking to news sources, digging up difficult-to-get facts, scooping other reporters, but find sitting down and writing the story laborious and sometimes even boring.

I think my career at the Post blossomed because as a Post editor told me once, "You're a producer." By that he meant that I almost always got the story by digging out the facts of a situation and writing in an interesting and sometimes compelling fashion. And doing it all in good time. I was a "producer" because I loved what I was doing.

# 40

## *"They're Taking Down What He's Saying!"*

After finishing my account of Billie Sol Estes and the farm problem and sending off the manuscript to my editor at Little Brown, I embarked on another extracurricular project—on the politics and economics of the defense program. This idea was suggested to me by Jack Fischer, the editor of Harper's magazine. During the nineteen thirties he had worked in Washington for the Associated Press and was always on the lookout for Washington pieces for Harper's. I had written a couple of articles for Harper's, one on the fight between the Agriculture and Interior departments over which one would run the U.S. Forest Service (Agriculture won out) and the other on a project being pushed by Senator Paul Douglas to require lenders to tell borrowers the true cost of consumer loans.

But the big story for me in 1964 was the presidential election. By the beginning of the year I had finished most of my work on the Harper's project on defense spending, which turned into a three-part series for the magazine. Later in the year I expanded the series into a book. Two books in as many years! That was pretty good.

Back to the presidential election, and the primaries. In February I was sent to New Hampshire to cover the first presidential primary of the year. The Iowa caucuses had not yet been discovered; that would come with Jimmy Carter in 1976. In 1964 New Hampshire was still unchallenged as the state where we would first learn something about what the voters thought of the candidates.

Henry Cabot Lodge, the former Republican senator from neighboring Massachusetts and the 1960 GOP vice-presidential candidate, was on his party's New Hampshire primary tickets along with Senator Barry Goldwater of Arizona. Both Lodge and Goldwater spent a good deal of time campaigning in New Hampshire and a close race was expected. Were there big issues between them? I guess so, but issues tend to get blurred even in primaries. Basically Goldwater was for cutting back sharply the federal government's role in American life, turning over some programs to the private sector, while Lodge represented the Eastern Republican establishment and tended to talk about the government not in terms of drastically cutting it back but rather that "we can do it better."

Lodge was the winner in New Hampshire. His victory was attributed in large part to his being a New Englander. But Goldwater did run a strong race, an indication that he was a force to be reckoned with in the 1964 Republican primaries. There was of course no opposition to Lyndon Johnson in the Democratic primary.

I remember many things from that primary from the new and beautiful hotel outside Manchester, New Hampshire, where reporters and candidates and their staffs stayed, to the beauty of the state itself even on the coldest, snowiest days. I also remember the story of one of the Goldwater supporters, an elderly woman, who said indignantly at a Goldwater rally: "Look! Those reporters are taking down what he's saying!" The Goldwater people did not like the press, to put it mildly, and that remark kind of sums up their feelings. On the other hand, reporters themselves liked Goldwater, even though many of them did not agree with his ideas. He was just a nice man who was always willing to answer even hostile questions. I have a picture on my wall showing myself at an informal Goldwater press conference in New Hampshire. The Senator is resting, sitting on a bed in his hotel room, and I am to one side, hunched forward to catch his every word.

A few days after I returned from New Hampshire our daughter Sally was born. I remember that it was a cold and icy on the night of February the twenty-third when she like all our other children was born in the Columbia Hospital for Women in Washington. Columbia, which traced its history to Civil War days when it sheltered wounded soldiers, is now gone.

Sally was a healthy baby. Even so, when Priscilla' pediatrician father visited us a month or so after Sally's birth he immediately went upstairs to see her to make sure she was all right. As a pediatrician he had seen too many babies with problems, particularly when the mothers were as old as Priscilla, who was thirty-nine when Sally was born. Priscilla's father found Sally to be in excellent shape.

In the spring of 1964 my book about Billie Sol Estes, entitled "Taxpayers' Hayride," was published and received some nice review in newspapers around the country. I appeared on a few radio talk shows to talk about it. "Taxpayers' Hayride" never became much of seller, total sales coming only to a few thousand copies, but it certainly was satisfying to have published a book and another one—on the politics and economics of defense spending—under way. I still wonder how I managed to do so much work, but I guess it's because when you are in your thirties and forties you have a lot of energy and drive.

In April I was on the political road again, first to Chicago to cover the Illinois presidential primary. Everyone knew Goldwater would do well in the Republican heartland, but the question to be answered at least in part in Illinois was: How well?

On election night I was able to work out of the city room of the Chicago Tribune, which was a good break for me because as a major paper the Tribune got returns fast and accurately in those days before computers. Even though editorially the Washington Post and Chicago Tribune were at opposite ends, the Tribune editors and political reporters treated me well and were helpful in everything from checking the statistics and explaining where the votes, particularly the early ones, were coming from in Illinois.

The early returns showed Goldwater running well, and as more and more returns kept coming in he did better and better. As the night wore on there was no question that Goldwater was quite popular in the Midwestern bellwether state of Illinois. The Illinois republican primary certainly boded well for the Senator from Arizona.

From Chicago it was not back to Washington for me, but across the rest of the country to Oregon where the next primary was coming up in May. I was happy to be going west; ever since my first trip west to Denver covering Kennedy in 1960 I had become more and more interested in that part of the country. I liked the people, the breath-taking mountains and just about everything else about the West. Some of the open country seemed like paradise to me.

The contest in Oregon pitted Goldwater against Governor Nelson Rockefeller of New York. Henry Cabot Lodge had dropped out of the Republican race, and Rockefeller had in effect replaced him. Oregon was the last primary before the grand finale early in June in California. In those days there were only a handful of primaries unlike today where all but a few states have primaries. And the Oregon primary was always considered significant. In 1948, for example, Governor Thomas E. Dewey of New York all but clinched the Republican presidential nomination by defeating former Governor Harold Stassen of Minnesota in the Oregon primary. Just before the primary Dewey debated Stassen; the issue was registration of the Communist party; Dewey said the communists should be regulated; Stassen argued that this was a free speech issue and that the communists should not be required to register with the federal government. Dewey's position was the popular one and helped him to win the 1948 primary.

In Oregon in 1964 there were a lot of political reporters including Walter Cronkite and David Brinkley and we all traveled up and down the state with the candidates. And sometimes Cronkite and Brinkley attracted more curious onlookers than the candidates themselves. The power of television was beginning to be felt.

Goldwater eked out a victory over Rockefeller, which was considered quite significant for Oregon because it was a state with a middle-of-the-road to liberal reputation even among Republicans. Wayne Morse was one of its senators, and he was considered quite liberal in Washington, particularly for being a Republican.

From Oregon it was on to California for me and most of the other political reporters. California would be the "big enchilada" for the Republicans because of its size and because of its importance in national politics. If Goldwater could take California he would be assured of the Republican nomination at the party's convention, which would be in San Francisco in July.

During the two weeks I was in California before the primary I spent a good deal of time in San Francisco but also traveled to Los Angeles, Sacramento and elsewhere in the state. I had a wonderful time; I saw a lot of the state; I think I wrote some good stories; and I covering a major story. Besides, I got to spend more time in San Francisco and was able to get to know the city a little better. The more I learned about the city the more I liked it. I often thought it would be great to live there someday. It had everything, the climate, the atmosphere, the food!

Because of the importance of the story, Ben Gilbert, one of the Post's editors, came out to help me with election-night coverage. We worked out of the Los Angeles Times news room—the Post and the Times having established a joint news service in 1962. The early returns indicated that it would be a close race between Goldwater and Rockefeller and as the night went on the race seemed to tighten.

Goldwater continued to maintain a slight lead as more returns came in, but should we call the race for him or say that it is too close to call? Relying on data from the pollster Lou Harris, who was then working for the Post and the Times-Post news service, Ben Gilbert and I decided late in the evening to file a story declaring Goldwater the winner.

We turned out to be right the next morning, but barely, and we received some criticism from Al Friendly, the Post's managing editor, for taking a chance and threatening the paper with an embarrassing headline like the Chicago Tribune's

"Dewey Defeats Truman" streamer of 1948. But we did turn out to be right, and could fly back to Washington holding our heads high.

I barely had time to get back home and have my clothes washed when I was on the road again. Republican Bill Scranton of Pennsylvania suddenly decided to challenge Goldwater for the nomination, and embarked on a quick flying tour of states where convention delegates were not yet tied up. I and most of the other political reporters who made the quickie trip with Scranton liked him. He came from an important Pennsylvania family—there is after all a Scranton, Pa.—and he had been elected governor twice. He was considered a good governor too.

But it was too late to stop the Goldwater juggernaut. And I think Scranton knew that. But he gave it a try, perhaps after being egged on by Rockefeller and Lodge. I don't really know about that, but I have always had that feeling. Unlike Rockefeller, Scranton did not give you the feeling that he was superior to mortal reporters. Try as he might, Rockefeller could not get down to earth talking with ordinary people. He always greeted reporters with "Hey, fellas, how are you doing," but the greeting never seemed genuine. Scranton, on the other hand, appeared genuinely to like reporters.

One thing I remember from the Scranton trip was having to spend a night in a hotel room in Minneapolis with a Chicago Tribune reporter who was famous for having written a story just before U.S. entry into World War II saying that the United States had broken the Japanese code which made it possible for Washington to intercept Japanese military messages.

The Tribune was anti-Roosevelt, which went far to explain its decision to publish the story, but it was viewed by many as a treasonous act. The Tribune reporter and I never talked about that story, and he was pleasant enough. He had trouble sleeping though and spent the night sitting on the toilet in the bathroom reading a paperback mystery while I slept fitfully in one of the beds. I always hated to have to double up with someone on a trip like that, but it was necessary at times when not enough rooms were available for everyone to have one for himself.

After the Scranton trip it was soon time to go to San Francisco for the Republican convention. Priscilla naturally wanted to come along, but who would take care of the children? Fred was sixteen, Steve fifteen, Suzie eleven and Sally not quite six months. First we thought of hiring someone to look after the children, but Fred, Steve and Suzie didn't like that idea. Why, we can do it, they said, and you could pay us what you would have to pay a sitter, couldn't you? Well, we thought about it and agreed to their suggestion after enlisting the help of Sue

Snyder, the daughter of our long-time friends Betsy and Jack Snyder. I think Sue Snyder was seventeen, and she agreed to drop by every day to check on things.

# 41

## *"Extremism in the Pursuit of Liberty"*

So, with some trepidation, we were off to San Francisco. We stayed at the Hyde Park Suites, at Hyde and Bay streets not far from Fisherman's Wharf. It was a comfortable place with a kitchen and living room as well as a bedroom as part of each unit. Every other day or so we checked with the children, and everything seemed to be going fine.

The Republican headquarters were at the St. Francis hotel, where I had stayed on my first visit to San Francisco a year earlier, and the convention sessions were at the Cow Palace just south of the city. I was one of four reporters sent to the convention by the Post. Russ Wiggins, the top editor, was also there to supervise the staff. The story was all Goldwater—no contest—but all of us reporters managed to find plenty to write about.

I guess there were some memorable moments, but the only one I—and most people who were there—can remember was the Goldwater acceptance speech in which he said "extremism in the pursuit of liberty...." was all right. Goldwater was being sharply criticized for being an extremist, and he was that, although some of the ideas he expressed in 1964 about less government in our lives were considered to be fairly mainstream in the later Nixon and Reagan years.

While I went to press conferences and attended convention sessions, Priscilla got acquainted with San Francisco and the Bay area. A couple of other wives of Post reporters were there, and they all teamed up to visit the Union Square stores, Chinatown, Fisherman's Wharf and Golden Gate Park as well as the Muir Woods and Half Moon Bay. Needless to say, a good time was had by all.

The convention was over all too soon, and within a week we were back to Washington and Chevy Chase. Fred, Steve and Suzie, with the help of Sue Snyder, turned out to be good baby sitters and even good cooks. The baby-sitting idea that they had suggested worked out surprisingly well. Priscilla was as taken with San Francisco as I had been, and after the 1964 trip we both said it would be nice to live there.

Next that summer came the Democratic convention, which was in Atlantic City late in August. I was among the Post reporters assigned to the convention, but a few days before the opening day of the convention I was suddenly told to go to New York. A big story was unfolding there—would Bobby Kennedy decided to run for the Senate from New York?

I had promised Fred and Steve that I would take them to the Democratic convention, but now I had to go to New York. Well, we hurriedly packed and the three of us drove to New York. I decided we should stay at the then quite new New York Hilton hotel, and we were able to get a room without any trouble. But what would Fred and Steve do while I dashed around after the Bobby Kennedy story?

I decided, and they agreed, that they should see the city. We had all been to New York a couple of years earlier; so they had some idea of the city. I suggested that they go to the World's Fair in progress at Flushing Meadows, now the site of the Mets' baseball stadium, and they did that. Another day they went down to Wall Street to visit the New York Stock Exchange. And so it went. Today I don't suppose you would dare send two teen-age boys on their own to see the sights of New York. But in 1964 I didn't really think they would have any problems, and they did get along all right by themselves.

As for me, I moved around Manhattan talking to Democratic politicians, trying to find out whether Bobby Kennedy was going to run for the Senate against Republican Kenneth Keating. For a couple of days it was a big will-he-won't-he story that consumed the New York papers.

Finally, Kennedy announced that yes, indeed, he was a candidate for the Senate. The announcement came just a day before the Democratic convention was scheduled to start in Atlantic City. So after writing the story of Kennedy's decision I was off with Fred and Steve to the convention. Atlantic City was an easy drive from New York.

We stayed in what was supposed to be one of the nicer hotels, but we thought it was pretty run down. This was before gambling came to Atlantic City and the whole place had a down-at-the-heels look about it, from the famous boardwalk to the hotels themselves. The people from New York and Philadelphia who once favored Atlantic City as a vacation spot now were taking jets to Florida and the Caribbean.

There were two big stories at the Democratic convention—competing delegations from Mississippi, one of which included blacks, and the question of who would be Lyndon Johnson's running mate. The Mississippi delegation that included Negroes was seated, and Senator Hubert Humphrey of Minnesota was picked by Johnson to be his vice presidential candidate. While I scurried around after these stories, I was able to get convention tickets for Fred and Steve so they could watch the action on the floor of the convention hall, which was also rather decrepit.

I had known Humphrey a bit ever since he first got into politics, running for mayor of Minneapolis in the nineteen forties. When he first ran he was teaching political science at the University of Minnesota, but I was never in one of his classes. I still remember covering a couple of speeches he made at the university during his first campaign for mayor, which was unsuccessful. He did get elected two years later and the in 1948 went on to the Senate, defeating a former St. Paul Pioneer Press political reporter, Joe Ball, who had been appointed to the Senate by Republican Governor Harold Stassen on the death of the incumbent. Ball then was elected once in his own right.

I thought Humphrey was a good choice for the vice presidential nomination. For one thing, it seemed to be his only chance at the presidency some day, after his failure in 1960 to defeat Kennedy in the Democratic presidential primaries. It was often said, however, that Humphrey was too nice and not tough enough to be president. Perhaps nice guys do finish last as baseball players, as Brooklyn Dodger manager Leo Durocher once said, but I am not convinced that is necessarily true. Humphrey was indeed a nice person and a tremendous orator. And he was on the liberal side of most of the issues of the time, ranging from civil rights to foreign affairs. So I think Johnson "done good" in choosing his running mate.

After Johnson picked Humphrey and both Johnson and Humphrey delivered their acceptance speeches, Fred, Steve and I drove back home, but I was not to stay even a day. After a change of clothes I was on the way to the airport to fly to California to cover the beginning of Barry Goldwater's campaign. For a long time after that trip I marveled at beginning the day at Atlantic City overlooking the Atlantic Ocean and ending the day in Newport, California where I could see the Pacific Ocean. I guess I was still a little Minnesota boy at heart and not quite able to get over the marvels of modern life.

The Goldwater press headquarters were at an up-scale motel in the decidedly up-scale town of Newport Beach just south of Los Angeles. It was the beginning of the Labor Day weekend and Goldwater was on a friend's yacht sailing not too far from Newport. So there was not too much for us reporters to do. Goldwater's press secretary held a news conference each morning, but he had little news to report.

On the Sunday before Labor Day one of the reporters suggested that we drive down to Tijuana, just over the border in Mexico from San Diego to take in a bull fight. I jumped at the chance and six or seven of us piled into two cars for the trip south.

The contrast between San Diego and Tijuana was unbelievable. The dirt, dust and roads in Mexico were terrible, but we managed to find the bull ring and get in just as the bull fights were beginning. Well, of course, the bull has no chance, the fights are gory and bloody, and the spectators, fueled by wine they poured into their mouths from goatskin bags cry for more bull bloodshed and boo bull fighters who end their contests too soon and without enough blood oozing from the bulls.

When telling people about my first and only bull fight I say, yes, it is worth seeing, once, but then you will be so disgusted with this spectacle that you will not want to go back for a second time. I am obviously wrong, because bull fights remain popular in Spain, Mexico and elsewhere in the world, but that is still my view of them.

But back to reality, or the semblance of reality that constitutes political campaigning. On Labor Day Goldwater officially began his fall campaign with a trip to his home state of Arizona, and then went on to Seattle, which was a hotbed of his support, and delivered a rousing speech in a packed to the rafters auditorium before a cheering, almost delirious crowd. It looked for a while as if Goldwater would catch fire, but of course he never did. From Seattle the Goldwater campaign worked itself back east, and I dropped off and another Post reporter took over the coverage.

I did not get back to the Goldwater campaign, but I did cover Lyndon Johnson's campaign for a week or so in mid-October. Truth to tell, it was a desultory campaign on both sides that fall. All the polls indicated that Johnson would soundly beat Goldwater, and he did. Goldwater was not much of a speaker, and the crowds he attracted, while sometimes quite large, were the faithful and already converted. On the political trail Johnson was more of a shouter than an orator, but as all presidents do, he did attract crowds eager to see a president in the flesh.

Toward the end of the campaign I did get out to California again. The purpose of the trip was to see whether Goldwater had any chance of taking California and also to look in on the senatorial campaign. California Governor Pat Brown had appointed Pierre Salinger, Kennedy's press secretary, to the Senate after a senator had died, and Salinger was seeking election in his own right. His opponent was George Murphy, a one-time movie actor and song-and-dance man. It was thought that Salinger could easily defeat an actor. This was before the rise of Ronald Reagan, although Reagan gained political prominence in 1964 with a much-praised television speech in support of Goldwater.

I spent two or three days covering Salinger and Murphy, and concluded that Salinger was in trouble. A not too tall, pudgy man, Salinger was said to remind people of the stock movie character who carried the machine gun in a violin case. Murphy, on the other hand, was a fairly handsome, debonair fellow who may not have been too smart politically but made a good appearance as he campaigned around the state. Murphy did indeed turn out to be the better candidate and defeated Salinger handily.

On election night I was in the Post city room, helping with the coverage of the results. Johnson enjoyed a resounding victory and the Democrats made some gains in the Senate and House. I did not really like Johnson, but I thought his political views were far superior to Goldwater's; so in general I was pleased with the election results. Later though I got to know Goldwater better, and respected him as a man who believed in what he said and was by no stretch a political poseur.

On my trip back to Washington from California I stopped in St. Paul for a day or so, and found that my mother had big news. She was going to remarry. She was very nervous telling me, because she thought I would disapprove. I did not; I was delighted. It was six years since my father had died and I knew that my mother was lonely.

Her husband-to-be was Frank Reberg, a man about her age who she had known and even dated when she was young and teaching in a country school house in Minnesota. Her marriage would mean moving back to Sauk Rapids, where she was born, but that seemed all right to me. Frank had worked for many years as a machinist in the St. Cloud "shops," the Great Northern railway yards where my grandfather helped build wooden box cars long ago and where box cars were still repaired.

Frank and my mother were married early in 1965 but I was unable to get to the wedding because of my work. It was an informal affair at the Evangelical church in Sauk Rapids that my mother had attended as a girl and a young woman. Frank had two sons, older than I, and my mother became particularly fond of one of them. My mother and Frank lived in a small but decent house in Sauk Rapids and I think they were reasonably happy. Frank died in 1972; so they had seven nice years together.

In January, 1965 I was traveling again, first to a Republican National Committee meeting in Chicago and then to a meeting in Miami Beach of an organization concerned with rural electrification and other public power issues. In Chicago the Republicans were trying to put themselves back together after the 1964 election debacle.

I have long since forgotten the details of the Miami Beach public power meeting, but I do remember that Florida was a much better place to be in January than cold and blustery Chicago. I guess there was more news in Chicago, but Miami, news or no news, was much to be preferred.

# 42

## *A Political Life*

Early in 1965 I was told by my editors that I had been selected as the Post's full-time political reporter, and I was elated. I had actually spent practically all of 1964 covering politics, and it had gotten into my blood. I guess I was always interested in politics since my University of Minnesota days, but as I covered more and more politics I became absolutely fascinated with the process. Sure, there are a lot of charlatans in the business, but, face it, charlatans are to be found everywhere.

What did I like about politics? First of all the people; they are of all shapes and forms but all of them love to talk and gossip and most of them are well-informed. Even the dullest of campaigns have some colorful moments and unexpected developments. And there is always an element of surprise in an election. The pollsters and other prognosticators are not always right. You never know what will really happen until all the votes are in. Also, I always enjoyed the camaraderie among the political reporters. Life-long friendships were made on the campaign trail.

But politics was not all my life in 1965. I found time to turn my Harper's magazine articles on the politics and economics of the defense program into a book, which was published later that year and called "Arms, Money, & Politics." Like my first book, it did not sell much but it received nice reviews. After writing two books in almost as many years and knowing first-hand the hard work that goes into a book, I vowed never again to speak ill of any book, no matter how unsatisfactory I thought a volume to be. And I have pretty much held myself to that promise over the years.

Two political stories stand out in my mind from 1965. One was in South Carolina and the other, by far the more important one, was in New York City.

I went down to South Carolina in the summer to cover a special election for the House of Representatives. A congressman had died, and there was an election to pick a successor. By then Strom Thurmond, the 1948 Dixiecrat presidential candidate, had been in the Senate for six years and had changed his party registration from Democratic to Republican and was a power not only in South Carolina but throughout the rest of the South. He was a staunch segregationist, and blacks were still kept from the polls in the South because of onerous and unfair voting restrictions.

I talked with Thurmond and the two candidates for the vacant house seat in Columbia, the capital of South Carolina. That evening I went to a big political rally in the baseball park in Columbia. I was sitting along the first-base side of the park, listening to Thurmond speak and suddenly heard my name. Thurmond was saying there was a Washington Post reporter in town named Julius Duscha, He pronounced it Dus-ka. The senator said he could not help but wonder why Post reporters didn't stay in Washington where they belonged and take care of their own Negro problems instead of coming to South Carolina and stirring up our Negroes, who of course he said were very happy. It was an embarrassing moment for me, but no one knew what I looked like and I never let on to those seated around me who I was. I've long since forgotten whether Thurmond's candidate won that special election, but I will never forget being targeted by Thurmond. As I write he is in his one hundred-and-first year, which I guess says something about him. He has since died, at 101.

As for New York City, I went there several times in the fall to cover the election for mayor. John Lindsay, a liberal Republican congressman, was running against the incumbent, Abe Beame, William Buckley Jr., the conservative writer, was also on the ballot.

Lindsay was looked upon as a rising Republican star who probably would be a presidential candidate some day, and he did try in a short and not very successful campaign in 1972 against the incumbent Richard Nixon. Beam was considered a political hack but four years earlier, to everyone's surprise he had been elected by defeating Mayor Robert Wagner Jr., whose father had been a distinguished senator in the nineteen-thirties and forties. But the son did not seem to have inherited much political savvy from the father and was considered a hack by many.

It was an exciting campaign. Lindsay was young, good-looking and personable. He also seemed to be in tune with the times and with New York's many problems. Beame was old and tired and clearly a man of the past in his approach to the city's problems. Buckley was a sideshow, adding a little spice to the campaign, but everyone agreed he had no chance of winning. He might indeed help Lindsay by taking some conservative votes away from Beame.

I followed the candidates around and learned a lot about New York's sometimes bizarre politics from the political reporters from the New York papers. In

1965 there were still six papers, the Times, Herald-Tribune, Daily News, Mirror, Post, World Telegram and Sun, and Journal-American.

Lindsay won the election handily, and much was expected from him. But for some reason he never lived up to his expectations. Maybe he was simply not the man most political reporters and other observers of politics thought him to be. Also, he had hardly been sworn into office in January of 1966 when New York was hit by a monster snowstorm and it took weeks for the municipal snow removal forces to dig the city out, and Lindsay never recovered from that debacle. In addition, he decided to take on the city's entrenched municipal unions, but failed to reduce their power. That fight also hurt him politically. A nice guy, but maybe nice guys do finish last.

In December of 1965 I found myself again I Chicago, this time to cover the annual convention of the American Farm Bureau Federation, the largest organization of farmers and a political power in Washington. Farmers and their wives do not exactly set a city on fire even when they descend on a place like Chicago by the thousands, but the convention made a little news by contributing to the on-going arguments in Washington on how best to keep farm prices at a level to assure decent incomes for farmers. It was an argument that began with the New Deal and continues to this day.

But what I remember most about that week I spent in Chicago was being able to see the musical "Gypsy" with Ethel Merman. On a cold, cold night I walked a few blocks from my hotel to the theater, which I suppose because of the weather, turned out to be half-empty. But I thoroughly enjoyed the show and as it turned out to be the only time I ever saw Ethel Merman on the stage. Such are the memories of political travel.

# PART VII

A Sojourn to California

# 43

## *More Than Just an Aging Actor*

The year 1966 was even more eventful. First of all, things were changing at the Washington Post. Mrs. Graham's management was taking hold and there were new faces both in the news room and in the business offices. Most importantly for the editors and reporters was the arrival of Ben Bradlee. He had been the Washington bureau chief for Newsweek and was now an editor at the Post in charge of the national staff. So changes were expected.

The Post's major problem was still money. The paper had surpassed the rival Evening Star in classified and retail advertising but the Star was still formidable competition both in news coverage and advertising. The Post's circulation was more than four hundred thousand compared with the Star's three hundred thousand, but the Star with its emphasis on local coverage and its conservative stance on issues was still viewed by the big advertisers like the retail stores Woodward & Lothrop and Hecht's as an important place to be. As for news coverage, the Star had many long-time reporters who were plugged in to places like the Senate which was still run by conservative southerners.

But the Post's money situation was getting better; in fact, the paper was actually making some money, and was sending its own reporters to cover more national and international stories. My political travels were a good example. When I came to the Post in 1958 no one traveled as much as I had in the last couple of years.

In 1966 my first big story was again in California. In January I flew to San Francisco and then went on to Sacramento to cover an important political announcement. The actor Ronald Reagan was going to run for governor. Reagan had been a radio baseball announcer in Des Moines, Iowa in the nineteen-thirties and late in the thirties had gone to Hollywood in hopes of becoming a movie actor. He succeeded to some extent, but never became a real star. In the nineteen-fifties as his movie career was fading he became the host of the General Electric

Theater on television, introducing weekly plays. Those television appearances probably made him better known than any of his movie roles.

His work for the General Electric Theater program expanded and he became a spokesman for General Electric, traveling the country for the company and speaking at conventions and other business meetings. Then in the 1964 presidential campaign he made a widely-praised television speech for Barry Goldwater.

That speech was his springboard into politics. He was also undoubtedly encouraged by the election of his fellow actor George Murphy to the Senate from California in 1964. If George can do it, why can't Ronnie?

During that January I spent some time with Reagan as he moved around California testing the political winds and then watched as he formally announced his candidacy for governor. He was in his mid-fifties, still a good-looking man and his personality was certainly likeable. A pleasant fellow, but was there anything more to him? That was the question everyone was asking. Did he just read his lines well, like any practiced actor? Or did he have genuine ideas of his own? When I got back to Washington I told my editors and reporter colleagues that this guy Reagan was more than just an aging actor. He had considerable appeal and could beat Democratic Governor Pat Brown, as likeable as he was.

Early in the spring of 1966 I heard about a new journalism fellowship program that was getting under way at Stanford University in California. The Ford Foundation had given a million dollars to Stanford to start a fellowship program that would be much like the Nieman program at Harvard. Some of the money would also be used to finance scholarships for journalism graduate students. I also learned that Stanford would be looking for a director and an associate director to run the fellowship program. I was interested. My trips to San Francisco had whetted my appetite for California, and Palo Alto, where Stanford is located, was a particularly appealing place.

As I began looking into the Stanford program I learned that Herb Brucker, the editor of the Hartford Courant, had been selected as the director of the new program but was looking for an associate director. I called Brucker and said I was interested. He knew my name and I guess something about me, and suggested that I come up to Hartford for a day so we could talk. So one day in May I flew to Hartford and had a long lunch with Herb Brucker. He was sixty-five years old, ready to retire from the Courant and probably would stay only a few years at Stanford. He was a pleasant man who was in charge of the paper's editorial page.

Herb told me he was talking to some other people about the associate director's job and that he would get back to me. He did, and offered me the job which

I accepted on the spot. Priscilla had encouraged me to go after the job and was pleased that I got it.

When I told Russ Wiggins and others at the Post that I would be leaving in August to go to Stanford, they wondered why I wanted to leave the good job I had at the paper but understood the attraction of Stanford and the chance to help shape an important journalism program.

I was one of the few Post reporters ever to leave a major assignment at the paper. My thinking was that I had no ambitions to be an editor and that I did not want to become in my fifties a worn-out reporter walking the halls of Capitol Hill with sore feet and a jaded appetite for the news. In the spring of 1966 I was just forty-one years old, and I didn't consider my writing days to be over. I was sure that I could continue writing as a free-lancer while helping to run the new fellowship program at Stanford. Perhaps there would even be another book or two in my future writing life. And who could ask for a better place to live than in Palo Alto? For these and I guess many other reasons, the move seemed to make a lot of sense to both Priscilla and me

# 44

## *Academia—And Journalism*

In July I went out to Los Angeles to cover the annual meeting of the National Governors Conference, and Priscilla went with me. Following the meeting we were planning to go to Palo Alto to search for a house. While I covered the governors, she enjoyed herself under the Los Angeles sun. The meeting was held in one of the new hotels, an idyllic spot.

Governors conferences attract political reporters not because of the meetings themselves, which are usually rather dull, but because of all the political gossip you can pick up from governors and their aides. And in 1966 Ronald Reagan was the talk of the conference. He was not yet a governor of course, but everyone wanted to talk with him. He held a press conference—at which one reporter whispered, "he looks mothy,"—but for the most part impressed the reporters and even some of the governors. The feeling was that, yes, he was a has-been movie actor, but perhaps a budding politician who could get elected governor and become a national figure, maybe even a presidential candidate some day.

But what I remember most about the governors' conference was a story I wrote about all the expensive gifts governors were given at these meetings, ranging from automobiles and television sets to jewelry. The gifts came from companies in the host state, and the practice had been going on for some time. But no one wrote about it until I did. Some of the reporters and I know that a lot of the governors considered me a party-spoiler, but to my reportorial instincts it was simply a good story.

I even impressed Mike Wallace, who was then just a CBS reporter. Sixty Minutes was still two years in the future. Wallace told me that I had uncovered a great story, and that he was going to look into the gifts further and do a piece for CBS News, which he did. So I felt I had done a good deed, and in the future the gift-giving practice was sharply cut back, as it deserved to be.

When the Governors Conference ended Priscilla and I flew to San Francisco and drove to Palo Alto to begin house-hunting. We had already negotiated a contract to sell our house in Chevy Chase and, surprisingly, we quickly found a very nice house in Palo Alto within walking distance of the Stanford campus. It was on a corner lot, had a big living room with a fireplace, a dining room, three bedrooms, and a porch behind the living room looking out on the garden and three bedrooms. The price was around forty thousand dollars, and we felt we could handle that. The contract to sell our Chevy Chase house was for around thirty-thousand dollars. We signed a contract for the Palo Alto house in just a day or two and were pleased about the transaction.

While in Palo Alto we met Chick Bush, a Stanford journalism professor near retirement who was temporarily in charge of setting up the Professional Journalism Fellowship Program, as it was called, that I would help run. Herb Brucker was still in Connecticut and would be arriving in Palo Alto late in August. The Stanford school year did not begin until late in September and Chick Bush and other members of the journalism faculty had already selected the first group of fellows who would arrive in mid-September. Chick Bush was a grand old man. He had never had any real journalism experience, but he was considered a fine professor, the kind that students always remembered and visited whenever they were in the neighborhood. Certainly not a forceful man, but a man who in his teaching did a lot for the journalism profession.

Then it was back to Washington and Chevy Chase to resolve some problems. Fred had graduated from Bethesda-Chevy Chase High School and had been accepted by the University of California at Berkeley. He had applied to Berkeley long before the Stanford job came up, and used to kid about our following him to California.

But Steve had another year to go in high school and had been named editor of the Bethesda-Chevy Chase student paper. We didn't want to take him away from that opportunity, but if he stayed where would he live. Finally we decided to ask our friends Pat and LaVerne Holt if Steve could stay with them. The Holts had a son Steve's age and their older son was off to college so they had a spare room. Steve also had a paper route, and was willing to turn over most of what he would earn on the route to the Holts to pay for his room and board. To our delight, the Holts agreed to the arrangement as did Steve. And it worked out fine. It turned out to be a very busy year for Steve, with a paper route, editing the school paper and everything else involved in being a senior in high school, but he managed.

Steve did go with us to California when we drove cross country. We stopped in Minnesota to see my mother, Frank and my Aunt Emma, and we also made a quick visit to Sioux City to visit Priscilla's folks. We also stopped in the Black

Hills of South Dakota to see the faces of the four presidents carved in stone—Washington, Jefferson, Lincoln and Theodore Roosevelt.

But what I remember most from the trip was our stop at the Grand Tetons in Wyoming. A Wyoming congressman that I had written about arranged for us to stay in a beautiful cottage in the park there, and we took time to explore that park and adjacent Yellowstone Park in Montana. I also remember a wonderful steak dinner in a restaurant by a lake with the Tetons above us. The congressman, whose name I have sadly forgotten, also gave me a memorable phrase that I have often used. After I wrote about him and his senatorial ambitions, which he never realized, he sent me a note saying, "As an old Wyoming rancher used to say, 'You done good.'"

From Wyoming we went through Salt Lake City and across Nevada and into California. We stopped at Lake Tahoe, my first visit there, for the night. We wanted to stay longer, but we could not because our furniture was due to arrive in Palo Alto just two days later, and it did arrive on time.

We got to California late in August; so we had ample time to get settled before my work would begin. I should have mentioned that just before we left Washington some colleagues at the Post threw a farewell party for me. The highlight of the evening was the presentation to me of a Post front-page "mat" which had my name in every headline. I still have the "mat" above my desk. In those days mats were made by pressing a thick, cardboard-like piece of composition paper on a page of type and then using the mat to make a plate to put on the press. The Post was reluctant to make changes in a mat such as they made for me, because it might embarrass the paper, and I was pleased that they made an exception to the rule for my case.

The office for the Professional Journalism Fellowships program was in a temporary building on one side of the Stanford campus. Though considered temporary, the building was nice enough, airy, with fairly large offices, and outside were flowers and shrubs tended by a full-time gardener, an older man who was on duty even on rainy days. Another nearby temporary building housed the journalism school staff, or rather the staff of the Department of Communications, as it was called. Journalism departments and schools have always had trouble convincing colleges and universities that they are legitimate academic endeavors. To bolster its standing at Stanford, the Communications department included researchers dealing with communications theories that were way beyond me, but a couple of the people chasing those theories were very nice and intelligent. One, Wilbur Schramm, had even published several short stories in the Saturday Evening Post in the nineteen thirties.

I had a corner office and Herb Brucker had an office down the hallway a bit. Separating us was an office for a secretary, Nancy Weston, whose father was a long-time pear rancher on the Peninsula. Today the ranch is part of the Great America Amusement Park.

As I settled myself into the office and got to know Herb Brucker better the first group of journalism fellows began to arrive. There were orientation sessions for them so the fellows—and Herb and I for that matter—could get to know Stanford. There were also meetings with faculty members who discussed subjects that the fellows could pursue. In general, the program was to be patterned after the Nieman experience, with fellows in effect given the run of the campus. We also organized weekly seminars for the fellows with faculty members like the Nie-mans' Tuesday afternoon beer-and-cheese sessions in the Harvard Faculty Club. Fortunately or unfortunately, our Stanford meetings did not include beer and cheese and were held in a room in our temporary building rather than in the very comfortable Stanford Faculty Club.

Everything seemed to get off to a good start, and I gradually was getting accustomed to the slower pace of academic life. Neither I nor Herb Brucker did any teaching as such, but we spent a lot of time with the fellows talking about journalism, its glorious past—of course the past is always glorious—and its uncertain future. In the nineteen-sixties newspapers were still the primary sources of information for most people, but television was developing rapidly and more and more people were watching its news programs.

Soon I was also doing stories for the Post. In November I helped a Post reporter, Bill Chapman, cover the results of the California election for governor, which saw Ronald Reagan beating the incumbent Pat Brown, to the astonishment of Democrats and the surprise of many political observers and experts.

In December and early in January I wrote stories for the Post about Reagan's preparations for taking office and about the beginnings of his administration after being sworn in early in January. The combination of helping administer the journalism fellowship program and keeping a hand in daily journalism appeared to me to be working well, and I was encouraged by Herb Brucker and others at Stanford to keep at it.

In 1967 I also did some work for the National Observer, the weekly newspaper started by Dow Jones, publisher of the Wall Street Journal, in 1962. Jim Perry, the political reporter for the National Observer, and I were good friends, and he encouraged me to do pieces for the paper. It was a weekly, published on Sundays, and was designed to give the kind of in-depth coverage to general news that the Wall Street Journal did for financial and business news.

Unfortunately, the National Observer never caught on and lasted only ten years. The stories I did involved education issues and some California matters of interest nationally. Fortunately, after the Observer closed, my friend Jim Perry moved on to the Wall Street Journal, where he covered national politics for many more years.

I continued to cover stories in the San Francisco Bay Area for the Washington Post, and even went down to Los Angeles on assignments a couple of times. One story I particularly remember was a feature for the Post Sunday magazine about the filming of "The FBI Story" for television. It was one of the big television series at the time. Suzie went with me to Los Angeles, and I still have a picture above my desk of Suzie and me talking with Efram Zimbalist Jr., the star of the series. What I remember about him is that he obviously wore a corset to appear thinner than he was, and that he refused to tell me how old he was. What I also remember from that little excursion is that Ford Motor Co. sponsored the series, so the FBI agents always drove Ford cars, while the bad guys they were chasing were in beat-up looking, yes, Chevrolets. And of course you know who always won. My story also appeared in the Los Angeles Times Sunday Magazine. I had a little fun with the series in writing the story, which I am sure the producers did not like.

Another story I did in 1967 involved Shirley Temple, yes, Shirley Temple. She of course was no longer a tousle-headed, dancing little girl. She was a grown-up now, a little pudgy but still with a nice face. She was running in a special election for Congress to replace a man who had died in office. I spent a day with her as she campaigned in the Palo Alto area, which was part of the congressional district. I found her to be a nice woman, a little uncertain in this her first foray into politics, but as I told many people afterwards, she was a "tough cookie". I guess you have to be tough to survive being a child movie star. But she wasn't tough enough to win the election. She was defeated by Pete McCloskey. Both he and Shirley Temple were Republicans, but he was on the liberal side and she was quite conservative politically. Later Shirley Temple went on to become a U.S. Ambassador to Czechoslovakia as well as a U.S. delegate to the United Nations. McCloskey was a maverick congressman who didn't last long in the House of Representatives but did challenge Richard Nixon for the Republican presidential nomination in 1972, unsuccessfully of course. The piece on the special election was written for The Reporter magazine, and was the last article I wrote for it. The magazine folded in 1968.

# PART VIII
## Back to the Capital

# 45

## *Back to Washington*

I kept busy helping to get the Professional Journalism Fellowship Program started and accepted on the Stanford campus. Herb Brucker, the director and my boss, was a nice enough guy, but not very forceful. And he was past sixty-five years old and at the end of a career that I don't think was that satisfying for him. In the nineteen-thirties he had taught at the School of Journalism at Columbia University, a prestigious enough place, and then had gone on to the Hartford Courant and to the presidency one year in the nineteen-fifties of the American Society of Newspaper Editors, a most prestigious honor. T the Hartford Courant, however, he was not in charge of the whole news and editorial side of the paper; he was just editor of the editorial page. And the Courant, although claiming to be the oldest newspaper in the United States, was not considered a major or important paper.

At any rate, I was enjoying th4e job at Stanford. Both Priscilla and I liked living in Palo Alto and the academic atmosphere at Stanford. Suzie seemed reasonably happy in junior high school. Sally was only two years old but there were other small children in our neighborhood for her to be with. Fred was doing well at Berkeley, and Steve seemed to be getting along fine living with the Holts and finishing high school as the editor of the school paper.

But as spring gave way to summer in 1967, I found myself increasingly restless at Stanford despite being involved in a new program and also being able to do a fair amount of reporting and writing as a free-lancer. I was still doing some traveling, interviewing applicants for the fellowship program with a trip through the Midwest, stopping in Minneapolis—and making a quick side-trip to Sauk Rapids to see my mother—and in St. Louis among other places. And in August I went to Boulder, Colorado, for the annual meeting of journalism educators. The meeting was held at the University of Colorado.

In Colorado Springs another life change began. While at the meeting I was interviewed for a job back in Washington. It was for the position of director of the Washington Journalism Center, a new program that had been established in 1965 by Willard Kiplinger, the founder of the Kiplinger Washing Letter, Changing Times magazine and some other specialized Washington newsletters covering such subjects as taxes and agriculture. I was interviewed by John Reyerson, a man close or just beyond retirement age who had worked for Kiplinger since shortly after the Washington Letter began in the mid-nineteen-twenties.

I still remember talking with Reyerson on the balcony of his hotel room overlooking the Rocky Mountains. It was a beautiful afternoon and the conversation went well as I talked about my background and he told me about the plans for the Washington Journalism Center. It was envisioned as a place for journalism students and fellows, for conferences and for research by journalism professors on leave from their teaching jobs. There was even a plan for the construction of a building housing the Center on some land Kiplinger owned in the Southeast Washington redevelopment area near the Potomac River. The plans were quite grandiose, but I was assured that Kiplinger was committed to them. Willard Kiplinger had died the year before, but his son, Austin, who was now in charge was said to be as committed to the project as was his father... And there was a Kiplinger Foundation with what seemed to be adequate funds.

I told Reyerson that I was quite interested in the job, and he said he would call me after he got back to Washington and talked with Austin Kiplinger. I think my problem at Stanford was partly that I did not have enough to do—there was really no need for two persons to run a fellowship program for fifteen or so journalists—and I also missed Washington. The Journalism Center job seemed to be a good way to get back to Washington.

A couple of weeks after returning to Stanford I did receive a call from Reyerson who said he and Austin Kiplinger would like to talk with me further, and when could I come to Washington to see them? I found time early in October for a quick trip, and spent a day or two talking mostly with Austin Kiplinger, who I found to be very likeable, astute and sophisticated. We apparently hit it off, because I was offered the job as director of the Washington Journalism Center. The only question was when I could start. We agreed that I should begin early in January. The salary was twenty thousand dollars, which was over five thousand dollars more than I was making at Stanford, and the job seemed quite interesting.

Back I went to Palo Alto. Priscilla was disappointed that I took the job and that we would be moving back to Washington after little more than a year at Stanford, but I think she understood my problems and restlessness. She was enjoying California and would have liked to stay longer. Herb Brucker was surprised that I wanted to leave and go back to Washington.

Se we had a lot to do that fall—selling our Palo Alto house, buying a house, hopefully, back in Chevy Chase and then actually moving. But before getting involved in all that I got a writing assignment.

And it was an important one. Ronald Reagan was nearing the end of his first year in office, and the New York Times Magazine was looking for an article on Reagan. Someone had suggested me to the editor of t he magazine, and when I got a call asking if I would like to try to do a piece on Reagan, I immediately said yes, I would.

From my Washington Post days I knew the people who had run Reagan's campaign for governor in 1966, had talked with both Republican and Democratic political figures in the state, and had some friends in the governor's office, particularly Lyn Nofziger, his press secretary.

I started calling these people, some of whom were in San Francisco, and t raveling to Los Angeles and Sacramento to see others. I spent some time with Reagan ad even interviewed his wife, Nancy. She gave me what I always thought was the best quote in the article. She said the "Ronnie didn't over-think things," by which she meant that he made up his mind on issues and other matters fairly quickly, but I know that to some who read my article the quote seemed to say that Reagan was not a thinker and made decisions somewhat haphazardly. The article was featured on the cover of the magazine and was the lead piece. So I felt pretty good about my first effort for the Times.

Back to family and domestic issues. We put our house in Palo Alto on the market and immediately got an offer for about the same price as we had paid for the house. Then Priscilla and I flew back to Washington for a weekend of house-hunting and found a place in Chevy Chase after only a day or two of searching. It was on Raymond Street east of Connecticut Avenue not too far from where we lived on Turner Lane. The house had four bedrooms, two baths and a powder room, a living room with a fireplace, a large family room that had been build on to the back of the house and a dining room. There was a patio looking into the back yard which stretched three hundred feet across a stream into some woods. The house and lot and location seemed to suit our needs well, and we quickly made an offer to buy it. This was a fast decision but I guess a good one because we lived in that house more than twenty years.

We left Palo Alto with mixed emotions early in January of 1968 and drove back to Washington, taking a southerly route hoping to avoid snow and ice, and we did. The weather was cold all across the country, but at least it was clear. Suzie flew back to Washington by herself so as not to miss much school, and of course Sally traveled with us.

We spent a couple of days in a motel on Wisconsin Avenue waiting for our furniture to arrive, and a few more days getting the house in shape to live in before I was off to work. When I arrived the Washington Journalism Center was temporarily housed on the corner of Twentieth and G Streets Northwest in a building that was part of the downtown campus of American University. But the university was closing its downtown facilities and consolidating all its activities on its main campus uptown at Nebraska and Massachusetts Avenues.

So one of the first things that had to be done after I arrived was to find new space for the Center. John Reyerson and I looked at several places and finally settled on part of the third floor of the building owned by the American Association of University Women. It was located in Foggy Bottom at 2401 Virginia Avenue Northwest at G Street just at the western edge of the George Washington University campus. The AAUW building was also close to the Watergate complex, consisting of apartment and office buildings and a hotel. We would be some distance from the National Press Building housing so many Washington offices of newspapers from around the country, but that did not seem to matter too much.

The AAUW building was less than twenty years old, clean and airy and the space we leased seemed to be more than adequate for the fellowship program that the Journalism Center was sponsoring. As yet there were not students, conferences or research operations. In March we moved out of the American University building, which had been sold along with other AU buildings in the area to George Washington University.

In the AAUW building we had room for our offices, for a conference room and for desks for the dozen or so journalists who were fellows at the Center. And I liked the location. We were out of the hustle and bustle of downtown Washington but within walking distance or short bus ride from the White House, the Mall and such departments as State, Commerce and Labor.

When I took over the Journalism Center its fellowship program was just over a year old. Under the program young journalists spent four months in Washington, working as interns in Washington bureaus or at the Washington Post or the Evening Star. As director of the Center it was my job to arrange for the internships and to organize seminars three or four times a week at which journalists, government officials and experts from such places as the Brookings Institution spoke to the interns.

My staff consisted of an older woman, Celia Kay, and a younger woman, Mary Kay Sextro, both of whom were at the Center when I arrived. They seemed to be all right, and I decided to keep them. They knew how the Center worked, and I did not. Celia had come to the Center after long experience as a secretary in

Federal government offices. She was our office manager and also did some of the bookkeeping. She had grown up in Minneapolis. Mary Kay was a school teacher who had come to Washington from a suburb of Chicago, but took a secretarial job at the Center after she was unable to find a teaching position. A year or so later she left the Center when a job as a teacher opened up in the District of Columbia schools.

# 46

## *Seventh Street—After the Riots*

Early on upon my return to Washington I was warned by two or three friends who knew of the beginnings of the Center that Kiplinger's John Reyerson really wanted to run the Center—he was secretary of the Center's board of directors, which was made up of some high-powered editors and publishers and chaired by Newbold Noyes, editor of the Evening Star and a member of one of the families that owned the Star. Reyerson, I was told, no longer had much to do at the Kiplinger Washington Letter, and was being kept on by Austin Kiplinger as a sort of retainer.

It became clear to me that the warnings about Reyerson were true. One day soon after we had moved in March to our new quarters in the AAUW Building he came by one afternoon, walked into my corner office, closed the door (which I always kept open) and said we had to talk. First of all, he began, you've got to get rid of that woman. He meant Celia Kay, my older assistant. He didn't say why, but I knew. She was Jewish and I had been told Reyerson did not like Jews. Then he wanted to know who I had been having lunch with and what we talked about. I had been getting together with some old friends and asking them about what they thought the Center should be doing. Reyerson demanded names and details about our conversations. I declined to give him names or details and he stormed out of the office.

A few days later I received a call from Newby Noyes. He said he would like to have lunch with me to talk about the Center. At that time I really did not know Noyes, but got to know him quite well in the next year in his capacity as chairman of the Center's board. We had lunch at the Sans Souci restaurant on Seventeenth Street just a couple of blocks from the White House, a restaurant long gone but then one of the best and fanciest in Washington. Art Buchwald, whose office was just around the corner, ate there every day.

As I suspected, Newby wanted to talk with me about Reyerson, who had complained to him about me, saying that I would not tell what I was doing as director of the Center. I told Newby about Reyerson coming to my office and our conversation. Newby was sympathetic with me, and after we had a long talk about the Center and what Reyerson's role should be, Newby concluded, see if you can work things out with Reyerson.

Before I had another chance to see Reyerson, I got a call from Austin Kiplinger who said in effect Reyerson was his problem and that I should just go about my business as director of the Center as I saw fit. By standing up to Reyerson and being honest with Newby I had solved the problem of who would run the Center early on. It was clear that I would run it, subject always of course to the general direction of Newby, Austin and the other members of the Board.

I may have been placing my job on the line, but I learned an important lesson—that you need to assert yourself to protect your job and most importantly your authority in the job. Throughout my years at the Center I think I continued to be a strong leader, always keeping the Board informed but also always letting the Board know what I thought was in the best interests of the Center and what I wanted to do.

The Board always backed me up, and also encouraged my desire to continue free-lance writing, understanding that the writing kept me in touch with the real world of journalism.

No sooner had I got back to Washington that I received a call from Nona Brown, who represented the Sunday department of the New York Times in Washington. She said "New York" would like an article about Democratic Representative Wilbur Mills of Arkansas, who was chairman of the House Ways and Means committee and considered one of the most powerful men in Washington. The editor of the magazine had liked my piece on Ronald Reagan and thought I might be a good person to try a piece on Wilbur Mills. I was delighted to be asked, and accepted the assignment immediately.

I spent a lot of time talking to congressmen who were on the Ways and Means committee and knew Mills well and to others on Capitol Hill and to lobbyists with frequent business before his committee. Then I talked to Mills at some length and still remember one conversation I had with him when he was getting a haircut in the House barber shop. Mills was particularly important at the time because President Lyndon Johnson was trying to get a tax bill through Congress to help pay for the Vietnam war, and all revenue legislation must originate in the House of Representatives, which further meant that the committee writing a bill would be Ways and Means with the exclusive jurisdiction it was granted by the House over taxes.

The article on Mills turned out well and was given good play in the magazine, which was carefully read in Washington as well as on Wall Street and in other financial centers in New York. And the article led to other assignments from Nona Brown and the magazine.

As I was working on the piece about Wilbur Mills the 1968 presidential primary season was beginning in New Hampshire, and to everyone's surprise Senator Eugene McCarthy of Minnesota had entered the New Hampshire primary in opposition to Lyndon Johnson. Even a greater surprise was how well McCarthy ran against Johnson on an anti-Vietnam-war platform. Johnson still won but not by much and in March announced that he would not be a candidate for reelection. Washington was stunned, even more so when Robert Kennedy, now a senator from New York, announced that he would be a candidate for the Democratic presidential nomination. Still another new candidate was Vice President Hubert Humphrey.

But soon the whole country was boiling. Early in April Martin Luther King Jr., the black civil rights leader, was shot to death in Nashville, Tennessee and riots erupted that night in Washington and other major cities around the country.

The next day I went to work as usual, but found Army troops stationed in downtown Washington. Rioting and vandalism continued particularly in areas where blacks lived. Looting was also widespread. I left the office in mid-afternoon as the situation seemed to be worsening, but I could not find a bus, and cabs had completely disappeared. What to do? How to get home? I did not want Priscilla to drive downtown to pick me up. That was too dangerous. And she might not even be able to make it to our office.

So I walked home that fateful afternoon. As I made my way up Connecticut Avenue, so did many others. From my office to our home in Chevy Chase was a good eight miles, perhaps nine, and much of it uphill. But I made it and considered myself lucky to get out without running into trouble. And all the way out Connecticut Avenue I did not see a single bus. Washington was paralyzed.

That evening people were warned on both radio and television to stay out of downtown Washington for the next day certainly and perhaps two or three days more. As I remember, I did not go to the office the next day, but by the following day Army troops had finally got the situation in hand and I went back to work, as did most others with jobs in Washington. I did not venture into the riot areas; the pictures on television and in the newspapers were enough for me. Serious damage had been done particularly on places like Seventh Street Northwest were blacks lived and whites owned most of the businesses.

Later though I would see the situation first hand, and on Seventh Street. A week or ten days after the riots I got another call from Nona Brown. She said that the New York Times Magazine editors would like a story on a block in Washington that had been particularly hard-hit by the rioting—who had lived on the block, what businesses were there and who ran them, where were the residents and business owners now, and what were their prospects. A big order, but if I could track enough people down it would make a good piece. As always, I accepted the assignment and quickly went to work on the story.

I began by trying to find the business owners. There had been a liquor store, a deli and a hardware store among others on the block on Seventh Street I chose as my subject. The owners of the stores lived in the suburbs and one by one I interviewed them. None was planning to return to the block. Most had insurance that would cover at least some of their losses. The business owners did not want to go back to Seventh Street because they knew they would not be welcome, and some were afraid for their lives.

The businessmen were easy to find, and the owners of the trashed and looted stores were all men. But how would I find the people who lived on the block, and were blacks? Some of the apartments above the Seventh Street stores escaped serious damage; so it was easy to find people in those apartments because they were still there. And they did not seem to mind a white man inquiring about their well-being and plans. Most planned to stay where they were. Many of them had lived on the block for a long time. The residents whose apartments were not trashed by the rioters told me where residents of apartments that had been badly damaged had gone.

I was lucky and was able to find almost all of the men, women and children who had been forced out of Seventh Street and were now living temporarily with friends or relatives.

Saturday I tracked down several of these displaced families, and Suzie, who was always interested in what I was writing about, went with me as I did my interviewing. She seemed to be as fascinated by the people and the idea of the story as I was. And I think Suzie being with me softened up the interviewing, with people perhaps more willing to talk than if I had been just by myself.

The article, which was pretty much straight reporting, came out well and was nicely displayed in the magazine with some good pictures taken by George Tames, the Times' chief Washington photographer who was an artist in the way he took pictures. I got a lot of compliments about the article, even years later, and just a few weeks before I sat down to write this account I got a call from a historian who wanted to refer to the article in a book she was writing about redeveloping areas of cities.

I came out of this assignment with a new understanding of the ghetto, if you will, and the people who lived in such areas. Most of the blacks I talked with had jobs and were upstanding citizens, if poor and if stymied by a lack of much education. The owners of the businesses, who were mostly Jewish, did not seem to be bad people exploiting their black customers. Like the rest of us, they were just trying to make a living.

# 47

## *"How is the Fat Jap?"*

I think as a reporter and writer I was lucky in that I was more of a generalist than a specialist. So I was given many opportunities to write about many different subjects. I stayed away from such areas as science, medicine and economics because I felt I did not know enough about such subjects to write intelligently about them. The generalist is often criticized for just being on the surface of things in his writing, but I have always answered that criticism by saying that the generalist is like the average reader and thus his writing does not become too detailed and can be easily understood by Joe Six Pack. Also, there is something to be said for the fresh look at a story that a generalist brings to an assignment. Maybe I am apologizing for my lack of knowledge in many areas, but I do think there is something to be said for a generalist writer like myself.

But back to the Washington Journalism Center. My predecessor as director, Ray Hiebert, had established a custom of having a dinner to honor the Center's fellows at the end of their stay in Washington. The one we had in the spring of 1968 turned out to be quite an occasion because our speaker was Dean Acheson, the former Secretary of State and one of Washington's "wise men." We invited many prominent journalists and other movers and shakers in Washington to these dinners, which were held at the National Press Club.

No one seemed to want to miss this affair. The Press Club ballroom was jammed. We got Acheson as our speaker thanks to Newby Noyes, who was an old friend of Acheson's. I have long since forgotten what Acheson talked about, but I know his subject was foreign affairs in general and the Vietnamese war in particular. Acheson was a supporter of the war. But I definitely remember that the event was a great evening and even made the papers. For one thing, it was the first time Acheson had given a speech at the National Press Club in almost twenty years, when he appeared on the same platform to say that perhaps the United States should no longer include Asia in its sphere of influence, a speech that was roundly criticized by the "China lobby" of the early nineteen-fifties.

During that spring the first journalism fellows to be picked under my direction were selected. The Center had an admissions committee that included an Evening Star editor and Gene Goodwin, a former Star reporter who was now dean of the journalism school at Pennsylvania State University and who became a good friend.

June of 1968 brought more tragedy to the country when Robert Kennedy was assassinated in the Ambassador hotel in Los Angeles on the night he won the California Democratic presidential primary. If he had not been killed he would have been the Democratic nominee for president. Could he have defeated Richard Nixon, who was nominated that summer by the Republicans and won the presidency in November? No one really knows. Unlike his brother Jack, Bobby Kennedy was a divisive figure in American politics. The outcome of a Bobby Kennedy-Nixon campaign probably would have been determined by what stand Kennedy took on the war in Vietnam, and how his position would have affected what Nixon said about the war. But speculation is fruitless.

Hubert Humphrey went on to become the Democratic candidate. He was formally selected at the party's convention in Chicago where there were near riots as opponents to the war in Vietnam clashed with police on streets near the convention hall. I was not at the convention, and I don't know that I wish I had been there. It was not a pleasant occasion and the rioting, most of which was seen on television, unquestionably hurt the subsequent Humphrey campaign against Nixon.

I did get a chance to cover some of the 1968 campaign. First, I was asked by the New York Times magazine to try a piece on Hubert Humphrey. I was going to spend some time traveling with the Humphrey entourage, but the trip I was scheduled to be on was cancelled at the last minute when Humphrey became ill. He quickly recovered, but instead of traveling with Humphrey I had to settle for a long interview in his vice presidential office in the Old Executive Office Building next to the White House. I knew Humphrey's press secretary, Bob Jensen, quite well and asked if I could bring Fred, Steve and Suzie with me to the interview, and he said he would check with Humphrey. He did, and Humphrey said yes. So early one evening the four us went to Humphrey's office. The children sat silent, and I am sure a bit awed, as Humphrey and I talked. I also spent some time talking with people in Washington who had worked with Humphrey over the years. I came away from the assignment still liking and in fact admiring Humphrey. I have always said it is too bad he never got to the White House. It is still my feeling that he would have made a good and decent president.

My other dip into the 1968 campaign involved another Times magazine article, this one about Spiro Agnew, Nixon's running mate. Agnew had been elected
governor of Maryland in 1966 largely through a fluke. The Democratic candidate was a perennially unsuccessful candidate who in 1966 ran on a platform
emphasizing that "my home is my castle," by which he meant he was opposed to
housing desegregation. The candidate, George Mahoney, lost the black vote in
Baltimore and the Washington suburban county of Prince Georges' and thus
threw the election in the normally Democratic state to Republican Agnew, who
had been the executive of Baltimore County, which encompassed areas outside
the city but did not include the city itself. It was said that Nixon selected Agnew
because he wanted a running mate who came from suburban America and also
that he did not want anyone who might outshine him.

I traveled with the Agnew entourage across the Midwest, through Las Vegas,
where Agnew actually stayed overnight, indicating how "Sin City" was becoming
more acceptable to Americans (Remember, Kennedy would not stay there overnight), and on to California. Nixon did not have to worry about Agnew outshin-
ing him. Agnew was not a particularly interesting man and not much of a
campaigner or speaker.

What I still remember from that assignment and trip was a remark Agnew
made when he came through the campaign plane as we were taking off from Las
Vegas. Both the press and the Agnew entourage were on one plane. The reporters
and some of the Agnew people, too, were tired and bleary-eyed after experiencing
too much of Sin City. One of the reporters was a Japanese-American who worked
for the Baltimore Sun, was somewhat overweight and was affectionately known
to his colleagues as "the fat Jap." As Agnew made his way through the plane chat-
ting with the press he saw the Sun reporter dozing in his seat and asked, "And
how is the fat Jap this morning?" Well, the remark was picked up by some other
reporters who were not familiar with what was a purely jocular reference among
the press corps in the Maryland capital of Annapolis, and a scandal erupted when
the story hit the papers and television. How insensitive could a vice presidential
candidate be? The story certainly hurt Agnew, and perhaps Nixon, too, but as
much as I didn't care for Agnew I felt sorry for the way he was attacked for what
was really an innocent remark.

I think the skirmish over the "fat Jap" remark was the beginning of the end of
the off-the-record status of certain, usually jocular, remarks on campaign trips.
From then on everything seemed to be on the record. Sure, some remarks by candidates as well as staff and reporters are still placed off the record, but if a remark

is juicy enough it usually manages to find its way into print. This development over the years has taken a lot of the fun out of campaigning.

Meantime, in the fall of 1968 the first group of journalism fellows that I had had a hand in picking arrived at the Center. There were twelve of them and they came with more experience—at least three to four years—than the previous groups, which included some young men and women with no meaningful journalism experience. One member of that fall, 1968 class was Brit Hume, who came from the Baltimore Sun, later worked with columnist and muckraker Jack Anderson, covered the White House for ABC News and now is a star anchor with Fox News. I will brag a little bit and say that I had a hand in advancing Brit's career when I recommended him highly for the job with Jack Anderson.

For this group I organized more seminars and tried harder to get some big names for the seminars—people like Washington Post editor Ben Bradlee, New York Times Washington bureau chief Tom Wicker, economists and political scientists from places like the Brookings Institution and a few government officials. I also found internships for the fellows at such places as the Washington Post, the New York Times bureau and local television stations. I was beginning to feel that the program was coming together.

As for personal and family matters, Steve had graduated from high school in the spring of 1967 and like Fred before him enrolled at the University of California at Berkeley. Both Fred and Steve came back to Chevy Chase for the summer of 1968 and we all went to Provincetown at the tip of Cape Cod in Massachusetts for four weeks. We rented a house at the edge of Provincetown, not much of a house, a place that needed a good deal of work, but it was an enjoyable vacation and gave us all a chance to see the Cape.

# 48

## *Being a Helping Hand*

Early in 1969 I received a call from one of the Ford Foundation program managers whom I had met while I was at Stanford. The Foundation wanted to do something to get more blacks into journalism. A commission headed by former Governor Otto Kerner of Illinois had issued a report on the riots in black neighborhoods after Martin Luther King's death and had concluded that one of many problems needing fixing was the lack of blacks in journalism. So, I was asked, would the Washington Journalism Center he interested in some Ford Foundation funding for a program to seek out blacks interested in journalism and train them? I said I thought so, but let me check with my Board. I talked with Newby Noyes, Austin Kiplinger and others, the Board met and approved the idea, authorizing me to discuss the proposal with the Ford Foundation program manager.

I went to New York and spent a day at the Ford Foundation, describing the Journalism Center program to two or three people there and listening to the Foundation's ideas for a program at the Center. After further talks and negotiations the Foundation worked out a plan for a grant of nearly three hundred thousand dollars for a three or four-year program to be run by the Center to get more blacks into journalism.

The grant was a windfall for the Center. It meant more money in general for our operations and it also meant that I could hire an associate director, preferably a black journalist, to help run the fellowship program and pay particular attention to the needs of the black fellows.

There was considerable envy among the heads of other journalism programs in the Washington area when the grant was announced, but I felt pretty good about it. Here I had been at the Center for little more than a year, and the Ford Foundation grant certainly helped to put the Center on the map. Bragging again a little bit; it was also a big vote of confidence in me by the journalism program managers at the prestigious Ford Foundation.

After getting the initial installment of the Ford Foundation grant the first thing I had to do was find someone for the associate director position. Newby Noyes quickly came up with a name, Clarence Hunter, a black reporter working for Newby at the Evening Star. I knew Clarence's name but I had never met him. So we got together and seemed to hit it off right away. He had some good journalistic experience, was personable and was quite interested in the job. So, with Newby Noyes' blessing, Clarence was hired.

Then came the organization of the program. Clarence and I decided that the blacks that came to the Center as part of the program financed by Ford should be part of the regular fellowship program that was already operating for journalists with some experience. And how to recruit interested blacks? We simply sent material to colleges and universities, with particular emphasis on black schools, and soon had a considerable number of applicants.

Our admissions committee interview the most promising of the applicants and we picked ten blacks with an interest in a journalistic career and ten young journalists with experience of at least three or four years. The first groups came to the Center in the fall of 1969.

The program continued for four years. We had some successes and some failures in both groups, but that was to be expected. I don't think there were any significant racial conflicts between the two groups, but it sometimes was not easy to meld the groups together. Some of the blacks were jealous of the achievements of the whites, many of whom were not much older than the blacks. Some of the journalists with experience wondered at times what the blacks were doing in a program with journalists who had already been out there making their way.

Some of the blacks went from the program to work on papers like the Washington Post and the Evening Star and a few later became sub-editors and even managing editors of papers around the country. And of course some simply did not make it and abandoned journalism for some other career.

As for the young journalists who came to the Center's program, a lot of them did quite well. Bill Keller was both a Moscow and South African correspondent for the New York Times, then the paper's managing editor and now is a executive editor. Another fellow, John Cochran, went to work first for NBC News in Washington and Europe, covering among other stories Solidarity in Poland and now works for ABC News in Washington. Still another, Ann Compton, covered the White House for ABC News, and another fellow was in Latin America for CBS News. Others worked for the Wall Street Journal, one, Les Gapay, in Washington, another John Berthelsen, in Asia. The list goes on and on.

It is satisfying to have a hand in picking talent and helping along the talented. Perhaps the high achievers who came out of the Center's journalism fellowship program might have succeeded as well without the program, but I like to think the Center gave their careers a boost and considerable help. I know the Nieman fellowship certainly did that for me.

Looking back at the fellowship program at the Washington Journalism Center, I sometimes wonder whether it was a mistake to throw the aspiring young blacks together with the upwardly mobile young journalists. It would have been much easier for us to have run separate programs, but I like to think that by putting the two groups together each group learned from the other. In a small way we tried at the Center to help bring blacks and whites together.

For the next five years I kept busy with the Center's fellowship program and with my free-lance writing. Also, in 1972 the Center embarked on a second program, which we called Conferences for Journalists, but more about that later.

The fellowship program fell into a pattern that seemed to work well. We had two groups of fellows a year, Each group stayed in Washington for about four months. There were fifteen to twenty fellows in each group, generally pretty evenly divided between young journalists with three to five years of experience and young blacks just out of college who wanted to be journalists. We interviewed the best of the applicants, most of the interviews taking place in Washington. But Gene Goodwin, the journalism professor from Penn State who was on our Admissions Committee, and I traveled twice a year to San Francisco to interview applicants from the West. The trips were brief, generally over a weekend, but they were always enjoyable and Gene and I became fast friends. I think most of our choices were good, but as is inevitable in any program, we did make some mistakes. I remember one young journalist who we chose. He turned out really to have serious mental problems and was a disruptive presence in the group. Another, a promising black, turned out to have spent several years in prison, for murder. He had not told us that in the interviewing process, and after I consulted with some members of our board we decided not to take him. Perhaps we were unfair; most everyone deserves a second chance; but I agreed with the decision not to take a chance on him.

Year by year we tried to expand our seminar program and we often had top, prestigious speakers including General Maxwell Taylor, who had commanded U.S. forces in Vietnam and was later Chairman of the Joint Chiefs of Staff. We also had John Mitchell, Nixon's controversial Attorney General; Robert Finch, Nixon's Secretary of Health and Human Services; Casper Weinberger when he was Chairman of the Federal Trade Commission under Nixon; former Secretary of Labor Willard Wirtz; members of the Federal Reserve Board; Senator Barry Goldwater; Representative Morris Udall; and many experts from such think tanks as the Brookings Institution and the American Enterprise Institute.

As for internships, we found them at the Washington Post, the Evening Star and the Washington bureau of the New York Times as well as Washington television stations and the Washington bureaus of the networks. Some fellows also had fellowships at smaller Washington bureaus and they often worked out better than the fellowships at the newspapers and larger bureaus. We soon learned that the most important factor in a fellowship was having someone overseeing the fellow who really cared and made sure that the fellow did some real work and was not just running errands for coffee and sandwiches.

My free-lance writing in those years ranged from the New York Times magazine and the Washingtonian magazine to smaller magazines like the Progressive, the New Republic and the Nation. Subjects ranged from profiles of Cabinet members and senators to articles about Washington columnists and the Sunday television news programs—NBC's Meet the Press, CBS' Face the Nation and a similar ABC program. It would be a decade or more before ABC burst through on Sunday morning with This Week with David Brinkley.

Profiles included two on Melvin Laird, who was Nixon's Secretary of Defense. I had gotten to know Laird when he was an important member of the House of Representatives from Wisconsin. He was an amiable man and understood how Congress worked and the politics and economics of the defense program. And he was quite a change from Robert McNamara, the technocrat. In the nineteen seventies I also did a piece on McNamara when he headed the World Bank. I got to interview him because I knew quite well his press secretary who had previously been press secretary to Senator Tom Kuchel of California. I could interview McNamara, my friend told me, only if I would promise not to ask any questions about Vietnam. When I saw McNamara it was some years before he issued his mea culpa about Vietnam in a book of his own. McNamara was a steely character who answered my questions about the World Bank precisely and with a tone that said, you'd better not disagree with me, bud.

I guess the person I wrote about at that time that I liked the most was Senator Mike Mansfield of Montana, who was then the Senate leader. I have mentioned that I met Mansfield at the Grand Tetons and had breakfast with him at the Grand Tetons Lodge. And whenever I saw him he always remembered that breakfast and never failed to talk a few minutes about it. In a way Mansfield was a difficult man to write about because he was a "yup" and "nope" person, a man of few words. It was said that every time he appeared on Meet the Press he set a record for the number of questions he was asked because his answers were so short and often just "yups" and "nopes," but he was such a decent and wonderful man that you could not help liking and admiring him. I spent part of a day with him and discovered that even though he was a national figure always assured of being reelected he still spent two or three hours every morning dealing with Montana business, answering letters from constituents and looking into problems involving his state.

Mansfield was also very close to Republican Senator George Aiken of Vermont, who was famous for saying that the best way for the U.S. to get out of Vietnam as just to say we had won the war, regardless of the situation at the time of such a declaration of victory, and then quickly pull out our troops. Mansfield and Aiken had breakfast every morning in the cafeteria in the New Senate Office Building, sitting together at a table in view of everyone in the cafeteria, as if they were just a couple of Senate aides. Could I sit in on one of their breakfasts? Oh my, no, Mansfield said, those breakfasts are just between George and me.

I also did a profile on Secretary of Agriculture Earl Butz, a controversial member of Nixon's Cabinet who later was forced to resign after saying on a public occasion, as I recall, that all Negroes are interest in is a soft pussy, a good pair of shoes and some fried chicken. I spent a day with Butz, flying out to North Dakota, where he made a speech, and back with him. He was a gregarious man, and we talked about farm problems and a lot of other political and economic matters. It was one of the few occasions when I used a tape recorder. I never liked tape recorders because of the time it took to transcribe what you had on tape to get at the few quotes that you would use. But I do think on this occasion I got Butz down quite well. I thought the piece was a rather critical look at him, but after it was published in the Times magazine I received a letter from an old friend of Butz who said it was best article he had ever read about Butz. Once again I learned that everything is in the eye or the mind of the reader.

As to my piece on Washington columnists, the most interesting interview I had was with David Lawrence, the first modern-day Washington political columnist. Lawrence had been an Associated Press reporter in Washington early in the nineteen hundreds and also had been close to President Woodrow Wilson. Soon after Wilson left the White House in 1921, haggard and a victim of a debilitating stroke, Lawrence began writing his column. He later started what is now the magazine U.S. News and World Report, but from the nineteen twenties into the nineteen seventies continued to write a column five times a week. There was speculation that by the nineteen sixties the column was being ghosted by one of his aides, but after I talked with Lawrence I think it was his, and only his, column to the very end.

When I first called his office seeking an interview, I was brusquely told by a woman, who I took to be his secretary, that I should know Mr. Lawrence never granted interviews. Well, I said, could you just ask him. She did, because a few days later I received a call saying that Mr. Lawrence would see me at six o'clock that evening. I arrived at his office shortly before six and was greeted by what we used to call a mannish woman. Abruptly, she told me in no uncertain terms to sit down and that Mr. Lawrence would be with me shortly. I noticed two young men at typewriters who shared the outer office with the secretary, who quite obviously ran the place. Now my suspicions were aroused. Were these young men writing drafts of columns?

Soon I was ushered into Mr. Lawrence's office, a large but not particularly fancy place. We started talking about the good old days of the Wilson Administration and before and about how much Washington had changed, mostly for the worst, in Lawrence's opinion. He was, I should note, a very conservative man and considered by many to be anti-black. It was said that the anti-desegregation stands reflected in U.S. News beginning in the nineteen-fifties were the reason the magazine sold so well in the South.

As Lawrence talked and I asked questions I soon discovered that he was happy to have a reporter like myself to come by his office. He obviously enjoyed reminiscing and relished the attention I was giving him. I concluded that he was a lonely old man, and later learned that his wife had died fairly recently and that his only son was a disappointment. After we talked for an hour or so he said it was time for him to leave for dinner. But just as was ready to break up our conversation the secretary came in to say that an editor was waiting to see him to get his approval of the cover for that week's magazine. It was then that I understood that Lawrence was very much in charge of both U.S. News and his column. Lawrence carefully looked at the mock-up of the cover as he and his associate discussed in minute detail the exact size of the type to be used on the cover. Lawrence was obviously a detail man.

Then as I got up to go, he asked me where I lived and how I got home. I told him I lived in Chevy Chase and would catch a bus. Oh, no, he said, you must ride with me. He lived in an apartment in the Wardman Park Hotel, not too far away just off Connecticut Avenue and his chauffer would be happy to take me up the Avenue to Chevy Chase. I protested that it was unnecessary to inconvenience his driver in that way, but Lawrence insisted that it was no trouble. So I came home that evening in grand style in David Lawrence's limousine. I apologized to the chauffeur for inconveniencing him and delaying his own dinner, but he smiled and said, oh, don't worry, this happens to me all the time.

# 49

## *Becoming an Enemy*

Thinking about my conversation with David Lawrence, I am reminded that although I always considered myself a political liberal—I guess you could call me a child of the New Deal—I also managed to get along just fine with conservatives. In interviews I think it was because I tried never to argue with the person with whom I was talking. I always tended at least to give the impression I agreed with whatever was being said, nodding my head, smiling, saying, yes, yes. I have always felt that you get the best out of a person by agreeing rather than arguing with him. Some may feel that this is the dodge of a chameleon, but I never thought so. At any rate, my way of at least seeming to agree worked well for me and got me some good interviews, stories and articles.

Another example of my, shall we say, soft interviewing technique came with another piece I did for the Washingtonian on the Sunday television interview programs. The first person I obviously had to see for that article was Larry Spivak who with Martha Roundtree invented the interview program with the radio version of Meet the Press in 1947. Roundtree dropped out of the program after a couple of years, but Spivak, who in the nineteen-forties was editor of the conservative American Mercury magazine, stuck with the radio program and in the early nineteen-fifties brought it to television.

On television Spivak took on the role of an angry man as he pursued senators, representatives and Cabinet members. The other members of the press who appeared with Spivak were generally more gentle in their questioning. In person, I discovered, Spivak was not such a terrible windstorm. He, like David Lawrence, lived in an apartment at the Wardman Park and kept an office in the same building. I spent most of an afternoon with him, and it turned out to be a cordial and most helpful time. He was full of stories and anecdotes about Meet the Press as well as his earlier life as a writer and editor. I also talked to the producers and moderators of the CBS and ABC programs, but Larry Spivak is the man I most remember. Many times afterwards I would run into him, and he always stopped to ask how I was and what I was writing.

Another fascinating person I wrote about at that time was Ralph Nader. I first met Nader when I was still at the Washington Post and he would come into the city room to see my colleague and his friend, Mort Mintz. In those days few people knew Nader and he was the quiet sort of guy who almost sneaked up on you.

By the time I first wrote about Nader in the nineteen-seventies he had become well known for his Nader's Raiders, the young men and women who worked for him uncovering governmental malfeasance, his crusades for auto safety—remember his book Unsafe at Any Speed?—and his efforts to reform congressional procedures, some of them quite ancient.

I think Nader is seen by most people as a nerd, but I and others who got to know him found Ralph to be not only brilliant but witty and sometimes downright funny. He also has always had tremendous insights into how an organization is run, whether it be a newspaper or General Motors. Incidentally a Washington Post reporter figured into the notorious shadowing of Nader ordered by General Motors, which had a big part in pushing Nader into the national spotlight. The reporter resembled Nader—tall, slim, quiet, purposeful—and was mistaken for Nader by a gumshoe hired by General Motors to follow him around to try to dig up some dirt about his personal life. Somehow the reporter discovered the man following him thought he was Nader, and told Ralph about it. Nader exploited the incident by telling reporters about it, and a scandal erupted. Later Nader sued General Motors, won a big settlement and used the money to finance his work exposing nefarious schemes like the shadowing by the gumshoe. How ironic can something be?

I wrote two pieces about Nader for the Times magazine in the seventies and, yes, they were favorable. I have always liked Nader and thought that what he was doing was for the public good. I used to say at that time that Nader could be a credible presidential candidate, but in those days he always said that he had no interest in electoral politics. He finally did run in 2000 and unquestionably drained votes away from Democrat Al Gore and is running again in 2004. If Nader had not been in the race in 2000 as the candidate of the Green Party Gore might well have won enough states to get a majority of votes in the Electoral College, and there would have been no recounts in Florida and no need for the Supreme Court decision giving the presidency to George W. Bush. Such are the ironies of history.

During my busy days of running the Journalism Center and continuing with my free-lance writing, our personal life was good, and busy, too. The only jolt came when Priscilla became ill in 1970 during a trip to San Francisco and Berkeley. The Berkeley part was to attend a convention of journalism educators. I was not really a teacher and the Journalism Center was by no means a journalism school, but it was felt that we should keep up with what was going on in journalism education.

So after attending the convention in Berkeley, we spent a few days in San Francisco, and on the day before we were to go back to Washington Priscilla suddenly complained of severe pains in the abdomen and kept to her bed. I was alarmed, and called a doctor who said oh, perhaps, it was just something she ate. But I think we both knew it was more than a stomach ache. Rather than stay in San Francisco for more medical evaluation we decided to go back to Washington the next day as planned.

Back in Washington our doctor said the pain was being caused by a growth and that an immediate operation was necessary. We both thought it might be a cancerous growth, and I can still vividly remember sitting by the telephone waiting for word from the doctor after the operation. Finally he called and said that he had removed a growth as large as a grapefruit, did not think it was cancerous, but because he had only once before seen such a large growth he wanted to have it tested a second time by a special laboratory. So, more anxious waiting, but in the end it turned out definitely not to be cancerous and within a few weeks Priscilla was as good as ever.

Also in the early seventies Steve was married and Fred was off to Japan to teach English. Steve met his wife, Carla, at Berkeley. They both worked on the student newspaper, the Daily Californian, of which he became editor in his junior year. Carla was from San Francisco and the wedding was held in a small Catholic church near the West Portal section of the city. Before the wedding Steve had taken some lessons in Catholicism from a priest. I think Carla's mother and father thought their daughter was marrying beneath her. We probably thought just the opposite. Her father owned a small pharmaceutical supply company and had wanted to be a physician. But he had made quite a bit of money and Carla grew up in the fancy Saint Francis Wood section of San Francisco.

For their honeymoon Steve and Carla traveled through western Canada, seeing Lake Louise among other places, and then went to Minnesota and Iowa to visit my mother and my Aunt Emma and Priscilla's parents and some of her relatives. I neglected to say earlier that Carla was of Italian descent. So it is not surprising that I still remember Steve telling me that when the two of them were in Iowa they visited the farm of an aunt and uncle of Priscilla's. "So," said the uncle to Carla, "you're from San Francisco. Nothin' but queers and Dagoes there, right?"

After graduating from Berkeley Steve went to work for the now long-gone Berkeley Gazette and Carla got a job doing public relations for an Oakland department store, also now long gone. Later Steve moved on to the Sacramento Bee and Carla worked for the Contra Costa Times. For a while they lived in Fairfield, which is about half way between Sacramento and Contra Costa County, which is across the Bay from San Francisco.

Upon graduating from Berkeley Fred went to graduate school at the University of Michigan, studying Japanese culture and history and the Japanese language. That prepared him for his decision to go to Japan to teach English. It sounded like a great adventure and we encouraged him to do it.

Meantime, Suzie graduated from high school and decided to go to Tufts University, a fine school in the Boston area. And Sally was making her way through elementary school. All four children were always good students and always eager to go to school.

In 1973 we made the first of three summer vacation trips to Maine. The first two years we went to Ogunquit, an old resort town only about twenty-five or thirty miles from the Massachusetts line and an easy drive from Boston.

A hundred years ago or more in the days before automobile travel Bostonians took a train to Ogunquit and stayed in big white clapboard hotels. The mother and children stayed all summer, and the father commuted weekends from his job in Boston.

We, however, rented one half of a modern duplex house right on the ocean. It was not particularly well furnished but it was adequate. There was also a swimming pool. And the view of the ocean was great. The house was owned by a couple who lived in Maine year-round, but moved from the house to a motel during the summer so they could rent out both floors. We paid $1,500 for the month we were there, which was a substantial amount of money in the seventies. We figured that the owners of the house paid most of their annual housing costs with the summer rentals.

While in Ogunquit we walked a lot and drove around Maine some. And some days we just stayed around the house and pool relaxing. It was a good life. One day we also bought a painting of the rocky coast of Maine from a part-time artist who had a shop in Ogunquit. His principal job was working for a defense installation nearby where he was a map-maker.

What I most remember about him was when it came time to pay for the painting I asked him if he would take a check. Oh, sure, he said. And did he want some identification? Oh, no, don't bother. I figure if someone gives me a bad check, he may need a painting much more than I do.

When we were in Ogunquit I was some sort of a celebrity. It was the time of the Watergate scandal. In 1972 the burglary of the Democratic National Committee offices in the Watergate Office Building had occurred. Two intrepid Washington Post reporters, Robert Woodward and Carl Bernstein, had exposed the Nixon White House connection to the burglary. And almost every day there were new developments.

By the summer of 1973 The Senate Committee headed by North Carolina Senator Sam Ervin was holding hearings and trying to get to the bottom of the scandal. One day a Nixon aide, John Dean, revealed to the committee the existence of the President's "enemies list." And guess who was one of the enemies? Yours truly. Yes, I was on the list and my name was read out on television along with the names of three hundred other journalists, writers, actors, and sundry others.

That evening I received a telephone call from my mother. She seldom called me; so I knew the minute I heard her voice that something was up and she was disturbed. She was indeed. A neighbor had told her that she heard my name on television. What did you do? My mother asked anxiously. I told her I was on Nixon's enemies list, and that I had done nothing wrong. In fact, I said, I considered it an honor to be on such a Nixon list. She was still a rock-ribbed Republican and to her Nixon was okay, if not perfect. I think I reassured her somewhat, but as I hung up I knew she did not consider her son to have been honored.

In the more than twenty-five years that have passed since the announcement and publication of the enemies list I have often said, only partly in jest, that it was the greatest honor I ever received. I heard from old friends going back to high school days who either congratulated me or wanted to know where I had gone wrong. I also heard from envious journalistic colleagues who wondered why they had not made the list. "I should have been on it," said my old Washington Post colleague Mort Mintz. "You're too nice to be on it." I guess Mort was saying that he was a lot meaner, especially to Nixon, than I ever was.

And how did I get on the list? I don't really know. In the spring of 1972, before the Watergate break-in, I had been asked by the Times magazine to try to do a piece on the Committee to Reelect the President, or CREEP, as it was called by Democrats, and on the Republican plans for that year's elections. I had called up a couple of the people whom it was later said had compiled the list in an effort to get interviews with them and John Mitchell, who had resigned as attorney general to be chairman of CREEP. That may have triggered my notoriety and put me on the list. However, I was listed as being with the Washingtonian magazine, not the Times or as a former Post reporter.

I basked in the "enemies list" limelight, seeing my name in the New York Times the next day (In its usual thoroughness the Times published the names of all of us enemies as given to the Ervin committee by John Dean). I also was pleased to see my picture in the London Sunday Times along with photos of most of the other "enemies". Later I received an official enemies list button from a man in California who had produced the buttons. He also encouraged me to see if I could find out whether the Internal Revenue Service had investigated my tax returns because I was an enemy. I never did follow through on that, but I don't think the IRS looked into my taxes.

Somewhat later, at the urging of my children, I did ask the Federal Bureau of Investigation if they had a file on me. After much back and forth I was finally told no file could be found on Julius Duscha. Needless to say, I was disappointed. I once did get a letter though from J.Edgar Hoover himself congratulating me on something I had written, but I knew such letters were ground out routinely by the FBI's extensive public relations operation, meant nothing and probably were never seen by Hoover, his signature coming from a machine.

When I was in Ogunquit that summer of 1953 I saw John Wood, an old friend from St. Paul days (He had been my successor as a copy boy at the Pioneer Press). He was now publishing a weekly newspaper in Maine and he wanted to run a story about my new distinction as an enemy. John's wife wrote the story which was most complimentary to me and ran with my picture under the head-line, "Julius Duscha, an 'Enemy' in Maine." Later that year when Priscilla and I were in San Francisco, my old friend Lionel Horwitz, who was the working for the Examiner, had a reporter talk to us. The reporter, Caroline Drewes, also wrote a nice piece which appeared under the headline, "What White House enemy list did to him," and was accompanied by an equally nice picture of Priscilla and myself.

# 50

## *"We Juliuses Better Stick Together"*

But enough of my notoriety, and back to the Journalism Center. Late in 1971 Evening Star editor Newby Noyes, who in addition to being on the Center's board also was a trustee of the American Press Institute, said at one of our board meetings that the API, which ran seminars on how to be a better editor, business manager, circulation manager, etc., was being asked to expand its program to include sessions on issues in the news and how better to cover them. But, Newby said, why doesn't the Journalism Center try such programs. His idea was to have a series of three or four-day seminars with each one focusing on a specific area such as economics, foreign policy, an upcoming political campaign, education, urban problems.

The board liked the idea and told me to go ahead with the planning of a few what came to be called Conferences for Journalists to see how they would work.

Clarence Hunter and I decided to hold the first one on crime and justice issues. I said above that I had written enough about Watergate. But there turns out to be a Watergate connection here too. In looking for ideas for a crime and justice conference Clarence Hunter and I had lunch one day with Sam Dash, a professor at Georgetown University law school and a former prosecutor in Philadelphia who later became chief counsel to Senator Ervin's Watergate committee. And one of the speakers at the conference was Attorney General John Mitchell, who later was deeply involved in Watergate and the subsequent cover-up for which he served time in prison. Small world, I guess you could say.

We decided to hold the crime and justice session in a conference facility on the top floor of the Watergate office building, six floors above the Democratic National Committee offices that were later burglarized. (Too many coincidences? Perhaps.) The conference came off well, and we next planned one on China. We scheduled it for February of 1972, a few weeks before Nixon was to make what turned out to be an historic trip to China. Our timing could not have been better, and this conference worked out well too. So we began scheduling conferences every month or six weeks. At first, at Austin Kiplinger's suggestion, we sought help from the Brookings Institution in organizing the conferences because Brookings had long experience in putting on such meetings. But after the first two or three conferences we decided we could do it all on our own.

There were other changes at the Journalism Center. Clarence Hunter decided he wanted to move on, and accepted a job as director of public affairs for Howard University, the mostly black school in Washington. I hired Arch Parson to succeed him. Arch was a pioneering black reporter who had worked for the New York Herald Tribune and the Washington Post. But Arch was restless and stayed at the Center for only a year or so before going on to the Urban Coalition. Arch was also a Nieman fellow, a member of the class of 1955, a year before I was at Harvard.

Finally, Charles Roberts came to work for me. Chuck was somewhat older than I was, but that was never a problem. He had a distinguished record as a journalist, beginning in Chicago and was Newsweek's White House correspondent for many years. He also had served in the Navy with the author of "Mr. Roberts." Chuck was not exactly the Mr. Roberts of the story, but he resembled him in some ways.

As the Center's conference program was revving up our fellowship program was winding down. It soon became clear that the members of our board liked the conference program much more than the fellowships. We were rapidly using up the Ford Foundation money and inflation was eating up the other funds available for fellowships, most of the money coming from the Kiplinger Foundation. So, reluctantly, we decided we would have to phase out the fellowships in 1974. That also meant that there would be no money for an associate director. It was a tough blow for me, and of course an even tougher one for Chuck Roberts, but there was simply not enough money available to pay both a director and an associate director.

After saying farewell to our last class of fellows in the spring of 1974, I concentrated on planning for a series of ten monthly conferences beginning that fall. To get ideas for subjects and speakers I called on old friends like Erwin Knoll, who had covered education for the Washington Post; Gersh Fishbein, another old Post reporter who was now publishing two newsletters on health issues; and Herb Morton, a colleague from Pioneer Press days who had gone on to get a doctorate in economics and was now director of information for the Bureau of Labor Statistics in the Labor department.

During the summer of 1974 we went back to Ogunquit and enjoyed another pleasant month on the Maine coast. I should mention that on one of those trips to Maine we found a lobster trap which we turned into a coffee table. Charles Pfund, an old friend who is an engineer as well as a patent lawyer, figured out a way for us to attach a piece of glass to make a top for the trap, which is made from wooden slats and has a rounded top. For many years the trap, which we painted black, was a conversation piece in our living room. We later found a second lobster trap, which Sally kept in her room. Fred now has the original lobster trap, and I think Sally still has hers. Priscilla's mother and father visited us in Ogunquit during that summer of 1974.

That fall Suzie was married to Bill Glaberson in a lovely ceremony in our backyard in Chevy Chase. My mother came for the wedding, which was just a few days before my fiftieth birthday. I think outdoor weddings are particularly nice. And we did have a beautiful fall day for Suzie's wedding.

In December we flew to San Francisco where I had work to do on a book on the campus press that I was writing with a lawyer. The idea for the book came from a friend who headed up an association of the presidents of state universities. There had always been controversy over the role of student newspapers at colleges and universities and in the book we tried to discuss the problems facing the campus press and possible solutions to the problems. I came down pretty much on the side of giving campus papers as much freedom as possible rather than tying the papers to a journalism school adviser. I think most colleges and universities like the idea of some ties because of fears that student editors would write stories embarrassing to the institutions.

We stayed in San Francisco for the Christmas and New Year's holidays, spending Christmas day with Steve and Carla who were then living in an apartment close to the Berkeley campus. We stayed at the Hyde Park Suites, at Hyde and Bay streets near Fisherman's Wharf. The Hyde Park had become our favorite place to stay in San Francisco not only because of its location but also because it was a very reasonable place. Unfortunately, it has now gone up-scale and become quite expensive. We spent Christmas eve by ourselves and I still remember a lonely dinner we had at the nearby DiMaggio's restaurant. The food was fine, but we were the only ones in the restaurant, and that is always dreary.

As I look back on the 1970's I realize that it was one of the most active writing periods in my life. In addition to the writing I have already mentioned, I did a piece for the Times Magazine on Patrick Buchanan, who was a speech-writer for Vice President Spiro Agnew and was thought to be the man who wrote "nattering nabobs of negativism" for a famous Agnew speech denouncing columnists—the "nabobs"—and other journalists who were critical of both Nixon and Agnew. I also did another piece for the Times magazine on dissent in America.

For the Washington Post magazine I did an article on the columnists Evans and Novak. I portrayed Rowland Evans and Robert Novak as a cottage industry. In addition to their five-days-a-week column they also published a monthly newsletter filled with political gossip, organized seminars for businessmen featuring important Washington political figures, and lectured throughout the country. In writing the piece I thought, hey, I am kind of a cottage industry myself what with running the Journalism Center and doing so much free-lance writing.

During that time I also wrote for the Sunday business section of the New York Times. Dick Mooney, the editor of the section at that time, was in my Nieman class and asked me to do the pieces. At that time, too, the Times was running quite a few Sunday business articles written by free-lancers like myself. One I remembering doing was an article on Julius Shiskin, then the commissioner of labor statistics in the Department of Labor. He was a wonderful, old-shoe type of man, who like so many government statisticians of that period, had come out of the Bureau of the Budget, now called the Office of Management and Budget. I remember Shiskin noting that I, too, was a Julius and saying that there were so few of us Juliuses around that we darn well better stick together.

Another economist-cum-statistician I wrote about was Alice Rivlin. A former assistant secretary of the Department of Health, Education and Welfare—now Health and Human Services, with Education split off into its own department—and then a Brookings Institution scholar, Alice had just taken the new job of director of the Congressional Budget Office when I interviewed her and wrote the piece about her and the new office for the Times. The office and accompanying Senate and House Budget committees were set up to give Congress more authority over the Federal budget and to thwart efforts by Nixon to overrule budget decisions made by Congress. The CBO office itself has since grown to a powerhouse on Capitol Hill. Alice Rivlin herself went on to become a member of the powerful Federal Reserve Board and is now back at Brookings.

I also did some other articles for the Washingtonian magazine, which was growing in both circulation and prestige. The magazine emphasized articles on how to live well in the Washington area, and has always been big on food and restaurant reviews, but it also has always had serious articles on major Washington issues and profiles on senators, congressmen and Cabinet members. In addition to the piece I did on Senator Mike Mansfield, I also did one on Senator Hugh Scott of Pennsylvania, the Senate Republican leader. I also wrote about the planning for what became the Kennedy Center for the Performing Arts and about a retired admiral who started one of the first think tanks questioning Defense department plans and decisions.

I even did a little work for television. In the 1970's there was a short-lived news program on public television in Washington, and I contributed a few pieces to it on press—or media—issues. The program was patterned after one broadcast in San Francisco during a newspaper strike. Reporters sat at a big round table and talked and commented about the news of the day. Ben Gilbert, the former city editor at the Washington Post, was the editor or the anchor of the program. He had left the Post after he had been passed over for a promotion to managing editor. I thought the program was fairly interesting, but it was expensive to produce and never attracted much of an audience. The idea though was much like the News Hour on public television today. I have never considered myself to be much of a talker; so I don't think I did very well on the few times I participated in the program. I have long since concluded that I am a reporter and a writer, not a speaker. I think that most writers are just that, not talkers, although some reporters have turned out to be pretty good talkers on television today.

Another writing project I should mention was a large contribution I made to a book looking at the possible Democratic candidates and the likely issues in the 1972 presidential elections. The book was published by U. S. News and World Report in a magazine-type format and was sold at newsstands.

At that time U.S. News was trying to get into the book business on a large scale, and I was asked to work on a book for them on the White House. The idea was to go through the rooms of the White House and describe the major events that occurred in specific rooms over the years. I did a lot of research for the book and even some writing, but it never saw the light of day when the Watergate scandal erupted and the editors felt there would be n o market for such a book. It was a disappointment to me, but the editors were probably right.

Meantime, things were going pretty well at the Journalism Center. Our conference program was becoming established, and some major newspapers like the Providence Journal and Bulletin, the Philadelphia Inquirer, St. Petersburg Times, Newsday and the Minneapolis Star and Tribune were sending reporters and editors to our conferences regularly.

Washington bureaus were also frequent participants. And we found that annual sessions on such subjects as politics, economics, health-care issues and urban problems attracted journalists year after year, some of the same ones coming back annually. Organizing the conferences kept me busy because I always tried to be up to date with important and current Washington figures as speakers. We also had good luck getting Cabinet and sub-Cabinet members.

My relations with the Center's board remained good. The board met only twice a year, and I always tried to keep members fully informed about what I was doing. If a particularly serious problem or crisis came up, I always kept the board, and particularly its chairman, fully informed. I also made it a point to come to board meetings with my own plans and proposals. I learned early on that board members are very busy with their own companies and affairs and however much they may have been interested in the Center they had little time to think about it. So rather than being faced with too many off-the-cuff and perhaps not clearly thought-out ideas from board members, I always had my own ideas.

Newby Noyes was succeeded as board chairman by Larry Laybourne, a long-time Time Inc. correspondent and executive. He was the corporation's Washington man when he headed our board. Unfortunately, he died too young of cancer after serving as chairman for only a couple of years. He was succeeded by Ted Koop, who came to Washington in the 1930's as an Associated Press reporter, then went to work as head of the CBS Washington news bureau and now as a vice president of CBS was its corporate Washington man. He was easy to work with and frequently we had pleasant luncheons at the now-gone International Club, of which he was one of the founders. Ted always noted that he hired Walter Cronkite for his first television job as a local anchor on WTOP, a station that was the Washington outlet for CBS and was then owned by the Washington Post.

Another way I kept up with things in Washington was through the Off the Record Club, a group of political writers who met regularly for lunch or dinner with a senator, congressman or Cabinet member. It was one of many such groups of reporters who find such small, informal meetings useful in getting to know important Washington figures. Members of the Off the Record Club included Bob Novak and David Broder who succeeded me as political reporter at the Washington Post. The meetings were always pleasant socially and often produced news.

# 51

# *Walking and Chewing Gum at the Same Time*

The year 1976 also was important from a personal standpoint. Steve and Carla decided to get a divorce, and Suzie's marriage to Bill Glaberson was coming apart. Of course Priscilla and I were disappointed with both situations, but such is life, I guess. Fred, however, was going to get married, to Hideko, a Japanese woman who had been a student in one of this language classes. But where should the marriage be? In Japan? Back in Washington? The compromise was to have the ceremony in Hawaii, a half-way point.

The date Fred and Hideko set was for late November, and the place was Honolulu. Priscilla, Sally and I flew out via Chicago for what was our first trip to Hawaii. Steve and Suzie came on their own. Hideko's parents and her brother also came to Hawaii. Despite language difficulties we all had a pleasant dinner before the wedding day. The wedding itself was in a pretty chapel where, it turned out, many Japanese were married daily. It seemed that Japanese like to fly off to Hawaii for weddings and honeymoons. After the ceremony we all had another pleasant dinner, probably with too much drinking, but, heck, it was a wedding, wasn't it?

The day after the wedding Fred and Hideko and her parents flew to another island where the newlyweds were to spend their honeymoon and the parents were to stay for a couple of days before going back to Japan. But the plans had to be abruptly changed. After the plane landed Hideko's father became ill and collapsed. Taken to a hospital, he was diagnosed as having suffered a heart attack. So Fred and Hideko spent their honeymoon helping nurse her father so that he would be healthy enough to go back to Japan. A month later he did make it back home, but died a year later.

Also in 1976 we began to go on house exchanges. Our San Francisco friends Dick and Suzie Kaplan had told us a year or so earlier about an organization in

New York called the Vacation Exchange Club that published an annual directory containing the names, addresses and other information about people who wanted to exchange homes. We registered with the club; information about us and our home in Chevy Chase appeared in the 1976 volume; and we decided to see if we could negotiate an exchange in California. We put together a letter further describing our home and location, made copies and sent several of them out to people in San Francisco and the surrounding area.

We found a couple in the Oakland Hills who were interested in an exchange and we negotiated an arrangement with them for us to stay three weeks in their house while they were in our house in July. We flew out to San Francisco on a night flight (night flights in those days were cheap). Arriving at five a.m. we had to spend some time in the San Francisco airport before taking the first helicopter flight of the day to the Oakland airport where we were met by the couple in whose house we would be living. (Helicopter flights like that one have long since disappeared.)

The Oakland house was modest but comfortable enough. There was no view of San Francisco bay, just a view of some barren hills. While there, we went into San Francisco quite often, drove around Oakland and Berkeley and enjoyed ourselves. The only drawback, really a slight one, was that there was a cat we had to feed. Neither Priscilla nor I liked cats, but this one lived outside; so all we had to do was put out food and water for him (or her?) every day.

Earlier in 1976 I had signed a contract with a publisher to write a book on Franklin D. Roosevelt's New Deal of the nineteen thirties. My idea for the book was to emphasize the people of the New Deal—Secretary of Agriculture Henry Wallace, Secretary of Labor Frances Perkins, Hugh Johnson, the head of the National Recovery Administration (NRA), Secretary of the Interior Harold Ickes and many others.

I had thought about trying to write such a book for a long time. Much had been written about the New Deal, but I felt that there was still room for a new look at the varied and interesting people who worked with Roosevelt. My literary agent, Julian Bach, thought it was a good idea too and after I put together an outline he found some interest among publishers. Julian was a major New York agent, whose authors included Teddy White. So earlier in 1976 I went to New York for a day to talk with several editors at major publishing houses, and a couple of weeks later Julian negotiated a deal with the venerable house of Henry Holt, former Holt Rhinehart. Holt is now part of CBS. The deal included an advance of $25,000, which was a pretty good sum of money in those days.

To research material for the book I read everything that had been written about the New Deal that I could put my hands on. I also was able to spend two or three hours some mornings at the Library of Congress where I was able, through a friend, to get a cubicle with a desk and a small bookcase where I could keep books for extended periods of time. Priscilla also helped in the research, going through books in the cubicle while I looked at newspaper files from the nineteen thirties that were on microfilm. It was not easy working on the microfilm machine but I persevered over a few years and got a lot of material.

I also decided that I should try to do some writing while we were on vacation and I began doing just that while we were in the house in the Oakland Hills. I brought my trusty portable Olivetti with me, set it up each morning on the dining room table and pecked away for two or three hours. At the end of our three weeks in Oakland I had made considerable progress and felt good about the project.

Something else I did in 1976—and a I keep asking myself how I managed to do so many things in those days—was to take four German journalists on a tour—I guess you could call it that—of the presidential election. This came about through Joe Stern, an old friend who was a Washington correspondent for the Baltimore Sun and now was the paper's editorial page editor.

Joe had been the Sun's Bonn correspondent some years earlier and while in Germany had met an expert on the country who was then the number two man in the U.S. embassy in Bonn. By 1976 the man had become head of the American Council on Germany which was located in New York and was sponsoring exchange visits between American and German journalists, businessmen, labor leaders and others. The man had asked Joe if he could squire a group of German journalists so that they could see how a presidential campaign works. Joe said that he did not have time to do that, but suggested that perhaps I could do it.

The German expert, whose name, I am embarrassed to say, I simply cannot recall, came to see me—to look me over, I am sure—and we agreed that I would take the journalists on the campaign trail. The three men and one woman who made up the group were nice people and fairly young. So how to proceed?

In 1976 Republican Gerald Ford, who had succeeded Nixon as President was running against Jimmy Carter, the little-known former governor of Georgia who to everyone's surprise had won the Democratic nomination. Senator Bob Dole of Kansas was the Republican vice presidential nominee and Senator Fritz Mondale of Minnesota as Carter's running mate. I knew Ford, Dole and Mondale to varying degrees but had never met Carter.

This was the first year since 1960 that the presidential candidates had agreed to debates. We were able to get to the Ford-Carter debate in Williamsburg, Virginia. We had to stay in Richmond, about fifty miles away, because of a shortage of hotel rooms in Williamsburg but did get seats so we could see the debate live, as they say today. And afterwards we were with the reporters in the press room where the candidates' handlers were trying to put a "spin" on their man. I can't remember who I thought won the debate, and I don't remember what the big issues were, if in fact there were any. But the German journalists found the debate fascinating, so different from anything done in campaigns in their country.

Vice presidential candidates Dole and Mondale also had one debate, but we were unable to get to that. So we had to settle for watching it on television. What I remember from that debate was Dole calling the Democrats "the war party" because World War I and II, the Korean war and the Vietnam war had all occurred under Democratic presidents. It was a cheap shot by Dole and I think it hurt Ford.

We traveled some with Ford and Carter and ended up in San Francisco where Carter made an appearance at Ghirardelli Square in a small place jammed with people and no doubt chosen to make television viewers think he was attracting large crowds, which in fact was not true. But such are the ways—or perhaps deceit is a better word—of campaigning.

Back we went to Washington for election night to watch the returns and see Carter and Mondale elected to the surprise of most people. A lot of us thought that Ford was defeated because he had pardoned Nixon for his role in the Watergate scandal. The pardon came after Ford had been in office hardly more than a month. I am sure it hurt Ford's chances of being elected, but I also think it was the right thing to do to try to end the Watergate imbroglio. I knew ford some when he was in the House of Representatives as a congressman from Michigan. As president he had only a couple of years so it is hard to judge what he would have done if he had a full term.

And now I remember one thing Ford said during one of the debates. He made a remark indicating that he felt people in Poland were doing fairly well even though the country was ruled by the Soviet Union. He was roundly ridiculed for the remark, but it turned out that Ford may have just been ahead of his time; Lech Walesa and the Solidarity movement erupted in Poland a few years later.

I suppose Ford was also hurt when he stumbled once or twice walking down steps from an airplane. Noting these mishaps, Lyndon Johnson was quoted as saying that Ford could not "walk and chew gum at the same time." What Johnson really said was the Ford could not "walk and fart at the same time."

# PART IX
## Politics

# 52

## *Germans and Cowboys*

On to 1980 and another election year. But before getting into politics I should say something about home exchanges again. This year we had three exchanges, the first one in Colorado and the other two in San Francisco. The highlight of the year, though, was Colorado. The state has become one of my favorites.

This time our exchange in Colorado was in Estes Park, which is not a state or national park but a community high in the Rocky Mountains. It is adjacent to Rocky Mountain National Park, but not part of it. The people we exchanged with lived in a suburb of Kansas City, Missouri, but they had this summer house in Estes Park. The house was quite new and was at about ten thousand feet in the mountains. The drive up to it was rather long, curvy and filled with switchbacks.

Once you got to the house you had to catch your breath because of the altitude. Something I have always remembered, too, is that whenever the telephone rang and you jumped up to get it you also had to catch your breath because of the altitude. Remember, we were at a height twice the five thousand foot altitude of Denver, where breathing is not easy either for a new arrival. But the air at those heights can be bracing and the view from our Estes Park house was indeed breath-taking.

We arrived in Estes Park just before the Fourth of July and were told that the old road crossing the top of the Rocky Mountains—the continental divide where water on one side runs east and on the other side runs west—had just been finally cleared of snow and was a beautiful drive. So we took the drive, and it was indeed spectacular—just a two lane road with snow still piled high on either side, and all this early in July!

Later we took the new, four-lane highway over the Continental Divide and got out of the car a couple of times to step on and examine the permafrost where the land never thaws out even in the summer.

During our stay in Estes Park we also drove around to other places in the Rockies, with each view being more spectacular than the previous one. There were other tourists, of course, but never too many. I think something else that attracted me to Estes Park was the fact that William Allen White, the famous editor of the 1920's and 1930's and Republican political figure from Emporia, Kansas, the Gazette was his paper, spent his summers in Estes Park. White was a hero of mine, as he was of many young journalists of my generation. I guess he is largely forgotten now, but he was a major journalistic figure from the nineteen twenties into the nineteen forties.

While we were in the house at Estes Park we often took walks up the mountain, to eleven thousand feet, and around a big rock formation. The walks were slow because of the altitude, but the stops we had to make meant that we could savor the spectacular views, always a little different from differing points of view. I should mention that in addition to Priscilla and Sally, a friend of Sally's—Tara—was with us that summer, and she enjoyed Colorado just as much as we did.

Another spectacular aspect of Estes Park were the thunderstorms. In the Rockies thunderstorms form late on many summer afternoons, and sometimes not so late. From the house we were in we could see storms miles away and moving toward us. First came the crackling of the lightning and then you could see the thunder bolts as the storms came closer. It was a times eerie and scary, but we were safe inside and could enjoy, if you will, the approaching storms. But they weren't so enjoyable when you were caught up in a one while driving, as we were more than once. But the storms do move quickly and a downpour, drenching and even flooding as it can be, is usually over quickly. I don't know whether I would want to live in Colorado—Denver, for one place, has become crowded and choking with smog at times—but our Colorado visits were memorable.

From Colorado we were off again to San Francisco. Our first exchange there was in a house near Mount Davidson. It was just an ordinary place and was at the edge of the summer fog belt. But again it was a good location for further explorations of the city and the Bay area. From there we went back to the Kaplan's house. That was not strictly an exchange as they did not spend time in our house in Chevy Chase, going instead to Europe. All in all, it was a good summer. Home exchanging seemed to be getting into our blood.

When we got back to Chevy Chase and Washington late in the summer, I received a call from my friend at the American Council on Germany asking if I would like to take another group of German journalists—three this time—to see the 1980 presidential elections. Would I! Of course! Among other things, this was a chance for me to see the presidential campaign first hand.

Meantime, I was busy organizing the fall and winter Conferences for Journalists. They continued to do fairly well and we were able to attract good speakers as well as journalists from major newspapers. But there were clouds on the horizon. A recession seemed to be on the way, and newspapers were starting to cut their travel budgets.

But I tried to put those concerns out of my mind late in October when the German journalists arrived. The presidential candidates were the incumbent Democrat Jimmy Carter and the former California Republican governor, and former movie actor, Ronald Reagan. Everyone knew Carter was in trouble because of the high inflation rate and the Americans held hostage by the Iranians in the U.S. Embassy in Tehran. Also, the failed attempt to rescue the hostages in the spring of 1980 hurt Carter.

Trailing the candidates, I and the Germans ended up at one point in Cleveland where one of three debates between Carter and Reagan was held. This was the famous debate where Carter said he had talked with his young daughter Amy about nuclear issues, a remark that I suppose was intended to be kind of homey but which ended up hurting Carter because it was interpreted to mean he was asking a child for advice about a serious problem. It was a faux pas as damaging to Carter as Gerald Ford's remark about Polish independence was to him in 1976. Presidential debates which are supposed to inform the electorate about serious issues end up being remembered for off-hand remarks or inconsequential matters that seem to be a slip of the tongue.

Dave Mazie, an old friend who worked with the columnist Carl Rowan, helped me squire the Germans around, as had done in 1976. Dave took them down to North Carolina a t one point to see Reagan campaign. And both Dave an I took them to New Jersey one day to see Carter. The event was in a rather small room where Carter answered questions from the a hand-picked audience. Carter was pretty good in such a setting, which was designed to be taped for television and for broadcast in the Philadelphia market which spills over into New Jersey. I always said the trouble with Carter was that when he smiled his eyes never smiled, too. Thus, he came through as cold and perhaps even calculating. As president, he was also too much of a micro-manager. Smart, yes, but without that all-important charisma that a presidential candidate needs.

Reagan, as I noted earlier, had that certain charisma. The German journalists and I followed him to California and Los Angeles where he ended the 1980 campaign. Before doing that, however, we traveled with Vice President Fritz Mondale and with Reagan's running mate, George Bush Sr. Like Carter, Mondale was also a stiff candidate, but I always liked him. Perhaps it was the Minnesota connection, but I think it was more than that. He was an intelligent, decent man but again no charisma.

Speaking of a lack of charisma, here was George Bush. In 1980 he favored small venues, usually in a high school gymnasium, where he stood in the middle of a crowd, hand-picked, answering soft-ball questions. The questions were predictable and the answers were generally from carefully scripted material easily adapted to the largely expected questions. That's one of the troubles with presidential, and other, campaigning today. Spontaneity has been squeezed out of politics largely, I think, because of television. TV covers everything now, and a slip of the tongue is quickly flashed across the country to the embarrassment of a candidate.

Although only a few reporters cover vice presidential candidates, Bush and his aides, including Vic Gold, an old friend from the Goldwater campaign and now a Bush adviser and speech-writer, carefully shielded him from the press. In the front of the campaign plane there was Bush and a few advisers who traveled with him, and in the back of the bus, so to speak, were the reporters chafing and complaining about the lack of contact with the candidate. The separation between candidate and media was particularly galling to the television correspondents whose reports on the vice-presidential campaign seldom made it to the evening news programs or even the less-watched but still important morning programs.

And as I had discovered in 1976 foreign journalists like my German friends were not much interested in vice presidential candidates. Their audiences wanted to hear about the top figures, the presidential candidates. Nor were the German journalists much concerned with the major senatorial and gubernatorial figures we came across in our criss-crossing of the country. It's not surprising I guess when you think of how few members of the German or even British parliaments that we Americans know by name or sight.

In 1980 I decided to end our traveling in Los Angeles because all the polls and all the political reporters seemed to agree that Reagan would be the winner. And he was. So we were in the right place at the Reagan Los Angeles headquarters where he did make a brief appearance after the returns appeared to be conclusive. It was a big story around the world. A former actor now to be president of the United States!

My trips with the German journalists also made me think more about the United States and how it is viewed in Europe. The journalists were impressed, perhaps even taken aback, at how large a country the United States is. They also were always looking for souvenirs to take back, souvenirs that were emblematic of America.

The one thing visitors can settle on as emblematic of America is the West of the cowboys. At least my German friends were always interested in taking back home cowboy hats, not the exact ten-gallon hats, but reasonable and smaller facsimiles. I thought about other symbols of America, but could not come up with anything better. In addition to the West I found the Germans also interested in the South—the romance associated with the old South, slavery, the Civil War, the civil rights movement, the World War II and post-war exodus of blacks from the South, desegregation, Martin Luther King Jr. and so on. We talked about that a lot between campaign stops.

We also had a lot of discussions about living standards in the United States compared with standards in Europe. America looked much more prosperous to the journalists than did Europe. They were impressed with the large houses here, the many automobiles, particularly two and even three-car families, traveling even by blue-collar workers, the salaries of American journalists and the perks they enjoyed. Journalists here, I realized, had considerably more status than they enjoyed in Europe, at least at the working reporter level.

# 53

## *Si and Joe*

It was also at this time that I got to know Si Bourgin and Joe Laitin well. I had met both of them earlier, in the nineteen-sixties, but we were just casual friends until the nineteen-eighties when we became good and close friends. The two of them had been friends for many years, going back in fact to the nineteen-fifties.

Si Bourgin is a tall, thin man with a wonderful soft way about him. He grew up in the tiny town of Ely, Minnesota, which is practically on the U.S.-Canadian border. It was originally an iron-mining town and is now a summer resort where people go on their way to canoeing in what is now called the Boundary Waters area. Si's family was the only Jewish family in town, and his father owned a clothing store.

Si went to the University of Chicago and from there went to Washington in the late nineteen-thirties, working at various journalism jobs until World War II when he enlisted in the Army. He served in Europe and was a member of the staff of Stars and Stripes, the soldiers' paper which was probably best-known for publishing the cartoons of Bill Mauldin. During the war Si also worked with such luminaries as Andy Rooney.

After the war Si worked for Time-Life and was based in Vienna, when it was a city divided between East and West. He traveled widely in Eastern Europe in the late nineteen-forties and the nineteen-fifties, covering many of the big post-war stories in Europe.

Later in the fifties he came back to the United States, left Time-Life and went to work for Newsweek magazine as its bureau chief in Los Angeles where he met and wrote about many movie stars, directors, producers and other important Hollywood people. From Los Angeles and Hollywood he came back to Washington, where he had started out working in the thirties. His return to Washington was in the early nineteen-sixties.

I first met Si at a party at the home of my friend Paul Green. Paul and Si had met while both were working on Stars and Stripes during the war. I saw Si a couple of other times at Paul Green's house but then lost track of him until the early nineteen-eighties when Paul suggested Si might like to sit in on some of our Journalism Center conferences. He did, and our friendship blossomed.

When Si came back to Washington he took a job with NASA' wrote about the space program and took some of the astronauts on trips around the country and on good-will visits abroad.

In the early nineteen-eighties Si was doing some work for the State Department and some other consulting, but he had time to come to our conferences. We also frequently had lunch and talked about everything. Si is one of the best-informed persons I have ever met, and one of the nicest.

I have often thought, and remarked to him, about how friendships made late in life are often better than those made early in life. Sometimes, it seems, early friendships disintegrate as people go their different ways and as one person becomes more successful than the other. I can think of several instances of that in my own life, and in the lives of others I have known. It's inevitable, I guess. But I know that Si will always be a dear friend while other friendships I made when I was quite young have ended.

The same was true of my friendship with Joe Laitin. I say "was" because Joe died two years ago. Joe was quite different from Si. Joe was short, chubby and a nervous fellow. Like Si, Joe was Jewish, but while Si grew up in decent circumstances in Ely, Minnesota, and went to the prestigious University of Chicago, Joe was a child of poor parents in Brooklyn who never finished high school.

Joe was able to get a job as a journalist in New York though. His first job was as a ship news reporter in the nineteen-thirties. In those days reporters were sent to meet the incoming ocean liners so they could interview important people coming to New York from Europe.

From the rather lowly position of a ship news reporter, Joe managed to get to Washington in the late nineteen-thirties and to a job with Reuters, the British news agency. Soon Reuters sent him to Honolulu. This was in the fall of 1941 when everyone felt the United States would soon be in World War II and there was concern about what might happen at Pearl Harbor.

Joe loved to tell the story of how he lounged around Honolulu and Pearl Harbor with nothing much happening. Finally in mid-November or so both he and his Reuters editors in New York decided they were wasting time and money in Hawaii, and so Joe came back to Washington. He had hardly arrived there when the Japanese bombed Pearl Harbor.

Like Si, Joe enlisted in the Army, but served in the Pacific. After having missed Pearl Harbor, he did not miss the end of the war and was on the deck of the USS

Missouri and witnessed General Douglas MacArthur signing the documents ending the war in the Pacific.

Si and Joe had met in Washington before the war, and later renewed their friendship in Los Angeles in the nineteen-fifties. Joe had gone to Los Angeles after the war, where he did many things—writing for The Big Broadcast, one of the last important radio shows; doing radio commentary himself; writing for magazines like Colliers and the Saturday Evening Post; and even teaching school to help make ends meet between free-lance writing assignments.

Tiring of the glitter of Los Angeles and Hollywood and the uncertainties of the free-lance life, Joe returned to Washington in 1962. Casting about for a job, he was told by a friend that Kermit Gordon, then the director of the Bureau of the Budget, now called the Office of Management and Budget, was looking for someone to handle the press for him. Joe talked to Gordon, and was hired. From Hollywood to a White House agency! Some leap! Well, Joe used to say, Washington at times is not so different from Hollywood. And he may be, no, he was, right.

I first met Joe in the nineteen-sixties when I was doing an article for the Washingtonian magazine on defense issues, and as the Budget's press man he introduced me to its defense expert, James Schlesinger who later became Secretary of Defense.

Our friendship blossomed in the nineteen-seventies and by the early nineteen-eighties we saw each other often, generally for lunch when we discussed all matter of things. In the meantime, Joe had risen fast. From the Bureau of the Budget he went to the White House itself where he was assistant press secretary during the Lyndon Johnson years.

When Richard Nixon succeeded Johnson in 1969 the Republicans kept Joe on and sent him back to the Bureau of the Budget. Later Joe went to the Department of the Treasury, the Federal Aviation Agency—always in what now were being called public affairs jobs—and finally when Schlesinger became Secretary of Defense to the Pentagon as Assistant Secretary for Public Affairs.

Joe was at the Pentagon during the Watergate years, and often told the story of one day going through the tunnel that connects the White House with the adjacent Old Executive Office Building when suddenly a man comes racing past him with a strange look in his eyes, followed by puffing Secret Service agents unable to keep up with him. Joe suddenly realized that the man rushing through the tunnel was the President himself. My God, Joe thought, what is the state of Nixon's mind in this crisis that could bring down the president.

As Joe told the story, he had instant access to Secretary Schlesinger and when he got back to his office he immediately called Schlesinger, told him what he had seen and of his concerns for the President's mental state. Schlesinger listened, did not say a word, just putting the telephone receiver down when Joe had finished talking. Later Joe learned that on the basis of what he had told Schlesinger, the Secretary immediately called the Chairman of the Joint Chiefs of Staff and told him that if the President ordered some sort of action not to do what the President wanted him to do but rather to call Schlesinger immediately and tell him what the President wanted done.

Schlesinger was concerned that Nixon might want the armed forces to conduct a coup d'etat to keep him in office. Nixon never did make such a call and finally resigned the presidency in 1974 and left Washington for California in disgrace.

Joe's tenure in government ended late in the nineteen eighties, but after that he served a term as ombudsman at the Washington Post (I had suggested him to Ben Bradlee) and as a consultant to the former chairman of the Federal Reserve Board.

Joe, Si and I frequently got together for lunch, and Joe started to write his memoirs. He had wonderful stories to tell, but for some reason he could not get beyond the stories and anecdotes in his writing. He asked for advice from both Si and me, and we thought we gave him a lot of ideas on how to turn the stories and anecdotes into a narrative. But like most writers Joe did not take well to criticism or suggestions and criticisms and the memoir never got written. Too bad, because he had a wonderful career and he had much to say about the world of reporting as well as Los Angeles and Hollywood and Washington and government.

Looking back at my late-blooming friendships with both Si and Joe, I think we became such good friends because all three of us had had successful careers, were interested in so much of what was going on in the world and could discuss events of the moment with common sense, good backgrounds and without rancor when we would disagree among ourselves.

As you can see from the above, Si and Joe had a great effect on me, and I think I had some effect on them. I still think a lot about how friendships develop, particularly late in life. I am not sure how all this happens, but in the case of both Joe and Si I am glad I got to know them so well even if it happened late in life.

I also must mention that Joe Laitin was responsible for the words of the astronaut who first stepped on the moon: "A small step for man; a giant step for mankind." When the astronauts were getting ready for their trip to the moon in 1969 many people in the Nixon Administration were asked to come up with appropriate words for the astronauts to send to the world. Joe said he came up with what turned out to be the right words one night at home with the help of his wife. The words now are part of our language and probably immortal.

In writing about Si Bourgin I should also mention that soon after the war when he was working out of Vienna for Time-Life and traveling frequently behind the Iron Curtain he met a young photographer named Bob Halmi in Hungary. He was so impressed with Halmi and his work that he recommended him to Life magazine's editors and he became a contract photographer. Later Halmi came to the United States, started making movies and today is one of the most important producers of television movies, often for the Hallmark Hall of Fame.

One more thing I should say about Joe Laitin, who was full of so many wonderful stories. While in Hollywood Joe attended a funeral of one of the powerful and hated movie moguls. The crowd at the funeral was huge. Among the mourners, no, spectators is probably the better word, was the comedian Red Skelton, who, Joe said, looked around and quipped, "Well, if you give people what they want, they will turn out for it!"

# 54

# *The Club That Stands for Brains*

But here we are still in the early nineteen-eighties, and I suppose I should tele-scope some of the events of those years. Family matters went along fairly smoothly. McGill University seemed to be a good fit for Sally and she was doing well. Suzie and Bob finally finished the addition to their house and both were still teaching in the small school near Saratoga Springs dealing with problem children. After serving as an assistant press secretary to Governor Jerry Brown of California Steve moved on to become director of a state job training program instituted by Brown. Fred was working for the Office of the State of California Labor Com-missioner and was back in school—law school this time. As for Priscilla and me we were busy going to the theater, having dinner with friends and home-exchanging. I remember Priscilla's brother Bill trying to reach us in the evening and when he finally did one night when we were home, saying, "Don't you peo-ple ever stay home." That was in the days before everyone had a telephone-answering machine. It was a busy and enjoyable life.

At the Journalism Center we continued to organize one and two-day confer-ences and got good acceptance of them and good attendance. Our best confer-ence size was about fifteen participating journalists. Sometimes we had twenty or more, which was nice from our budgetary standpoint but maybe too many par-ticipants for everyone to have a good chance to ask questions.

My long-time principal assistant, Celia Kay, retired, but we managed to find good people. Arnette was one, Grace another, and Murielle the best of all. Muri-elle was from Switzerland and tremendously efficient as well as being a pleasant person to work for. She was joined later by Francoise, who grew up in France. They made a good team. The Center's board continued to give me good support while still letting me run the Center. I have always been grateful for that because I knew of too many boards where a member or two wanted to run the program they were overseeing rather than letting the director they had hired be the direc-tor.

And there were always extra-curricular activities. In addition to administering the Thomas Stokes Award for what was now called environmental writing, for a few years we took on the judging of the annual contest sponsored by the Education Writers Association. That contest had a lot of categories and a lot of entries; so we had to pick several judges. But I looked on it as a useful project encouraging better journalism.

Also for a time I was in charge of organizing a series of dinners for Nieman fellows who were in Washington. There were about sixty fellows in the capital, and we would typically get forty or fifty to a dinner. Among our speakers were Henry Kissinger and Louis Lyons, the long-time "curator" of the Nieman program who was retired when he spoke to the Washington group.

I also served for several years on the board of Science Service, which publishes the weekly magazine Science News and is best known for administering the Search for Science Talent, a program seeking outstanding high-school science students. The ten best students are awarded college scholarships at what a dinner in March in Washington. Glenn Seaborg, the Nobel laureate and University of California at Berkeley distinguished professor, was the chairman of the Science Service board, and there were other important scientists on the board as well as two or three of us grubby journalists. I was honored to be on such a prestigious board and always enjoyed our bi-monthly meetings in the old building on N Street that served as the headquarters for Science Service. I also was on the board of a committee that was part of the Newspaper Guild and that made an annual award for the best newspaper criticism. It was called the Lowell Mellett Fund, named in honor of a distinguished journalist from the nineteen-thirties and forties. Sometimes the award went to an author of a book; other times we honored a journalist for a series of articles.

Another activity I enjoyed was the Off-the-Record Club. This group of political reporters had regular lunches and dinners with senators, representatives, Cabinet members and other political figures as guests. It was a way for me to keep in touch with the political world.

In the early nineteen-eighties my old Washington Post colleague Carroll Kilpatrick suggested to me that I should join the Cosmos Club. I was flattered that he even thought I could qualify for membership in such a famous club. The Cosmos Club was started in the late eighteen hundreds and was patterned after the men's clubs in London. Among the founders of the Cosmos was Gilbert Grovenor, who was also the principal founder of the National Geographic Society.

From its beginnings the Cosmos Club has had many scientists as members. As the club grew it also admitted writers, journalists, lawyers and government officials as well as physicians. The club house is in an old mansion—called the Townsend mansion for its first occupants—on Massachusetts Avenue just west of Dupont Circle. It is a beautiful place with a ballroom that is considered one of the most stunning rooms in Washington. The wood-paneled library, filled with books many of which were written by club members, is also one of the most beautiful rooms I have ever seen.

With Carroll Kilpatrick's encouragement I decided to apply for membership. To become a member, it helps to have written books, and I had done that. I also needed personal recommendations from at least twelve club members who knew me personally, and I was able to round those up. I was accepted as a member in nineteen-eighty-two. And Priscilla and I made good use of the club, dining there often, attending lectures, special events like steak or crab nights and the monthly Book-and-Author suppers. More often than not the author was a club member.

I always have liked to tell people what is said about what are probably the three most prestigious clubs in Washington—the Metropolitan Club means social standing; the Chevy Chase Club signifies money; and the Cosmos Club stands for brains!

Later I became quite active in the club when I was asked to edit the club's monthly bulletin, which I and fellow club member David Richardson turned into a little magazine, but more about that later.

# 55

## *From Seattle to a Convertible*

From San Francisco and the Democratic convention we went to a second house exchange in that year of 1984 in Seattle. There we found ourselves in a nice, fairly new house not too far from downtown Seattle. I remember many things about our stay in Seattle, but probably most importantly I remember that there was absolutely no rain while we were there. Was this really Seattle, where everyone knows it always rains or mists. Yes, it was. Seattle does get a respite from rain in the summer months. While we were there people were beginning to talk about a drought. A drought? In Seattle?

Drought or not, we had a good time in sunny Seattle, visiting the old town called Pioneer Square, going to the site of the nineteen-sixties World's Fair with its Space Needle, watching boats going through the locks that connect a lake with Puget Sound and eating wonderful sea food.

One evening we had a long dinner with the mayor, that's right, the mayor. I'm reaching for his name now, and I am sure it will come back. The mayor started out as a television journalist, became very well known, decided to get into politics and won in his first effort. I knew him because he was a fellow at the Journalism Center in the early nineteen-seventies.

His brother, who was his campaign manager, was also a fellow at the Center. Both were smart and personable. My friend was reasonably successful as mayor, but when he tried to run for the Senate he failed. He jumped into a Senate race quickly after longtime Senator Henry (Scoop) Jackson died suddenly. After that my friend went to Harvard to help run a program in the Kennedy School of Government, and I have now lost track of him.

Our evening with the mayor began at his office where he produced a little libation for us. From there we went to a restaurant atop a building with a grand view of Puget Sound. We ate well, drank a bit, talked a lot and had a great time. The mayor's brother joined us for dinner and added to the merriment. Aha! The name of the mayor—Charles Royer. How's that for memory, recall, or something. His brother—Robert Royer. Where do those things come from that suddenly pop into your head?

There were also several other Journalism Center fellows in the Seattle area, and we invited them all to a party one night at the house in which we were living and had a great time talking about both the past and the present, with emphasis on politics, particularly the upcoming Reagan-Mondale fall campaign.

While in Seattle we also took a trip to Vancouver Island and Vancouver itself. To get there we took a ferry boat through the San Juan Islands, and that boat trip was almost better than our destinations. The islands are spectacular; some are fairly large, others rather small, but all are green, picturesque and so inviting.

As for the city of Victoria on Vancouver Island it was a little too touristy for us. The famous old hotel there—and its equally famous afternoon teas—were just too, too much. The hotel lobby was so jammed at tea time that we did not even try to have tea.

We did stay in a funny old hotel just outside Victoria. The room we had was enormous and strangely decorated. It was almost spooky, but we didn't see any ghosts and enjoyed our night there. Another attraction on Vancouver Island is a huge garden fashioned in what was once a stone quarry. A man and his wife with money built the garden. It had every flower, shrub and tree imaginable and is truly spectacular as well as huge. Well worth a visit.

But the city of Vancouver was our favorite. It is even more spectacular than San Francisco or Seattle. Almost surrounded by the Pacific Ocean and by mountains, Vancouver affords wonderful views wherever you look. The city is clean, quite walkable and its buildings are diverse and almost as interesting to look at as the water and the mountains. Unfortunately, we only were able to spend a couple of days in Vancouver as we had to get back to Seattle because my Aunt Honey had made plans to come up from Oregon to visit us. But, fortunately, Priscilla and I did get back to both Seattle and Vancouver a few years later for editors' conventions.

As director of the Journalism Center I attended the annual conventions of the American Society of Newspaper Editors (ASNE), the Associated Press Managing Editors Association (APME) and the National Conference of Editorial Writers (NCEW) and the American Newspaper Publishers Association (ANPA).

The ASNE usually met in Washington first at the Shoreham hotel and later at the Marriott at Fourteenth and E streets, the site of the original Washington Post building. The other organizations generally met in different places each year. As a result, I got to go to cities like Denver, San Francisco, Fort Worth, Louisville, Boston, both Charleston, West Virginia, and Charleston, South Carolina, St.

Paul and Minneapolis. Phoenix, Honolulu, Philadelphia, Hartford, Connecticut, New York and Providence, Rhode Island.

The convention programs kept me in touch with new ideas circulating among editors. My attendance at the meetings also was a way of showing the flag for the Journalism Center, meeting editors I had only talked with on the telephone. And wherever I went I also made time to see the cities, the Churchill Downs race track in Louisville, the beautifully restored houses in Charleston, South Carolina, the Liberty Bell in Philadelphia, Pearl Harbor in Hawaii, the cowboy museum in Fort Worth, and on and on.

In my travels I always made sure I got a least a fleeting look at whatever city I was visiting. I never wanted to spend all time in a hotel room or a meeting room. I also liked to walk around cities because that is the way to get a genuine feel of a city. I remembered from my Nieman year a foreign correspondent who talked to us saying that whenever he got to an unfamiliar city he walked about it as much as possible because he felt that was the best way to get a feel for the city and even the country where it was located.

But back to 1984 and the presidential campaign. Again, I took three German journalists around to see the last couple of weeks of the presidential campaigning. We saw Mondale in Baltimore and Buffalo, New York, among other places and traveled with Reagan in the West ending up again in Los Angeles because I was certain Reagan would be reelected. We also traveled with Vice President Bush in the Midwest and South. I also remember going up to Millersville, Pennsylvania, to watch Reagan speak to a college audience. He appeared in an auditorium at Millersville University, and the stage from which he spoke was filled with bales of hay and corn stalks. At Reagan's back was a large painting of a farm scene. It was all for television and indeed on television it looked as if Reagan was actually in a farm field. The Reagan handlers were geniuses at making fakery look real.

The German journalists and I spent Election Day at the Universal Studios Theme Park in Hollywood where we went the usual tourist route seeing back lots, old sets with faux southern mansions and make-believe New York street scenes. Movies are an indelible part of the American story, and the German journalists thoroughly enjoyed the Universal tour and its purported back scene look at movie making.

We spent election night at the Reagan headquarters in Los Angeles and got a glimpse of Reagan himself when he appeared to make a short statement after it was apparent that he had defeated Mondale, soundly in fact. Mondale only carried his home state of Minnesota and the District of Columbia.

Mondale turned out to be a disappointing candidate. He was certainly no Hubert Humphrey, although he had come up in Minnesota politics during the Humphrey years and was a Humphrey protégé. Mondale had none of Humphrey's sunny personality, and was wooden as a campaigner. He was a good man, but not a good politician and unfortunately you have to be that particularly when you are running for president.

So there we were with another four years of Reagan, not a pleasant prospect as far as I was concerned. In my view Reagan went a long way largely on his personality. I don't think he ever worked very hard at being president, but people overlooked that. They liked him as a person and didn't seem to be bothered by his short office hours and disinterest in details.

Before leaving 1984 I should note that it was the year we became sporty and bought a convertible. Convertibles had all but disappeared when Chrysler, in 1983, brought them back. We got a red Dodge convertible, and had a ball with it, taking weekend trips throughout Maryland and Virginia and even up to Pennsylvania. Second childhood? Perhaps, but fun.

# PART X

## Seeing Europe from the Ground Up

# 56

## *Loch Lommand in the Rain*

Soon, 1988 was upon us, and that meant another election year. But before we get to the election, I must report on a few other matters. One involved the Cosmos Club. One day I was asked to have lunch with president of the club.

When I arrived for lunch I found not only the club president waiting for me but also a couple of other officers. What was this? I soon discovered what was up. The club was going through many changes and one of them was to turn its anemic monthly bulletin into something of which the club could be proud, perhaps even a magazine. I was asked if I would take over the editorship of the magazine, called simply the Cosmos Bulletin. I was flattered, but quickly said, sure, I'll do it and give it my best.

It was not an easy job, but together with a new-found friend David Richardson, a former Time-Life and U. S. News and World Report correspondent in Europe, the Middle East and Latin America, we began to turn the Bulletin into a real magazine. Dave and I decided we should cover Club events—luncheon and dinner speakers, award ceremonies, book-and-author suppers—and also have profiles of particularly interesting club members.

We started slowly but soon developed what I thought was a pretty good publication. The Bulletin is printed on small pages the size of the Readers' Digest and we only had thirty-six or so pages to work with each month, but we managed to pack quite a bit into it. The club has its own print shop, located in the basement of the club house. At the time, the printer was a man who had spent many years with the Evening Star before coming to the club. He was a nice man, very cooperative and the Bulletin looked good.

As editor of the Bulletin I was also privileged to sit in on the monthly meetings of the Board of Management, which oversaw all of the club's operations, and at those meetings I learned a lot about the club, its operations and its distinguished history. Again I was flattered to a part of the inner circle that ran such a storied club. Also, the meetings were very civilized. They started at about five in the evening and at the side of the meeting room there was always a nice bar which even included freshly mixed manhattans, then my drink of choice. At six-thirty or so sandwiches and coffee were brought in for the hungry board members. Yes, those cats knew how to live.

And each spring brought spring training. We had become regulars at the Yacht Harbor Inn and Suites overlooking a pretty yacht basin in Dunedin, Florida. We continued to go largely to see Philadelphia play at nearby Clearwater and Toronto at Dunedin. We also managed to see St. Louis at St. Petersburg once or twice too. Priscilla's sister Barbara and her brother Bill and his wife Mickey also joined us each year for spring training. What began as a lark became a ritual of spring for all of us. People used to ask me what do you do besides go to baseball games. What do we do? The day begins with a leisurely breakfast followed by a trip to a newsstand to get the New York Times and the n reading some of the Times before it is time to go to the ball park. The game is over and it's time to return to the Yacht Harbor Inn for cocktails and then it's out to dinner. What do we do? That's what we do.

That spring I attended Washington's Gridiron Club dinner. It is one of the social highlights of the year. People would kill to get an invitation. I was a guest of Chuck Bailey, a long-time Washington correspondent for the Minneapolis Tribune, editor of what became the Minneapolis Star-Tribune for ten years or so and chairman of the Journalism Center's board for a few years. The Gridiron Club is made up of fifty or so prominent Washington journalists and its only reason for being is an annual dinner at which Washington luminaries are kidded in songs and sketches. The dinner is held in the ballroom of the Statler-Hilton hotel and is limited to about five hundred guests. It is a white-tie-and-tails event. So it is pretty fancy and classy.

What I remember most about that year's Gridiron is going into a room before the dinner to meet Chuck. The room, like so many on Gridiron nights, was fitted out with a bar, and the drinks were free. As I moved toward the bar, I saw what seemed to be a familiar face. The man held out his hand, and said Hi! I'm Lee Iacocca. Of course he was the president of the Chrysler Corporation, the savior of it, who was appearing frequently on televised ads asking people to buy Chrysler and Dodge cars. I told him that I was the proud owner of a red 1984 Dodge convertible but was disturbed that Chrysler was planning to change what I had thought had become a classic, sculptured look. Well, you know, said my new-found friend, you have to keep changing things in the automobile business. I guess he was right, but I was still disappointed in Chrysler's plans. Then my friend said how about a drink and I said fine. So he "bought" me a drink. (They were all free of course).

The Gridiron program was long, boy, was it long. Some of it was good; some was not, President Reagan was there—presidents skip Gridiron dinners at their peril—and made a short, light, sometimes funny speech, as is the custom at those dinners. Afterwards I thought that some of the jokes and song parodies of the Capitol Steps satire group were better than the Gridiron offerings, but it was still fun to be at a Gridiron dinner, all fancied up in white tie and tails, rented just for the evening.

That summer we spent some time in London before going way up north for a home exchange in Aberdeen, Scotland. In London we stayed in a second-rate hotel that had gotten a good notice in the Washington Post or New York Times travel section, but it turned out to be third rate and we were eager to got out of London even though we did as usual enjoy the London theater for a few nights and matinees.

We went to Scotland on the train, the fast and luxurious Royal Scotsman which whisked us through the English and Scottish countryside to Edinburgh in just a few hours. From Edinburgh we took a local, not at all luxurious train to Aberdeen, an old, old city on the North Sea that had become the center for the off-shore oil business that was booming and had turned Aberdeen into a corporate headquarters.

The house where we stayed in Aberdeen was I guess you could say middle-aged, not very fancy but like so many other exchange houses adequate for our needs. We found Aberdeen an interesting old city with many ancient buildings. It also has one of the oldest universities in the British Isles. But it is a gray, cold and rainy place, as is most of Scotland and Ireland and much of the north of England itself.

One Sunday soon after we arrived we drove a bit south of Aberdeen to an old fishing village where we had lunch in what had once been a hangout for fishermen. Sitting next to us were a middle-aged man and an older woman, whom we took to be his mother. As we were talking to each other tring to puzzle out some items on the menu, the man leaned, over to our table, asked if we were Americans and then explained the puzzling menu items to use.

It turned out that he was an editor of the Aberdeen newspaper and had visited the United States many years earlier when he was just out of college. So as we ate we talked about newspapers, Scotland and America and after a bit he asked if I would like to write a column for his paper about my observations of Scotland and Aberdeen in particular. I said sure. After I had written the piece we went by the newspaper office to deliver my observations and received a tour of the plant. The piece I wrote was not very profound, remarking on the grayness of Aberdeen, the seeming penchant of the residents for red and other brightly-colored cars and the friendliness of the people. Our editor-friend invited us to dinner a couple of times. On those occasions he was accompanied by his girl friend. One of the dinners was in a restaurant said to be one of the oldest, if not the oldest, in Scotland.

Balmoral castle, where Queen Elizabeth and other members of the Royal Family spend part of each summer, was not far from Aberdeen and we visited it one day. We did not see the Queen. She had not yet arrived for her summer visit.

We had been told that a visit to Scotland is not complete without taking in the Isle of Skye. We decided to follow this advice even though it meant driving clear across Scotland, and we were warned that some visitors to Skye never saw much of the island because of the rain and fog that often bedevil the place. But we decided to take our chances.

On our way we stopped at an old fishing lodge on Loch Lommand—you know, the lake that is supposed to harbor a huge monster—Fish? Animal? Human? The fishing lodge had been converted into a delightful inn. Although it rained all the time we were at the inn, we had a wonderful time there. It was being run by two young Australians, the man being the chef, and the woman the manager and general factotum. Before dinner you went to the lounge for drinks, and the chef came by in due time to describe the evening's menu. When our table was ready and the soup was already on it, the woman who was the manager came by to escort us into the dining room. The meal was superb, and beautifully served. I had lamb, being in Scotland, and Priscilla had fresh fish, probably caught that very day in Loch Lommand. After-dinner drinks were served back in the lounge.

The next morning the rain was finally beginning to stop. We had learned by then not to let rain interfere with our plans in Scotland. Rain is just a normal part of life there, and nothing seems to stop because of it, even if it is a hard, drenching, bone-chilling rain.

So after a most satisfying breakfast we were off to the Isle of Skye. Actually, it was not as far away from Loch Lommand as we had thought it would be, and before lunch time we were parked waiting for the ferry to take us on the short trip to Skye from the mainland. Now there is a bridge linking the mainland to Skye.

Once on the island we had lunch at a restaurant near the ferry terminal and then started driving around the island. We soon learned that there were probably more sheep than people on Skye. Every so often the sheep blocked the road and there was nothing to be done except to wait patiently for the sheep to move on.

There was no rain but the sky remained overcast as we explored the island. It is a barren place and there is not that much to see. But there is a fairly large mountain that dominates the scenery, and that is an interesting sight.

But as we returned to the ferry terminal for the trip back to the mainland we said that at least we had the satisfaction of actually seeing the Isle of Skye without rain or fog obscuring the view. Is it worth all the time and trouble and driving we took to get there? Marginal. The old fishing lodge that had been turned into that wonderful inn was much more interesting.

Our journey back to Aberdeen was uneventful, and a few days later we went to Inverness, which is the town at the northern tip of Loch Lommand and is near the site of one of the most famous battles between the clans in Scotland. The battle was centuries ago but it is still remembered and commemorated. On both the Skye and Inverness trips we saw remnants of the crofter's cottages that were smashed and often burned by the English in the eighteenth century during the infamous "clearances" which drove out the crofters—the farmers—so that the English could run sheep over the crofter's lands and make much more money than they could get from leasing the land for farming. When you see those ruins of cottages you can surely understand the enmity that continues between the Scots and the English. Many of the crofters fled to Ireland, and their descendants are now the Protestants in Northern Ireland.

One other trip we made, more than once, took us to a restaurant on the northern coast of Scotland that had been featured in a New York Times travel/food piece. It was famous for its fish, and not only was the food good but the restaurant itself was one of those charming places in an old, old stone building right by the sea.

Our home exchange in Scotland was a great success despite the rain and sometimes clammy days. There is something about Scotland that seems to grab you and hold on to you. I'm not sure I would want to live in that climate, but I could go there again, and in fact did, as I will relate later, and enjoy it every bit as much.

But as always the time comes to go home, and as invigorating as travel can be it is always nice to get back to the familiar surroundings of home. So it was back to organizing conferences and then, in October, there were three more German journalists on my doorstep wanting to see the 1988 presidential election.

When the first German journalists came in 1976 they spent time at Harvard listening to professors talking about American politics, but the later groups came directly to Washington, wanting the action of the campaign trail rather than academic discussions.

In 1988 it was George Bush Sr. versus Michael Dukakis, the governor Massa
chusetts. Republican Bush had been Ronald Reagan's vice president and Dukaki
had been a reasonably successful Democratic governor. Neither candidate hac
much of that seemingly necessary charisma.

As his vice presidential candidate Bush picked a young senator from Indi
ana—Dan Quayle—and a long-time senator from Texas—Lloyd Bentsen—wa
Dukakis' running mate.

The German journalists and I first caught up with Bush at a rally in a subur
ban high school in a Chicago suburb and then followed him to two rallies i
Michigan. From Michigan we flew to Atlanta and then to Columbia, Soutl
Carolina where we caught with Quayle and followed him west to Oklahoma anc
then back to Washington. The Germans were not much impressed with eithe
Bush or Quayle. Nor was I. No one could figure out why Bush picked this youn
senator, who he barely knew, was considered naïve and was ridiculed for his lacl
of experience and seeming lack of basic knowledge about the country and th
world. But there he was perhaps soon to be just a step from the presidency itself.

After getting back to Washington we soon headed up to Boston to catch u
with the Dukakis campaign. We were lucky to get on a trip west in the wanin
days of the campaign. On the way to California we stopped in South Dakot
where Dukakis gave a speech to a group of farmers. Coming from Massachusett
I don't think he knew much about farming, but an agriculture speech is necessar
and someone had written the right things for him to say.

Our destination was California, and the big event there was a train trip fron
Bakersfield up the valley to Stockton. That was a great adventure for all o
us—the train itself, the several stops en route where we could get a good look a
Dukakis on the stump and the camaraderie on the train itself with all the newspa
per and television correspondents. Unfortunately for Dukakis, by then it wa
generally agreed that Bush was the sure winner. And he was. Dukakis turned ou
to be not exactly a stirring candidate; not that Bush was either. But Bush was bet
ter known and considered a man who could assume the Reagan mantle and con
tinue to bring good times to the country.

Something that I, and many others, will always remember from that campaig
was the debate between the two vice presidential candidates. The young Indian
senator tried to compare himself with John F. Kennedy. The Texas senator wa
appalled. "Senator," he said, "I knew Jack Kennedy and you are not a Jacl
Kennedy."

As things turned out this would be the last time for me to take German jour
nalists on the campaign trail. I wished I could have done it again, but with m

impending retirement that was not possible. I think I gave them a good look at—and some understanding of—presidential politics and campaigning—and made some friends in the process.

But then it was back to Washington, more Journalism Center conferences and another Gannett lecture. Our lecture series had worked out quite well, and I no longer trembled ahead of time in fear that no one would show up. They became a bit of a Washington tradition with journalists and others who attended them looking forward not only to the speaker but also to the camaraderie before, during and after the lecture.

And we had some outstanding speakers over the years including David Broder, Walter Cronkite and Katherine Graham. All had important things to say about the particular state of journalism at the time they spoke, and nearly every lecture made some news and was published in a journalism review or some other important publication.

As 1988 turned into 1989 it suddenly dawned on me that this would be my last year at the Journalism Center, with my sixty-fifth birthday coming up in the next November. Soon there was talk about who would succeed me. The job was considered something of a plumb, and indeed it was. So several prominent Washington journalists were indicating and interest in the position. But there was still a year to go, which meant organizing more conferences and making sure that we got the best possi ble speakers and enough attendees. Major papers continued to support our program, and that was always gratifying and encouraging.

And then there was my work as editor of the Cosmos Bulletin. I would often drop off at the club in the morning to take care of some Bulletin matters before going on to the office. Or I might leave the office a little early and spend some time at the club before going on home. The job added to an already fairly busy schedule but I enjoyed it and got compliments on it.

In the summer of 1989 we had two home exchanges. The first was in San Francisco in a large apartment at Geary and Franklin streets, just across from the new, very modern Catholic Cathedral. We were taken with the location, although it was near some not too desirable areas, and thought about it as a place to live when we would make our move to San Francisco the following year. So we checked out apartments in the building and a couple of nearby buildings.

After the trip to San Francisco we went back to Washington for a short time and then were off to London for our second exchange of the year. The house in London was south of the Thames river and in a very ordinary neighborhood. And it was a rather messy place. But we made do.

We also decided to visit the Cotswolds where we had never been before. Before our trip there we had dinner with an American who working for Reuters news service in London and, anxious to get back to the United States, was a candidate for the directorship of the Journalism Center. (He didn't get the job.) Over dinner he suggested places to stay in the Cotswolds. The Cotswolds, once a center for the raising of sheep and the sheep trade, are dotted with charming villages and small towns and are a favorite with tourists coming to England.

We followed one suggestion made by our friend, and found the inn he had recommended to be charming and just right. The room was snug, the food was good and there was a brook and tiny falls across the way. Again, as in Scotland, the evening began with drinks in the lounge, the chef coming through to tell us about the menu and then being escorted into the dining room when our table was ready. That was living! Everything was just right.

We enjoyed touring the Cotswolds. The villages and towns are historic, quaint and just plain beautiful. Most of the old buildings are built from a yellowish stone native to the area, and seem to have improved with age. There are always too many tourists and tourist buses, but what can be done about that? We are tourists, too.

Back in London we took in theater and more sightseeing. I could go to London for two weeks just for the theater, seeing a play every evening, two on matinee days. The London theater is marvelous and the actors seem to be better than their American counterparts. Or is it just the English accent?

# PART XI
## A New Life

# 57

## *A Death in Hamburg*

Back to Hamburg and the worst days of my life. Our trip was coming to a close and on this particular evening we packed up, thought about what a wonderful summer we had had and went to bed early because we had to get up at six a.m. to get to the Hamburg airport for our flight to London and then on to San Francisco.

As I was drifting off to sleep, I suddenly heard Priscilla. Strange noises were coming from her throat. I leaped up, looked at her and shouted: "Priscilla! Priscilla! What's the matter?" There was no response.

I shook her. I shook her again. Again there was no response. Her eyes did not open. Her mouth did not move. When I tried to lift her, neither her arms or her legs responded. Finally I carefully put her back on the bed, threw on a bathrobe and went across the hall and knocked on the adjoining apartment door.

When a man opened the door I told him that I needed help. Something had happened to my wife. Could he call an ambulance, please? The man—and his wife and grown daughter who were also at the door by now—ran into our apartment, looked at Priscilla and the man immediately went back to his apartment and called for an ambulance.

Medics arrived very quickly, rushed into our apartment, asked me to get out of the bedroom and, as they told me later, tried to revive Priscilla. After an interminable time, about an hour I guess it was, they came out and one of them said: "I am sorry, but she is gone. There was nothing we could do. My guess is that it was a heart attack."

Priscilla was dead! I couldn't believe it. She had been so alive just a few hours earlier. What to do? There we were in far away Hamburg. The medics told me that someone else would come to pick up the body, take it to the morgue so that the cause of death could be determined for certain. It was a heart attack, I was later told.

Meantime, I got on the phone to call first Fred and then Suzie to tell them the terrible news and to ask them to call Steve and Sally and certain friends in Washington and California. Then I tried to sleep, and I guess I did rather fitfully for an hour or two.

Soon it was morning and I dressed and was invited to have breakfast with the people next door who had been so helpful. They said that they thought the first thing I should do is go to the American consulate because they understood that deaths of U.S. citizens abroad had to be reported to an embassy or consulate.

The daughter of the people next door drove me to the consulate where I found the consulate general, a woman, very helpful. She guided me through the necessary paperwork and then when I asked about funeral arrangements gave me the names of a couple of mortuaries. One was not too far away and I walked there. I later wondered how I made it, so shocked and grief-stricken as I was, but I made it, walking around one of the Hamburg lakes and thinking about the wonderful times Priscilla and I had had that summer. And now it was all over, everything was all over.

At the mortuary I talked with a nice woman who had enough English so we could communicate. I told her that Priscilla and I had agreed that we wanted to be cremated. She said that could be done, but that it would take a few days under German law. Given the history of Germany under the Nazis a waiting period certainly was understandable.

After making all the necessary arrangements at the mortuary, I went back to the apartment, picked up all our luggage, called a cab and went to a hotel that had been recommended by the consul general. But what to do next? I talked again with Fred and Suzie as well as Steve and Sally and they all agreed that there was nothing more I could do in Hamburg and that I should come home. I had already made arrangements for Priscilla's ashes to be shipped to California. So I called United Airlines, told them what had happened and was able to get a seat on flights the next day. That evening I had dinner with a woman who was a friend of the people we had exchanged with and with whom we had had dinner when we first arrived in Hamburg. She had heard of Priscilla's death from the exchangers, who were still in San Francisco and I had called. I don't think I was very good company, but it was nice to have someone to talk with.

Both the flight to London and then the flight over the Arctic Circle were very full, but at least I got aisle seats. On the flights I keep replaying the night Priscilla died and kept thinking, why her? Why now? Why at the still relatively young age of sixty-seven years? Why her, and why not me?

We had been married forty-six years. Being married at the age of twenty-one you could almost say we grew up together. And all in all it was a good marriage. I had been relatively successful as a journalist and a writer. We had done many things together, and never tired of each other's company. Our children were doing well. And now as I sat on those planes our life was like a movie unrolling before my eyes.

Death, I must admit, is something I never thought much about, never in fact wanted to think about. My father died when I was in my early thirties. I was saddened by his death, but it was just as I was going to work at the Washington Post and I guess the excitement of the new job in a way overwhelmed my sorrow at my father's death. My mother was in her nineties when she died, and I have written she wanted to die. I have also mentioned the column I wrote about never thinking I would heave a sigh of relief at my mother's death.

The deaths of parents are hard to take, but nothing is harder to deal with than the death of a spouse. On the few occasions when I thought of my death or Priscilla's death I always thought I would be the first one to die. Is that the way most husbands think? I don't know, but I have a feeling it is.

Was this God's will that Priscilla should die when she did? I don't know whether there is a God or not looking over us. I think not. Nor do I think there is a hereafter. If we live on at all after death, I think it is through our children, how we have taught them, what ideas we have instilled in them.

When relatives and friends sympathized with me over Priscilla's death and said, anyway, she's in heaven now, I know I hurt the feelings of some, without meaning to, by saying no, Priscilla's life ended when she died.

# 58

## *Loneliness—And Friendship*

Slowly but surely I began to adjust to life alone. I think I have always been fairly self-sufficient and I fairly easily fell into the habit of making my own meals. I made it a practice to get out of the apartment every day and that meant having lunch out with a friend like Lionel or Dick Kaplan or even by myself. I also went out to dinner fairly often.

During the day I worked on our Defense Advisory Newsletter, talking by telephone to people involved in the issues, attending seminars and meetings that were held in San Francisco, Oakland, down the Peninsula and in San Jose. And of course there was the actual writing of the newsletter. I did practically all the reporting and writing and Steve did the editing and put the whole newsletter together ready for a printer.

Unfortunately, the newsletter was never a success and we were forced to abandon it after a couple of years. We failed, I think, for a number of reasons. I am not sure we were able to target a market. We did not have much money to circulate sample copies of the newsletter to prospective subscribers. And we were too far away from Washington to keep up adequately with developments in the Pentagon and the Commerce and Labor departments concerning defense conversion issues, although I did continue to go to Washington every six months or so.

If it was any consolation to us, a Washington newsletter publisher that specialized on Pentagon issues also tried a defense conversion publication and it too failed. So I guess the answer was that the market for such a publication simply did not exist.

Meantime, life went on. I resumed going to spring training where I was joined by Priscilla's sister Barbara and her brother Bill and his wife Mickey. And, in 1994 Priscilla's cousin Evelyn Crawford, who lived in San Francisco, also went to spring training with us. We all had a good time, and there is something to be said for carrying on what had become kind of a tradition.

In 1994 I also met Erica, at, of all places, my eye doctor's office. One day when I was scheduled for a field-of-vision test Erica was operating the machine. She was a nice-looking, blonde woman of about sixty and was from Romania. We talked about her heritage and my Polish-German background and I suggested we have dinner some time to continue our discussion, and she said Why not?

So began a friendship that lasted a couple of years. Erica's father had been the eye physician to King Leopold of Romania, who fled when the Nazis overran his country in 1941. Erica and her family stayed in Romania through the war. Afterwards she came to the United States and ended up as a saleswoman for medicines and equipment needed by eye doctors and traveled through the West visiting physicians. When I met her she was working part-time in my eye doctor's office and trying to organize tourist trips to Romania and other Eastern European countries, without much success though. And she had been married three times, but never had any children.

We seemed to hit it off, had dinner fairly often, went to the theater occasionally or to a movie and did other things together. I enjoyed the companionship and I think she did too. She was an intelligent person and good company. But when she suggested after we had known each other for a couple of years that we should get married, I did not think so. As much as I wanted to remarry I did not think Erica was quite right for me. Why not? Well, I am not quite sure I can put it into words. At any rate, we stopped seeing each other in 1996. I think we parted amicably, and in fact a couple of months after we split Erica invited me to a house in Marin she had moved into from her apartment, and over a nice dinner she prepared it seemed to me she was trying to renew our friendship and try again to entice me into marriage, but it never happened.

To continue with personal matters, at about the same time I met Erica I also became acquainted with Jack Worswick, who had become the resident manager of our building at 2200 Pacific Avenue. Jack was close to my age and had come to California from a small town in Wisconsin where he had run a store that rented equipment ranging from farm implements to wheelchairs and lawn mowers. He had also traveled throughout the United States raising money for a Lutheran home for the retarded in Wisconsin. Jack's wife had died about the same time as Priscilla. So as midwesterners we had some things in common. His three daughters and a retarded son lived in Northern California and that was an important reason why he moved to California from Wisconsin. He was born in a suburb of Chicago and had spent most of life in Illinois and Wisconsin.

Jack was lonely, and so was I; so we would have lunch together once a week or so, go to baseball games—I had tickets to Giants and A's midweek day games—and some times just have a drink together and talk about our lives. Unfortunately, as I write, Jack is seriously ill, needing oxygen twenty-four hours a day to keep breathing. It is sad indeed to see someone, particularly a friend, tethered to a tube. Jack is no longer the resident manager and now lives near his children in Santa Rosa.

Priscilla's cousin Evelyn was also a comfort to me. She is about my age, perhaps a little older, and is a widow. She likes to go out to dinner, as I do, and we managed to eat out a couple of times a month. Her hairdresser is a gay man and he and his partner have dinner out every night and keep up with the ever-changing restaurant scene. So Evelyn always had a good recommendation for dinner.

And now we are in 1995. I am doing much better in putting Priscilla's death behind me and looking at my new life as a kind of a new adventure. I certainly have had no lack of female companionship, which has been nice, and I have kept busy with everything from the defense advisory newsletter, short as its life was, to reading the papers and magazines to keep up with the world. The solution to life I guess is to keep busy. And that I did.

Spring training was on my agenda again in 1995 and again I enjoyed the ten days in Florida. And that spring I received an offer for a home exchange in Paris. I t sounded good and I asked Fred if he and his family would like to come along. They thought about it and decided to go to Paris. So early in July we were off for a couple of weeks in Paris, and as it turned out elsewhere in France.

Our exchange in Paris was an apartment east of the center of the city. We exchanged with a man and his wife. The man was a writer and had published a couple of books of fiction. One room of the apartment was jammed with books and was so full of books and other things that we could not use the room. The apartment was small, but we all managed to find a place to sleep. We were in a neighborhood where there were many Algerians, but we were close to a subway, or Metro, stop so it was relatively easy for us to get to the center of Paris. There was also a Sunday market practically at our door, and it was filled with very good and very fresh fruits and vegetables as well as some wonderful barbequed chicken.

In addition to taking in the famous sites of Paris we drove to the Loire valley and stayed in a nice little hotel for a couple of nights. It was right at the castle that straddles the Loire river. On another excursion we drove to Normandy and saw the beaches. I had never been to Normandy before; so that was a particularly enjoyable trip for me. All in all, it was a good exchange despite the inadequacies of the apartment.

And before I knew it 1996 was upon us, and it was time for spring training again. Bill, Mickey and Barbara were there again in Florida and we enjoyed the baseball games as well as the camaraderie. After spring training I went to Washington, staying a the Cosmos Club and seeing old friends. I had dinner a couple of times with Francoise, but saw my friend Jeannie only once. She was ill, and it was serious, cancer of the lymph glands. A couple of times when we were trying to get together, she called at the last minute to say she was too sick to make it. She was being treated with chemotherapy and radiation, and it was all taking a toll on her.

And then it was back to San Francisco, but no home exchange that summer. I received some offers, but decided I did not want to go off by myself. So I stayed home, saw a lot of Giants and A's baseball games and continued to see Erica. But by the end of the summer we had broken up. As I said earlier, I thought it was the right thing to do, but I must admit I missed female companionship. I guess man is not meant to live a life alone; nor I guess is woman, for that matter. But that fall there came a big change in my life.

# 59

## *Suzanne Enters My Life*

I met Suzanne Van Den Heurk. After our first casual meeting at a party, I called her a couple of days later and suggested we get together for dinner and we agreed to meet at the Waterfront restaurant, which is on the Embarcadero at the foot of Broadway. I arrived a bit early and waited for her in the bar. She was somewhat late, and sometime later said that she had sat in her car wondering whether she should go in to meet me. Needless to say, I was glad she came in.

Suzanne was then a beautiful brunette, now a gorgeous blonde, with sparkling eyes and an even more sparkling personality. She is about five feet, seven inches tall, has a great figure and dresses beautifully. When she enters a room everyone looks at her.

As we ordered drinks and dinner, we began to talk about each other. I of course told her about my experiences as a journalist, and especially about my days at the Washington Post and my free-lance writing since then. I also told her about retiring, moving to San Francisco and about Priscilla's death four years earlier.

Suzanne told me she had been born in the south of Turkey—within sight of Cyprus on a clear day—that her father was a French doctor who had come to Turkey to open a hospital and clinic with his brother, also a doctor, and that her mother came from Yugoslavia. Suzanne had a charming accent, not quite French and not quite Turkish.

I also learned that she had gone to school in Switzerland and then to Paris where as a girl she had been a model for the famous designer Madame Chanel. At the age of seventeen Suzanne married a Turkish man and they came to the United States, more precisely to Berkeley where her husband attended graduate school.

Suzanne cast about for something to do, and ended up working in a dress shop in Berkeley where she got interested in the business. Soon she was operating her own dress shop in Piedmont and living in Montclair in the Oakland hills.

During the last ten years or so Suzanne had been designing and manufacturing women's clothing in San Francisco and had her own label Suzanne Van Den Heurk.

Suzanne had been divorced about twenty years earlier and Van Den Heurk was the name of her second husband. She had three sons, two of whom where twins, and a daughter by her first husband. She and her second husband had also been divorced.

The more we talked the more I thought she is some woman. She is beautiful, talented, fun to be with, younger than I am by eight years or so but close enough in age.

Pretty much from the beginning I thought this is someone I would like to be with for the rest of my life. We continued to see each other, often meeting at her business on Eighth street south of Market. I met her children—Nil, Farris, John and Jim—and she met Fred and Steve and we got to know each other better and better as we went out to dinner often, went to the theater and saw movies together.

In the midst of all this I also started doing some writing for David Cole, whom I had met a few years earlier at an editors' convention, and who had recently purchased a news letter called News Inc., which covered the business of the news business, as its slogan had it.

The first article I wrote for him was on newspaper ombudsmen, a subject I knew quite well from my days at the Washington Journalism Center. He liked the piece, and I went on to do other articles about the press for him pretty much on a monthly basis. He did not pay much, but I enjoyed the work and the pieces ran two thousand words; so you had room to turn around and say something. Thus, as 1997 began I had found a wonderful woman and had begun a satisfying writing task.

In the spring of 1997 I went to spring training again, and until the last day or so it was the usual pleasant experience with Bill, Mickey and Barbara. But on the day before we were to leave, Barbara did not show up as usual for breakfast. We knocked on her door, but got no response. Finally Bill went to the motel office and got the manager to come with a key to open the door. Once we got into the room we found Barbara lying on the floor. We called an ambulance and she was taken to the hospital where doctors aid she had suffered a stroke.

When we visited her later in the hospital she could talk fairly well but could not move her left side. Bill called a couple of her children and a daughter came down to Florida from Michigan and a few days later took her home. Fortunately, she was able to travel on a regular airplane flight.

It was all a harrowing experience. As I write Barbara is still alive; I write to her occasionally; but she never replies. I feel for her. She was a school teacher, had been divorced and never had much of a life. She had four children, but her relations with them were never good. Now Barbara is seventy-six years old and living in a nursing home.

I had missed Suzanne a lot while at spring training and was glad to get back to San Francisco. We were becoming closer and closer. I particularly remember when a Saudi prince—yes, a Saudi prince!—she had met in New York came on his private plane to Oakland and Suzanne spent part of a day with him. Before coming back from Oakland Suzanne called me and said let's have dinner. We did, and Suzanne said the Saudi prince was not for her, despite his wealth and his desire to marry her, but I was.

A couple of weeks later while we were having dinner at Vannessi's on Nob Hill, I asked Suzanne to marry me. She wanted to marry me as much as I wanted to marry her, and she immediately said yes.

I was so pleased I could not wait to tell friends, and I think it was that very night when I called Jerry and Janice Waters in Bethesda to tell them, knowing that Janice would quickly spread the word. And she did. I hardly put down the phone when I heard from Pat Holt. "What's this I hear about you getting married?"

After twenty years or so as a retailer Suzanne decided to become a fashion designer. It was a bold move, but it turned out to be a good move. She moved to San Francisco and opened her design business by taking some space in a big building on Third street. After a couple of years there she moved to Fourth street where she occupied a two-story building with space for manufacturing as well as for her designing. In fact, she lived on the second floor of the building.

Soon her clothes, under the Suzanne Van Den Heurk label, were in Nordstrom's and Saks Fifth Avenue. She held the first trunk show in the new Nordstrom's store in downtown San Francisco. And not only were her clothes featured on Saks stores but also in a Saks catalogue sent to people throughout the country.

Suzanne took a special interest in leather, and trade-marked a colorful leather jacket. Her designs were always imaginative and very colorful. She was indeed a star.

On her frequent trips to New York as a designer she stayed at the Waldorf Astoria where she displayed her creations for buyers from major stores. At the Waldorf she also met a lawyer for Imelda Marcos and eventually Imelda Marcos herself. Suzanne still keeps in touch with her. It was also at the Waldorf that Suzanne met the Saudi prince I have previously mentioned.

When I met Suzanne she had been involved in trying to sell her clothing on one of the television channels that features clothing and accessories for women. Suzanne herself frequently appeared on the television program which was broadcast from Minneapolis. Unfortunately, the television plan did not succeed.

I was dazzled by Suzanne and her ventures in "the rag trade." I had never before known personally such a glamorous woman and I had known little about the design and clothing business. It was a whole new world for me.

But our lives did have some similarities. We both started out on our own when we were very young. I was not quite eighteen years old when I became a full-fledged reporter at the St. Paul Pioneer Press. Suzanne was married at seventeen, had been a model for Madame Chanel in Paris even before that and had become interested in the fashion business soon after arriving in the United States at the age of seventeen.

# 60

## *From Las Vegas to Vienna*

I have always thought that the newspaper business and writing itself were fairly glamorous, but after meeting Suzanne I knew that the fashion business was far more glamorous and exciting. I guess we both learned from each other's careers, and I still have much to learn from Suzanne about the glamorous fashion business. Also, she has been an entrepreneur not afraid to take chances while I am somewhat conservative in that regard. For example, I though over the years of trying to bee a free-lance writer, but I always hung back because I never thought I could make a living at free-lancing.

Suzanne even spent some time in the Philippines visiting Imelda Marcos in Manila and traveling with her around the country. When she describes those trips, I must confess being envious. Suzanne has also been to Hong Kong and, briefly, to Korea and Japan, places I have yet to see but still hope to visit some day.

Suzanne has also spent time in Chicago and Dallas, where she had buyers' offices. I too have bee in those cities, but only on short, reporting visits.

And now to our wedding. Suzanne suggested a June wedding, on her birthday, if possible, which is on June 28. And she thought we should do it in Las Vegas. Why not? Suzanne has an old friend, Gail, now living in Las Vegas, and called on her for advice. We started with the date. The twenty-eight did not work out for Gail; so we switched to June 21.

Our friend Gail booked us a room in the Grand hotel, which is next to the huge, new MGM Grand. We arrived in Las Vegas a day or two early and the first thing we did after checking into the hotel was go to City Hall to get a marriage license. We were told that we might have to stand in a long line—because marriage is such a big business in Las Vegas—but when we got to the office there was little wait, and fewer questions. All that seemed to matter was our thirty-five dollars which was the cost of the license.

The ceremony was conducted in a chapel in the hotel by a minister who was officiating at ceremonies all day. Ours was scheduled for four-thirty in the afternoon and it was made clear that we were expected to be out of the room by five o'clock to make way for the next couple.

The minister was nice enough and did not give off an air of boredom after having officiated at ceremonies all day. Fred and Suzanne's son John were best men and Suzie's youngest daughter Lizzie was the flower girl.

Also attending the wedding were Suzanne's son Jim and Fred's two daughters, Steve and his wife Wanda Lee and Suzie and her two daughters. I confess to being nervous and did stumble over a few words, but Suzanne was flawless and was beautiful as ever.

Suzanne's old friends Tom and Velda Berkeley were in attendance as were Gail, of course, and Jack Worswick, the resident manager of our building and a woman friend of his from Wisconsin. And Priscilla's brother Bill and his wife Mickey were also there, coming all the way from their home in North Carolina. Sally, Henry and Amelia did not attend, because of the long trip from Massachusetts and also because they had met Suzanne on a trip to San Francisco in May. Suzanne's daughter Nil and her family were in Europe on a previously scheduled trip and her other son Farris was tied upon business in San Francisco.

After the ceremony and after slipping the minister the obligatory twenty dollars, we all went to dinner in a private room at the hotel. It was an end to a wonderful day.

The next day we checked out some of Las Vegas, including the New York, New York hotel which has small replicas of such New York landmarks as the Statue of Liberty and the Empire State Building, Caesar's Palace and some other hotels. The weather was very hot, and that limited our sightseeing.

I had not been to Las Vegas in almost forty years and was amazed at how it had grown. There were many more hotels and restaurants and tourists, even in the desert heat of summer. In the intervening years Las Vegas had become respectable. Why, even my mother and three of her sisters—all very conservative Minnesotans—had been there and enjoyed themselves. I don't think my mother did any gambling, but I know that two of her sisters did, and one in fact who was now living in Oregon was a frequent visitor to Las Vegas and Reno.

Our time in Las Vegas was short but sweet. Everything went off fine and we joked about our thirty-five dollar marriage, referring to the cost of a marriage license in Nevada. We announced the wedding to our friends with a card which proclaimed Extra! In old-fashioned newspaper style and said "Stop the traffic on

Seventh Avenue!!! Stop the presses!!! Fashion designer weds ink-stained journal-ist."

So back we came to apartment 7-D at 2200 Pacific Avenue and settled in. Suzanne was winding down her business and I was continuing to do articles for the News Inc. newsletter. And we were planning for our honeymoon trip.

In the spring I had agreed to a home exchange with a couple who lived just outside Vienna in what would now be called a suburb but was in fact a village that was founded in the fifteenth century and was originally the center of a vine-yard area.

So in September we were off to Vienna, stopping on the way for a couple of days in Washington and staying at the Cosmos Club. The couple we were exchanging with were in Washington when we were there; so we had a chance to meet them at the Cosmos Club.

The man was a psychiatrist—naturally, we said, all physicians from Freud's Vienna must be psychiatrists!—and quite a distinguished one who was going to give an important lecture while he was in the United States. It is always nice to meet the people you exchange with, and we had a pleasant chat with the doctor and his wife.

They lived in an apartment on the main street of the village, not too far from the center with its shops and restaurants. The apartment was rather dark, but it met our needs as we planned to do quite a bit of traveling. His study was jammed with books, on his desk, on tables, on shelves and on the floor, but there was plenty of room for us elsewhere in the apartment.

To get to the center of Vienna we walked a few blocks to catch a bus which took us to the end of one of Vienna's subway lines and it was a fairly short ride on the subway to the city center. Vienna is a beautiful city and we did the usual sight-seeing, traveling some on a trolley route that took us around the city center and gave us good views of the famous castle, theaters, opera house and other notable buildings.

After seeing some of Vienna and otherwise orienting ourselves to the city and the village we were in, we set out on a motor trip to Salzburg. I guess you could best describe Salzburg as the music city.

Our trip took us along the Danube river. The views were often spectacular and the villages we went through were always picturesque. We stayed in a nice hotel just outside Salzburg and drove into the city to sightsee. Salzburg is not too large a city and it has a charming pedestrian street filled with interesting shops and restaurants.

After a couple of days in Salzburg we headed back to Vienna via the lake country east and south of Salzburg. Our friend Si Bourgin who had spent several years in Vienna as a Time-Life correspondent had suggested we visit the lake country because he thought it was one of the prettiest areas in central Europe. And he was right. Not only are the lakes gorgeous, but they are situated in the midst of some spectacular mountains.

On the way back to Vienna we also stopped at a hotel where we stayed in a room overlooking the Danube. It was picture-perfect as we looked out our window and watched the boats go by. We still get brochures from the hotel inviting us back. And maybe we will make it some day.

Back in Vienna we did some more sightseeing and planned for trips we wanted to take to Prague and Budapest. We decided to go to Prague first and to travel by bus. We had been asked by our exchangers not to take their car into Eastern Europe because so many cars were stolen there.

The bus ride was all right because you got a good look at the countryside. The trip took most of a day and we were met at the bus station in Prague by a representative of the travel agency that had arranged our trip and he took us to our hotel which was a bit out of the way but close to a subway station. The man was an American and we talked with him about the fairly large number of young Americans who were in Prague and how inexpensive it was to live in the city.

Prague is considered the most beautiful city in Europe. It escaped bombing during World War II and is used from time to time by movie-makers filming stories centered in Vienna in the eighteenth and nineteenth centuries. "Amadeus," for example, was filmed there.

We explored Wenceslas Square, which was the site of the demonstrations that ended Communist rule in Czechoslovakia. We also took a tour of the city that included the old Jewish cemetery and that ended in the old town square dominated by a clock steeple. We also bought some crystal at a shop in Old Town.

Our next excursion was to Budapest. To get there we took a boat down the Danube. It was not a very large boat, but it was a fast boat that skimmed along on the surface of the Danube. It was certainly a different way of traveling and was a relatively quick way to make the trip from Vienna to Budapest.

Budapest is a larger city than Prague. Budapest is in fact two cities. Buda on a hill on one side of the Danube and Pest on flat land on the other side of the river. On the Buda side is an old castle that is now the headquarters of the Hungarian government. There is also a cathedral. Other buildings now used by the government surround the castle and the cathedral.

On the Pest side is what is now the Parliament building. Near it are hotels, restaurants and pastry shops. We went to one of the most famous, if not the most famous, pastry shop. The nineteenth century interior of the shop was magnificent, as were the pastries, I should add.

Back in Vienna we did some more sightseeing and also drove to a wine restaurant on top of a hill from which we could see Vienna and the Vienna woods. And then it was time to go back to the real world, stopping in Washington again on our way to San Francisco.

# 61

## *From Beaconsfield to Edinburgh*

And soon it was 1998. I continued to do some pieces for the News Inc. newsletter, and Suzanne worked at keeping her business going. We went to the theater, continuing our ACT membership, and to movies.

The highlight of the year was a home exchange in England. We exchanged with a woman who had a beautiful house in Beaconsfield, a suburb west of London about half way to Oxford. The house was quite new on a street of equally nice houses. We were within walking distance of the town's shopping area which had in addition to the usual news agent, butcher, bakery and other small shops a shiny supermarket where meat, fish, cheese, breads and pastry where displayed in such a gorgeous way that you simply could not buy some of each. We took a train into London, the trip taking about half an hour. On one train trip we met a British Army officer who was taking courses at a military installation in Beaconsfield to prepare him for an assignment in the British embassy in Moscow.

On our trips into London, which brought us to Paddington station where it was easy to transfer to the Underground, we did some sightseeing and took in some theater.

Among the plays we saw were the musical "Chicago" and the comedy "Art". There is no substitute for the London theater. The acting is always superb, the theaters are comfortable and not too large and you always leave with a good feeling of having seen theater the way it is meant to be.

I even did some work in London. The editor of News Inc. suggested that I try to see some of the top people at Reuters, the venerable British news agency, and before we left for London I was able to arrange some interviews, including a lunch with the number two man at the Reuters headquarters on Fleet Street. The article I wrote emphasized how Reuters was evolving into a financial information company but still with emphasis on news-gathering.

The highlight of our trip was a tour we took of England by car. The car was part of our home exchange, and as the driver I managed to survive operating a stick-shift car and being on "the wrong side of the road," as we Yanks say when we drive in England. I thought I did a pretty good job as the driver, but Suzanne was always concerned about whether I was too close to the side of the road.

We set off from London up the eastern side of England. Our first stop was Cambridge, where we wandered through the old quads and peeked inside some of the equally old buildings. On entering one quad we had a "small world" experience. The man at the entrance who supervised the quad area including the rooms for the students noticed that we were Americans. Where are you from? San Francisco. Oh, I'm from Minnesota. Minnesota? Yes, went to the University of Minnesota. So did I. Well, it turned out our new-found friend graduated from the U of M, married an English woman and eventually settled in Cambridge. We talked some of the good old college days and parted as fellow Minnesotans still remembering the nice times of now long ago.

Cambridge is a beautiful place with its yellowish stone buildings, its green-carpeted quads and the river flowing just behind the buildings. To my mind, Cambridge is far more attractive than Oxford (more about that later) even though I think Oxford is always uppermost in American minds.

From Cambridge we drove north seeking a place to stay for the night. We ended up in an old hotel overlooking the North Sea. Our room was huge, the hotel was half empty, it being October. And we spent a pleasant night.

The next day we were on the road again, moving through interesting countryside and old villages and towns. The serene English countryside is so different from crowded and bustling London, and as much as I like London in many ways I prefer the picture-perfect villages, even though a lot of them mask pretty dreary living conditions and some downright poverty.

That night we did not have good luck in finding a place to stay. We tried several nice looking inns, but they were full. So we ended up in a not very desirable place in a rather isolated area. But after a day of driving we were tired enough that I suppose we could have slept most anywhere.

The next day we made it to Edinburgh and decided to stay in the Balmoral hotel, a luxurious establishment named after the castle in Scotland where the British royal family spends the month of August and was a favorite of Queen Victoria. The hotel is in the center of what is still called the new part of Edinburgh, a commercial area developed in the eighteenth century.

Edinburgh is a wonderful city, cosmopolitan but not too big, full of historic cites as well as up-to-the-minute shops.

The old town encompasses a mile-long street that begins at the top of a hill where the remains of Edinburgh's original castle still stands and ends almost at the doorstep of still another castle at the bottom of the hill. It is a rather touristy street now with many shops and some restaurants. But the shops and restaurants are in old stone buildings, many of them dating back centuries. The street is well worth most of a day. We had drinks in the old tavern near the old castle. This is the tavern where the Dr. Jekyll and Mr. Hide story by Robert Louis Stevenson is said to have originated, Mr. Hyde supposedly being the owner of the tavern who became the evil Dr. Hyde after midnight.

While we are still in Scotland a word should be said about the Scots themselves. The clichés about them being stingy and stand-offish are, in my opinion, simply not true. I think, based on my own experiences, that the Scots are a warm people, happy to have visitors from America or wherever and eager to please their visitors. And their food is good and hearty, even haggis the much-maligned sausage-like delicacy served in a bag made from a calf's stomach. I have tried it and I am here to say that I like it.

After a few days in Edinburgh we set off west and south on our way back to Beaconsfield. We decided to drive back on the western side of England, which we found every bit as attractive as the eastern side, although on our first day coming back we ran into a heavy rain storm. We ended up that night in a large, modern hotel in the countryside. It seemed to be a place designed for tour groups, but that didn't bother us. We had a nice room and a fine dinner. While we ate we looked out windows at as pretty a rural scene as you could imagine. There were even lambs that practically rubbed their noses on the windows.

The next day we set our sights on the Cotswolds and toured several of the villages. I suppose the Cotswolds are the prettiest parts of England. The area, which is west of London and encompasses Oxford, is the England you picture in your mind, with villages seemingly unchanged for centuries and farms where you expect to see farmers using horse-drawn plows to work their fields.

The Cotswolds were originally the center of the British woolen trade, with fields filled with sheep and the villages centers for sales of wool to the wool processors, dyers and weavers in cities like Manchester. But late in the eighteenth century the raising of sheep shifted to Scotland, and since then the Cotswold villages have languished but become more and more picturesque and more and more a destination for tourists.

We decided to skip Oxford on our trip back, as we were getting tired of being on the road and figured we could do Oxford later, as we were so close to it in Beaconsfield.

The Sunday after we returned to Beaconsfield we took a walk to seek out a pub in the countryside just outside our suburb. As we were walking in what we thought was the direction of the pub, we met a man going in the opposite direction. Are we going in the right direction to find this pub? Yes, said the man, but I am going to a much more interesting pub to meet some friends. Why don't you come with me?

The pub he was heading for turned out to be one of the oldest in England. It claims to be THE oldest, our new-found friend said, but so many pubs claim that distinction that I wouldn't pay attention to that.

It turned out that our friend had been in the United States a lot, working for Xerox, and had just retired. At the pub we met his wife and some friends. Part of the pub was indeed old, and the door to the oldest part was low, reflecting heights of people long ago.

After an enjoyable afternoon in the ancient pub, our new-found friend asked if we had toured Oxford, and we said no, we were planning to take such a tour this week. Well, he said, I am an Oxford graduate and would love to give you a deluxe tour. We accepted his offer immediately.

A few days later he came by our house in his car and we were off to Oxford. We spent most of the day there, exploring the dormitories, the classroom buildings, the churches and of course the Bodleian library. I still think the setting for Cambridge, with the river flowing behind the buildings, is more spectacular, but Oxford is beautiful, too. As we toured Oxford with our friend, I could not help but think how wonderful it would have been to be a student there. Rhodes Scholar? Sure, but just an ordinary undergraduate would have been fine, too.

After our tour our friend took us to a pub alongside a stream. We sat outside and had a late lunch. All in all, it was a great way to see a great university. And our friend seemed to enjoy the tour as much as we did, going back as he was to his college-days.

# 62

# *The Changing World of Politics*

As I have relived my boyhood in Minnesota and my adult years covering Washington and national politics, I am struck by how much everything in life has changed, and particularly how politics and political campaigning have changed.

Change is inevitable, of course, and the sixty years I have been involved in politics, most as an observer and commentator, is indeed a long time. So I should not be surprised by how different things are in the first decade of the twenty-first century compared with the nineteen-thirties and nineteen forties.

As a final summing-up let's take a look at some of the specific changes and try to evaluate them in terms of their effects—good or bad—on America's political life.

## Political Parties

We still have the same two major political parties—Republicans and Democrats—as we had sixty years ago, and third parties still spring up every presidential year. But the Republicans and Democrats put far less emphasis on party labels.

As I recall, George Romney, the automobile manufacturing executive, was the first major candidate to practically ignore his party affiliation when he ran for governor of Michigan in the nineteen-sixties. He was a Republican running in a Democratic state so he had good reason to skip over his party affiliation. And he won election because, I think, of his good business record and his warm personality.

Since then more and more candidates have run on their names rather than their particular party identifications. And some candidates have simply announced that they are members of one party or the other without having any previous political experience. President Eisenhower was the best example of that trend. The parties still support whatever candidates are nominated, of course.

Parties are still important, but not nearly as important as they were sixty years ago. The parties still hold conventions, still raise money for campaigns and still issue statements by their chairmen and publications and programs. But in campaigns the center of gravity has shifted to the staffs assembled by the candidates. The White House is the center of politics as well as policy-making for the winning party in a presidential election and the leaders of the Senate and the House of the losing party are the principal spokesmen for their party.

## Choosing the Candidates

Sixty years ago candidates were truly chosen at the party political conventions. There were no state primaries. James Farley, who was Franklin D. Roosevelt's chief political operative, traveled the country to talk with Democratic Party leaders in the late twenties and early thirties. Farley's contact and work paid off in Roosevelt's nomination for president at the 1932 Democratic convention in Chicago.

Primaries first became important in 1952, when Tennessee Senator Estes Kefauver went to New Hampshire and won that state's Democratic primary on the basis of the fame he had achieved during Senate hearings on organized crime in the United States. But it was still the Democratic convention that mattered in the end. The delegates nominated Governor Adlai Stevenson of Illinois.

It was not until 1960 that the primaries became significant. That year Senator John F. Kennedy of Massachusetts entered primaries from New Hampshire to Wisconsin, Oregon and California and back to West Virginia to demonstrate his popularity and won the Democratic presidential nomination at the party's convention in Los Angeles.

By the 1970's most states were holding primaries and conventions became largely social events ratifying the decisions made by voters in the primaries. By the time of the conventions the selection process was all over. The primaries were hailed as a victory for democracy. The people had taken the nominating power away from the party bosses who used to dominate conventions and had the final say on who would run for president. We were all better off? Or are we?

## Primaries—Good? Or Bad?

I have watched the development and growth of primaries and have covered many primaries over my long political reporting career. Primaries are fun to cover. They give you an opportunity to get close to candidates as the candidates themselves are honing their campaign skills. Few reporters are usually around. Crowds are small. There are meetings over coffee in the living rooms of ordinary people.

Sometimes issues are raised that neither candidates nor reporters have thought about or even considered to be important. All of this is to the good.

But who turns out for the intimate meetings and the state primary elections that follow? For the most part the voters who come to the meetings and then later come out to vote on a primary election date are the true party believers, which means the people on the left in the Democratic party and those Republicans on the right. The turnout of voters from the extremes of both parties skews the results. Candidates that have the greatest appeal to the extremes tend to win the primaries and then the party nominations. Goldwater beats Rockefeller. McGovern is chosen over Muskie. Reagan over Bush Sr. Bush Jr. over McCain.

There are of course exceptions to the rule, but the exceptions are mostly on the Democratic side—Carter, Clinton, Gore, Kerry. It is also true that candidates move toward the middle of the political spectrum as they come out of the primaries and advance toward the possibility of being nominated. And it has often been said that the middle is always moving in American politics even as the candidates strive to be considered reasonable middle-of-the-roaders.

But it is often difficult for candidates to shed an extremist label that they had pinned on themselves to win party primaries. Goldwater never shed such a label; nor did McGovern.

Now let us go back to "the good old days" when conventions actually chose the candidates. The delegates to the conventions were usually chosen by state party conventions and were generally long-time party stalwarts. In some states like New York, New Jersey and Illinois party "bosses' controlled the delegations. Sometimes the bosses were mayors—like Daley of Chicago—other times they were state or county chairmen, as was the case in New York. But they were always men who were not ideologues but men who above all wanted to win.

So when the conventions met they looked to candidates who had wide appeal and were viewed as likely winners. The fringes of the parties did not dominate those conventions as they have tended to dominate primaries. The delegates—and, yes, the bosses—above all wanted winners. And winners were men of the center of the parties. And the system worked pretty well for a long time.

I don't suppose we will ever go back to the old convention system, but I still would like to see a decline in primaries and a return to some extent of the old days. Perhaps I am just being nostalgic. But I don't think so.

## Personalities and Politics

The personality of candidates has always been important, even in the days before mass communications when the only opportunity voters had to see a candidate was to attend a rally or meeting at which the candidate was speaking.

Today television dominates political campaigning. Candidates make quick stops at airports so they will be seen on local television news programs because they had campaigned in "our" city or state.

Political activities are designed for the evening network news programs. Candidates also are eager for exposure on the Sunday morning interview programs, the morning shows, the late-night programs and even the Oprah shows. And then of course there are the television commercials bought and paid for by campaigns.

All of this emphasis on television affects the personalities candidates are seeking to project. You must talk softly and smile, smile, smile. Teeth must be straight and pearly. Answers to questions must be short and pithy. You must dress nicely at all times. Your wife and children must have that all-American look. You must not be too fat or too skinny.

Today a Franklin D. Roosevelt or a Woodrow Wilson would have to have something done about his teeth. A William Howard Taft would have to see Jenny Craig. A Thomas Dewey or a Theodore Roosevelt would have to get rid of those moustaches.

Candidates hire consultants to advise them on how to speak so they come over just right on television. Other consultants offer advice on how to dress and even on how to walk and how to approach voters for an old-fashioned hand-shake.

All of this emphasis on appearance and how one talks is important to some degree. But often a voter will get a feeling that the candidate and his ways are all too contrived. My own feeling is that we would be just as well off it candidates just presented themselves as they really are. There was nothing contrived about Harry Truman and he did all right.

Political candidates are not movie stars, although we did elect one movie star president. All of us would probably be better off if candidates and public officials paid less attention to how they appear on television and gave more attention to issues of substance.

I hope that someday someone will come along who will just be himself as he campaigns for president. That probably is too much to hope for, but it would be refreshing.

## Political Consultants

When I started covering politics sixty years ago there were no political consultants. The Eisenhower campaign of 1952 did get some advice from Madison Avenue advertising agencies, but it was minimal. As I recall, most of the advice concerned television advertising. There was no day-in and day-out strategizing by professional consultants.

I first became aware of political consultants in the 1960 campaigns. Louis Harris, the pollster, had left the Gallup Organization and working as an independent pollster was questioning voters for the Kennedy campaign. He was not slanting his polling; he was trying for an accurate record of the views of voters. Then Kennedy could use the information to tailor his campaign speeches to issues appealing to voters.

Pollsters who work for candidates do not like to be thought of as consultants to the candidates, but they are in fact are advisers. They often interpret the polling results in ways favorable to the candidates for whom they are working.

Today every package put together by a consultant for a candidate includes a polling component. (More on polling later.) In fact, the rise of the political consultant can be traced in large part to the sophistication and boom of polling techniques in the nineteen-fifties.

My first good look at consultants came in 1964 when both the Goldwater and Rockefeller campaigns made extensive use of consultants in their hard-fought battles in the primaries for the Republican presidential nomination.

In the years since then consultants have become as important if not more important than party organizations. When someone considers running for President, the Senate or the House, governor, mayor or even a city council seat (for dog-catcher, too?), the first thing the potential candidate does is hire a consultant. Political consultants even have a national organization; so it is easy to find one.

The first thing a consultant does is take a hard look at the would-be candidate and his likelihood of winning the office he covets. Would he make a good candidate? What are his political assets" His liabilities? Can he raise the money that will be needed? Is he willing to work hard at campaigning? What about his family? And on and on.

Once a candidate takes on a consultant, his new adviser maps out campaign plans and develops what he hopes will be a winning strategy. Typically the consultant also commissions a poll to determine what voters think of the candidate and what seem to be winning issues for him. Then a campaign plan is developed—where to go, and when, what to say, what not to say, where and from whom money is likely to be raised, how and when to seek endorsements from public figures and organizations that would help the candidacy.

And perhaps more importantly, the consultant deals with television. The only time most voters today see a candidate is on television. So the consultant tries to devise "sound bites" or longer statements that will play well on television news programs. Efforts are made to get the candidate on every kind of television program from the heaviest news and interview programs to lighter fare where the audience will include many people who seldom watch news programs.

Then there is television advertising, those 15 and 30-second spots that irritate many of us, but serve the useful purpose of getting people familiar with a candidate's name and his positions on key issues in the campaign. Consultants follow the rules of Madison Avenue—one message repeated over and over again to drive it into the heads of voters. It works for Wheaties, why shouldn't it work for Joe Candidate? And it usually does.

So the consultant organizes and to a considerable extent controls the campaign, day by day, week by week. The candidate of course must go along with the tactics and strategy. He is to a certain extent relieved of the detailed planning and execution of a campaign and has the final say on what the consultant proposes as the campaign.

So are we better off or worse off now that consultants have become so important in our politics? I am of two minds about consultants. On the one hand, they do bring discipline and order to a campaign and through polling and other means throw a spotlight on issues of genuine concern to voters.

On the other hand, candidates can become putty in the hands of consultants who may mold political views to suit their own pre-conceived ideas of what should be a campaign when the candidates themselves may be closer to the people have better ideas.

But like so much else in American politics today, the consultants are with us and are likely to remain an important part of the political landscape for a long time to come.

## Money and Politics

One of my lasting memories of the Truman campaign of 1948 is money—or rather the lack of it. I was paid every week, around 100 dollars as I remember. I know it doesn't seem like much today, but it was pretty good for a whipper-snapper in his early twenties. In fact, I was making more than a lot of young reporters of those days.

But the Truman campaign lacked money for such things as the all-important radio broadcasts (no television then) planned for each week in September and October. Broadcasters demanded their money in advance, and if they didn't get it, sorry, Buster, no air time for you.

More than once it was touch and go until a few hours before a scheduled broadcast when one of the campaign money raisers found a donor with ready cash and the country could hear Harry "give 'em hell" that evening.

Today money pours into presidential campaigns by the millions. How much do campaigns cost—$100 million?—$200 million—$300 million? No one knows for sure but it's plenty. Some of the money comes from the Federal government, both for the primaries and the general election, but just as much comes from ordinary folks and special interests.

Both parties have done a good job of seeking small contributions form Joe and Josephine Voter, but the real money comes in real chunks from special interest groups—unions, business, special interest organizations. Some of the money goes directly to the campaigns, but as much goes to political action committees and other organizations set up to funnel funds, sometimes secretly, to campaigns.

Money, as the California politician Jess Unruh once said, is "the mother's milk of politics." But it also can be, and has been, a corrupting influence. When the money comes from a union, a business or a special interest like the National Rifle Association or even the Sierra Club, the donor is in effect trying to buy a piece of the candidate. And often the purchase is consummated.

I am in favor of public financing of political campaigns, with a section in the law providing a candidate show his viability by raising some money on his own to qualify for government support. Public financing would not solve all of the problems caused by money in politics, but it would go a long ways and be a big help.

## Debates

Now for some good news for a change. Debates have become a part of presidential campaigns and of many senatorial, congressional, gubernatorial and mayoralty campaigns. And this is all to the good. Although the debates do not generally fit the Lincoln-Douglas mode of direct confrontation, the debates do bring candidates together on television so that voters can have an opportunity to judge them side by side.

The first modern debates were in 1960 between Kennedy and Nixon. There were three debates and Kennedy was judged to have won them on television, but Nixon was thought to have come over better on radio. Unfortunately, presidential debates were not held again until 1976 when Carter and Ford met three times as did vice presidential candidates Mondale and Dole. Since then there have been presidential and vice presidential debates every four years. There have also been numerous debates among candidates in the presidential primaries.

On the state and local levels debates have become quite common. It is hard for a candidate to duck a debate; if a candidate does refuse to debate, he faces the possibility of his opponent buying television time to "debate" an empty chair.

If I had my way I would dispense with reporters—or anyone else—asking questions and just have the two candidates sitting there questioning each other over a cup of coffee. I am told that German candidates do it this way—over a glass of beer.

## Polling

George Gallup and Elmo Roper pioneered public-opinion polling in the nineteen-thirties. Both Gallup and Roper had backgrounds in advertising. They devised and tested their ideas that a relatively small sample of voters and/or consumers could be questioned and that their answers would reflect the larger universe of which they were a part. Working-class Democrats would vote for their party candidates. Businessmen were generally Republicans and their voting preferences could be predicted on the basis of a sample of businessmen.

Although the bread-and-butter of the polling business was concerned with determining consumer preferences for products, Gallup and Roper became immediately famous for their political polls. So did, it should be mentioned, the Literary Digest, a long-forgotten magazine that conducted a poll in 1936 predicting that Republican Governor Alf Landon of Kansas would defeat Franklin D. Roosevelt, running for his second term. Roosevelt trounced Landon, winning 46 of the 48 states, and the literary Digest went out of business. It had made the mistake of polling by telephone at a time when many poor and lower middle-class voters could not afford phones.

In 1940 and 1944 the polls accurately predicted Roosevelt's reelection but in 1948 they stumbled again, finding that Dewey would defeat Truman. Roper even quit polling early in September saying that it was a waste of time to continue because the outcome of the election was a foregone conclusion. Gallup continued his polling through the third week in October. His polls found Dewey ahead by a comfortable margin, but Truman gaining on him. Gallup should have kept asking questions because of course Truman won in one of the biggest upsets in American political history.

Today polls are everywhere and are generally more accurate because the pollsters have become more sophisticated in determining and drawing their samples.

They also have more polling history to draw on in analyzing the results of their sampling.

But polls may soon be in trouble again. Beginning in the nineteen-seventies the pollsters abandoned door-to-door sampling, because with more and more women working it was hard to find anyone at home except in the evening. So the pollsters began relying on the telephone. But now more and more people just have mobile phones, and their numbers are not in any phone book. So pollsters may be missing a lot of people.

Today polls are everywhere. All the major newspapers and television networks conduct national polls. Many papers, large and small, survey voters on state issues. Private organizations like the Mervin Field poll in California provide some papers with polling results that are highly respected.

Polls are certainly useful. They provide valuable information to voters as well as candidates. For the most part they are a good mirror reflecting what is on the minds of voters. But the polls also can unduly shape positions taken by candidates.

I still like candidates that have formed their own views and are willing, even eager, to present them because they have thought long and hard about issues. I prefer a man or woman of ideas that come from gut feelings, not someone who is being molded excessively by what the polls happen to show. But the polls are with us to stay, for good or ill.

## Some Further Thoughts

I could go on and on with my reflections about how things have changed over a long life or observance of and fascination with politics, but perhaps enough is enough and I will conclude with just a few more random thoughts:

The Hatchet Men. Vice presidential candidates have seldom been in the spotlight. One vice president is said to have remarked that his only real job was to get up in the morning and check on the president's health. Another is reported to have run on a platform declaring that what the country needs is "a good five-cent cigar."

But vice presidents are important. Sometimes they become presidents—Truman and Johnson when presidents died; Nixon and Bush Sr. after running on their own. And no vice president has been as important and powerful as Dick Cheney, the No. 2 man for Bush Jr.

Unfortunately, as campaigners vice-presidential candidates all too often are relegated to roles as hatchet-men doing the dirty-work for their running mates. It seems that we no longer can come up with warm and charming vice presidents like "The Veep" Alben Barkeley.

Press Conferences. There has been a steady decline of press conferences, both during campaigns and after candidates are elected. As an old newspaperman, I value press conferences highly because they give reporters a good look at office holders and let the office holders know what is on people's minds as reflected in the questions asked by the reporters.

Unfortunately, in an increasingly scripted world, public officials try to avoid press conferences. The officials don't know what questions will be asked and often don't have answers to unexpected questions.

Nevertheless, I still think that all major public officials, and perhaps even some minor ones, should have regular press conferences, preferable weekly but at least twice a month.

White House Staffs. It is hard to believe that when Roosevelt entered the White House in 1933, he really had no staff—just a couple or three secretaries and two or three assistants he had brought with him from his campaign. After his reelection in 1936 he did announce that he was hiring seven or eight young assistants "with a passion for anonymity." The White House staff remained small even when Truman succeeded to the presidency in 1945. He still had only seven or so on his staff and met with all of them every morning, handing out assignments after first asking who was caught up with his work and was free to take on a new assignment. My, how things have changed.

Today the White House staff numbers in the hundreds. Some deputy assistants to the president never have met the man. And the large staff leads to mischief. Many on the staff don't have enough real work to do so they get involved in trying to micro-manage departments and agencies or, worse yet, petty politics, or even still worse, in something close to the scope of Watergate.

A president needs an adequate staff, but not an over-blown one. I hope the next president takes a hard look at the staff problem and realizes that departments and agencies can best be run by Cabinet secretaries and agency directors not by young, politically-ambitious men and women fresh off the campaign trail.

An Informed or Docile Public? Finally, or at last, you may say, I am concerned with the decline of interest in public affairs when there is so much information available.

For the most part newspapers and magazines are better than ever; there is much good information available on radio and television news programs; and the internet is full of factual material, and of opinions to consider. But who is reading, listening and watching?

Newspaper circulation is in a free-fall. The audience for the evening news programs on television has been in decline for close to twenty years. News magazine subscriptions are stagnant. Cable news audiences are small. The radio audience is still there but it is difficult to find much news on most stations.

When I was growing up in the thirties newspapers were my window on the world. I may have learned as much from newspapers as I did in school rooms. Today young people don't read newspapers, and apparently they don't watch much television news. Where do they get their information? Or don't they care?

I have no answers to those questions. But I am concerned. Our world gets more complicated, presidents and other officials accumulate more power, and the public pays less attention. It is a worrisome situation, and on that unfortunately pessimistic note I end.

# Epilogue

✦

## Changes—For Good and Bad

When my father was born in 1876 there were no electric lights, no automobiles, no airplanes, no movies, no radios, no television, and few effective or life-saving drugs. The vast majority of Americans still lived on farms. Roads were dusty, dirty and muddy. Most Americans lived out their lives where they were born or close to their birth place. Life was hard. Men worked twelve or more hours a day, often at back-breaking labor. Women worked just as hard and as long in their kitchens, at their washtubs, in their bathrooms if they had any and in the rest of the rooms of their houses trying to keep them neat and tidy. There were no vacuum cleaners or other kinds of cleaners other than soap and water. People with money did have horses and sometimes carriages to convey them about cities and the countryside. But what messes the horses made!

When I was born forty-eight years later in 1924, there were airplanes but routine air travel was still in the future. There were automobiles, but no traffic jams. Movies were still silent. Radio was just beginning to become a mass medium. Television was still twenty-five years away. So were life-saving drugs. Twelve-hour working days and six-day working weeks were still the norm. Women did have washing machines and the lucky ones had refrigerators. A company named Hoover was revolutionizing home cleaning by manufacturing vacuum cleaners. Horses and buggies were still around but rapidly being replaced by automobiles.

If there is a constant in our world today it is change. Change—in the material things in life, in the way we live both materially and spiritually, in what we consider important, in how we view ourselves as well as others, in setting our goals, in what we consider moral and immoral, in what we consider a good life.

In looking back over the seventy-five years of my life for which I have some memory, I have tried to think of a lot of the changes I have seen as a person and as a journalist. There are so many, and in thinking of them I am sure that I have omitted some. Many, perhaps most, of the changes that I have seen have improved lives, but many have not. In reviewing and assessing these changes I hope I do not come out as a fuddy-duddy seeming to resist change. What I hope I am saying is that I am taking a thoughtful look at changes and evaluating them in sensible ways. I know that many will disagree with my conclusions and I may in fact change my mind as I re-read what I write and ask others to review my thoughts.

## Where the Living Is Easier

I will start with the home. Women no longer need put in twelve-hour days cooking and cleaning, washing and scrubbing. The automatic washing machine and dryer have replaced the wringer, the tub and the scrubbing board. The refrigerator and the automatic stove have replaced the ice box and the gas stove that had to be lighted with a match. Prepared foods in cans and boxes have made it much easier and faster to put together a meal. Frozen foods have brought fruits and vegetables to us year-round. Instant this and instant that have changed everything from coffee-drinking to the cooking of potatoes or rice.

It is much easier, too, for a woman or a man to keep a home looking nice. There is the vacuum cleaner, of course, and all manner of other sweepers and magical cleaners that make almost every spot disappear.

There is central heating with natural gas, electricity or oil. No more does a family have to shovel dirty and dusty coal into a furnace. And air-conditioning. How did we ever get along without it? Air-conditioning is more responsible than any other single change for the economic development of the hot and humid South and the dry and hot Southwest as well as making life much more tolerable in the humid Eastern and Midwestern summers.

## Workplace Amenities

Work has changed dramatically, and for the good for the most part. Fewer than ten per cent of Americans are living and working on farms today, and tractors and other machinery have made farm life and work much easier. Yet these relatively few farmers produce bountiful harvests and most Americans have plenty to eat, even too much as obesity grows as a health problem.

In factories and offices the work week has steadily declined. Hardly anyone works six days a week any longer. Most of us work a forty-hour week and thirty-six or even thirty-two hour work weeks are increasingly common. With the decline in the work week productivity has increased.

Workers are also paid much better and have health insurance and other benefits paid for by their employers. There are still tough, dirty jobs in places like steel mills, but there is no dispute that life on an assembly line or in an office is far better today than it was when my father was born or when I was born.

The role of women in the work force is probably the most dramatic change in work during my lifetime. When I was growing up few married women worked and the single or married women who did work were confined for the most part to office jobs as secretaries or stenographers, to clerking in department stores or to teaching. In the space of my lifetime women have increasingly found places in the law, medicine, management, police and fire departments and on and on. Women are working everywhere, even in military combat.

And so are blacks, Hispanics, Asians and other minorities. This too has been a sea-change like the new role of women in our society. And all of these changes have come within my lifetime, seventy-nine years, a short time really when you look back to a period like the Middle Ages when time stood still and nothing changed for centuries.

## Getting From Here to There

As a young man my father saw the beginning of the end of the horse-and-buggy days and the start of the automobile era. And in my time the automobile—and airplane—era came to fruition. Most of these two developments were good, but not entirely.

The combustion engines in automobiles and buses displaced horses and street cars as the primary methods of transportation in cities and automobiles and buses and airplanes all but ended passenger train service.

I grew up in a family that had no car, and I can still remember how pleased my mother and father were when I had saved enough money to buy a car when I was still in high school. The car meant that we all could go for Sunday drives in the countryside and take many other trips within both St. Paul and Minneapolis and to Sauk Rapids, the small Minnesota town where my mother was born and where both my parents grew up.

I can also remember my first rain ride as a young reporter from St. Paul to Milwaukee and other train rides to and from Chicago and Washington. My first airplane trip was from Chicago to the St. Paul-Minneapolis Airport in 1949. I flew in one of the first jet airliners in Richard Nixon's 1960 presidential campaign.

But with the automobile came traffic deaths, 50,000 or more in a year, and countless more injuries. And the airplane brought us the bombings that killed so many innocent people in World War II and since, and the terrorist attacks in recent years.

Would I prefer to have lived in the horse-and-buggy age? Probably not. But I think it is useful to remember the downside of "progress" as well as its benefits. It is nice to jump in the car and run an errand close by or take a long trip on the freeways at eighty miles an hour. It is also wonderful to sit back in a jet airliner and fly in five or six hours across the country. But everything in life has a cost.

## Communicating With Ourselves and the World

When I was growing up a long-distance telephone call placed by my mother in St. Paul to her mother seventy miles away in Sauk Rapids was a big deal. You dialed the operator, told her where you wanted to call and she said, thank you, I will call you back when I have reached your party. Maybe fifteen minutes later the call would be ready, hook-ups having been made every fifteen or twenty miles.

Today we pick up the phone and dial London or Paris directly. Cell phones are everywhere. Written material can be sent by fax machines with the speed of the spoken word. And the Internet is even faster. The whole world is literally at our fingertips.

Instant communications are all to the good, although at times we would all like a little silence and privacy. The ringing of a cell phone in a restaurant or on a bus and the subsequent conversation for all to hear can certainly be annoying.

## Becoming Informed and Being Entertained

Television has replaced newspapers as the primary source of daily news events. Television has also replaced radio, movies and the theater as the principal source of entertainment. In addition, the largest audience for sporting events is the television audience.

Yes, a lot of people still read newspapers, go out to movies, the theater, sporting events, dances and other forms of entertainment. But television reigns supreme as the center of entertainment most evenings and most weekends.

There is much mindless material on television, but most mass media ranging from, yes, newspapers and magazines to radio and movies have always aimed much of their material to the lowest common denominator in the audiences.

Television redeems itself by bringing its audiences right to such events as presidential State of the Union addresses and other governmental matters, to the scenes of disasters and other heart-rending events and to interviews and close-ups with important people throughout the world. And some of the pure entertainment can be classy and good.

I guess one of the things that most bothers me about television is that it takes people away from reading, from family time and from just good conversation. And it is appalling to learn how many hours children, even the youngest, spend watching television. But television is here to stay and to affect all of us for good or ill.

## Educating Ourselves

The world, at least the developed world, is much better educated that when I was a boy. In the block on which I grew up I was the only child to go to college. Perhaps ten per cent of high school graduates sixty years ago went on to graduate from a university or college. Today the number is approaching forty per cent. And post-graduate education is increasing, too.

But high schools often turn out too many youths who are close to illiterate and not fit to work even in a MacDonald's restaurant. Anyone who hires people can tell you how many times applicants have to be turned down because of the lack of speaking, writing or simple arithmetic skills. And how discouraging it is to talk with such people who because of their poor education will never make it in the world.

There are indeed more high school and college graduates than in my day, but there are also a disturbing number who are graduates in name only. I don't have an answer to this ominous trend. I think it has to do mostly with the deteriorating role of the family in today's world.

## The Changing Role of the Family

I think the family is the most important institution in civilized society, yet it seems to me that the family has deteriorated over my lifetime. More and more married women are working Divorce has become common place. Single mothers are no longer a fairly isolated phenomenon. Television has taken a big bite out of family time. Many families no longer eat their meals together or even talk together.

All of these changes in the family are a result of many factors—including the speeding up of life in general, and the need or perceived need of both the husband and wife to work at full-time jobs outside the home.

I may be overly pessimistic about the dangers resulting from the changes in family life. For every family that has been harmed by these changes you can find one that has been faced with the same changes and is doing just fine. But I am old enough to remember that it was shocking to find so many single mothers among blacks, but now such situations are becoming more and more common throughout society.

As I said earlier, not all changes in life are for the best, and I think the changes in family life are a good example.

## What Society Accepts—and Rejects

Great changes during my lifetime have involved attitudes toward sex. When I was growing up I don't think I ever heard the word sex. When I started working as a newspaper reporter, I was told that the word rape could never appear in print. You said a woman was attacked. When I first started going to movies, sex was referred to in such a quiet way that even as a high school boy I don't think I caught on to what was being talked about. In fact, I am sure I didn't.

Now sex is everywhere—in the movies, on television, in books, magazines, newspapers. Is this good or bad? I do not consider myself a prude, to use an old-fashioned word, but I am so tired of the gratuitous sex scenes in the movies and the use over and over of four-letter words in movies. If writers can think only of those words, they are not fit to be called writers.

Children and youth are needlessly exposed to the dirty words and sexual situations. And to what purpose? I certainly don't know. I guess I don't want to go back to Victorian days, but I do question whether there is any good reason—even a teasing one—for sex, sex, sex, everywhere.

## Proper—and—Improper Language

Another sea-change that bothers me is what is considered proper language today. In my boyhood I was forcefully told by my parents not even to say darn, let alone damn. Even "cheegees" because it was said to be a swear word for Jesus.

Today the coarsest and most guttural of language is heard everywhere and often from the mouths of the most sophisticated people. Children use the worst of the bad words. I find all of this most distasteful.

I guess my comment is the same as what I said about the writers for the movies. If what we used to call a "swear word" is the best you can do, then you have no imagination.

Language standards seem to have entirely disappeared. Am I just behind the times? I don't think so. Again I think I am arguing for civility in both our private and public lives.

## Toward Healthier and Longer Lives

I guess it's time to "accentuate the positive and eliminate the negative," as an old popular song put it. The changes in health care and medicine in my life time have truly been spectacular. Penicillin, antibiotics, improvements in treating everything from high-blood pressure and heart attacks to cancer have been miraculous.

I have personally had the benefit of two eye operations that were not available when I was born—surgery to replace a detached retina and surgery to remove cataracts in my eyes. Without these operations I would be blind or close to it today. And without the medicine I have taken over the years to control my high blood pressure I would probably have died long ago of a heart attack.

Are there downsides to the achievements of modern medicine? I suppose you can say that in some cases lives are extended too long and people linger in a vegetative state. For the most part though modern medicine has indeed been miraculous. That can be seen as so many people live longer and longer lives, well into their seventies, eighties and even nineties. Look at me—seventy-nine going on eighty!

As lives have been extended programs such as Social Security and other public and private pension plans—and Medicare—have made life much easier for us "geezers." In many ways retired men and women have gained the most from the New Deal reforms of President Franklin D. Roosevelt. As modern medicine has prolonged life Social Security and other pensions programs have made the "sunset years" much more enjoyable. And so has Medicare, the part of the Social Security system that helps us retired folk to get adequate medical care. In my opinion we still need universal health insurance, but I am confident that will soon come.

## A Pause for Some Reflections

I don't think there is any question in my mind that my life in the last three-quarters of the twentieth century and the beginning of the twenty-first century has been better than the lives of the millions of human beings who preceded me and my generation on this planet earth. I say this despite the Great Depression of the nineteen thirties, the horrors of World War II and subsequent wars in China, Vietnam, Africa, Europe itself, and now Iraq. As for living in the age of nuclear bombs that can literally blow up the whole world, all I can say is that in many ways they have kept the peace among the United States, the former Soviet Union, now Russia, Japan, China and other major powers.

The changes in transportation and the development of instant communications have brought everyone at least in the developed world closer together, and that on balance is all to the good.

But is life too fast? Probably. I sometimes wonder why we all seem to be in such a hurry and so impatient. I think we all would do well to slow down and smell the roses from time to time, as we used to say.

I have said nothing here about changes in government and politics. That is such a big subject and was such an important part of my working life that I have decided to devote a separate chapter to those changes. Stay tuned!

Now for more comments on other changes in my lifetime:

## Shopping and the Consumer Economy

I have seen the demise of the small corner shop and of personal service and the rise of the supermarket and the Wal-Mart economy where supposedly I am saving money but where I get no service whatsoever.

My mother did her grocery shopping on the telephone, calling up Michaud's every day or two, getting Eddie on the line and telling him what she needed while he let her know what was particularly good that day. Strawberries are at their peak, Mrs. Duscha. There's a special on pork, and the meat looks excellent.

When my mother went to the Emporium or some other downtown store, the clerks often knew her by name and her likes and dislikes. All that is gone in our increasingly impersonal world.

## How We Dress

When I went to high school I wore a tie, a clean shirt, a nice sweater and neat trousers. Today there seem to be contests among high school students to see how sloppy or outrageous they can dress.

Dress has become extremely informal in my lifetime. Some of this of course good. It never made much sense for me to attend baseball games in suit and tie as men once did. But outsize pants dragging on the street? Skimpy T-shirts so belly buttons can bulge out?

In my boyhood it was shocking to see a woman in slacks. Today it is commonplace and slacks seem in fact to be more popular than skirts.

My father never left for work without his hat. I even had a hat shortly after I graduated from high school. Today few men or women wear hats or anything else to cover their heads.

## A Few Words on Music

I have a deaf ear and cannot sing, or dance for that matter. But I do appreciate classical music, love the musical theater if it isn't rock and roll and remember with affection Glenn Miller, Tommy Dorsey, Bing Crosby, Frank Sinatra and the other greats of the swing music era.

But when I hear rock and roll and particularly so-called music like hip-hop I cringe and turn off the radio as quickly as possible. I don't want to hear rap songs using the coarsest of language and urging me to kill the police or "dis" women.

Popular music has often been on the edge of civility, but the changes in such music in my lifetime have in my opinion been mostly for the worst in society and I am disturbed the way teen-agers hang onto the words of these "artists" and repeat them over and over again. Again, civility has disappeared in another corner of our world.

## Drinking and Drugs

Early on I learned about drinking—and its evils—but I never heard of drugs until I was probably in my thirties. My father had a beer with "the boys" when he finished work and before he came home. In our basement he kept well-hidden a bottle of whiskey—"schnapps" he called it—which was brought upstairs and opened only when a particularly good friend visited. My father would send me to the "Jew store" on an occasional Sunday to buy for him a bottle of cheap beer which cost, I think, only a nickel. My mother strongly disapproved of drinking and cocktails were never served in our house.

I had my first taste of beer after I had graduated from high school, and my first hard liquor maybe in my second year of college. Cocktails before dinner became a part of my life after I was married. Today I still like a glass of wine at the end of the day.

In my lifetime cocktails have become commonplace. Alcoholism is as big a problem as ever, but there has been a decided shift from hard liquor to wine. Drinking is much more acceptable, and beer, wine and liquor are more easily available than they once were. For example, I never knew of a grocery store that sold "spirits" when I was growing up.

As for illegal drugs, as I said earlier I never heard of them until I was quite grown up. Now drugs can commonly be found in high schools and even junior high schools, or middle schools as they are now usually called. The drug culture is another appalling development that may be destroying more lives than even alcohol. And no one seems to know what can be done about it. Drugs are one of the true tragedies of our time.

## Moving From Place to Place and From Job to Job

When I was growing up people stayed put for the most part. It was not uncommon to live out your life in the house where you were born. Once you had what seemed to be a good job you stuck with it until it was time to retire.

But not any more. People move around the country much more than they did fifty or sixty years ago. People who stay put seldom remain in the same house all their lives. There are now "starter" houses and people then upgrade themselves to bigger and better houses.

Economists who study employment patterns say that people today should plan on having three or four jobs in a lifetime and even to move from one trade to another or from one profession to another.

This new mobility is one of the important effects of a much more prosperous country than the times of my boyhood where a man often was so happy to have a job, any job, that he seldom thought of moving on to some other work. On the whole, a mobile lifestyle and economy are probably all to the good, but a decline in loyalty to a company or a trade or profession is a disturbing trend.

## The Changing Countryside

Farmers and others who lived in the country even as late as the nineteen thirties generally were isolated. Farm houses were often far apart; trips into town would take a day when the only transportation was a horse and buggy. Often farmers with few resources had to walk back and forth to town.

Today the few farmers who are left—ten per cent or so of the population—are connected with the world just like us city-dwellers. They have automobiles, television, computers to keep up instantly with he commodity markets. They vacation in Florida in the winter and enjoy their swimming pools in the summer. The changes and improvements in country living in my lifetime have been spectacular and all for the good.

## Declining Regional Differences

It is still possible listening to a person's accent to know whether he or she is from New England, the South or even Minnesota. But it is getting harder to spot regional trends and differences as people move around so much more than in the past. Cities like Boston, New York and Atlanta have a lot more "outsiders" than native born citizens.

The diffusion of regional differences is probably inevitable in the increasingly mobile society that we have today, but I think it is unfortunate. Some will say that the disappearing regionalism helps unite the country. Perhaps. But it seems to me that it also takes something away when the uniqueness of Georgian, Bostonian or Minnesota ways disappear into a national melting pot.

## The Migration of Blacks and Other Minorities

Another great change in my lifetime involves the migration of blacks within the United States and the movement of Latinos and Asians beyond the Southwest and California.

Black migration north and west began during the labor shortages of World War II when employers desperate for workers were willing to hire blacks despite concerns about whether they would perform well in all sorts of skilled and unskilled jobs. The blacks did do well and began to prosper. Today America has an ever expanding black middle class.

What a change. I did not know a black in high school. Why? There were none. When I started working as a reporter, I soon learned that blacks—Negroes as we then referred to them—never made it into the paper. Even black crime up to and including murders was kept out of print. "Forget it," the police reporter would say. "It's just another nigger murder." I did not in fact know or meet a black until I got to the Washington Post in the nineteen fifties.

There were a few Chinese in St. Paul and Minneapolis, running restaurants and laundries, of course, when I was growing up. The only Latinos I ever heard of in those days were migrant workers who lived in shacks in the countryside when they came through to work at harvest time.

Today many Asians and Latinos are prospering throughout the country as they, like blacks, assimilate into the middle class. There is still prejudice against minorities, but it continues to decline as the minorities climb into the middle class and prove themselves to the rest of us.

## Anti-Semitism—Yesterday and Today

In the nineteen thirties St. Paul and particularly Minneapolis were considered hot-beds of anti-semitism. This stain on the reputation of the Twin Cities was written about and commented on in national publications. I guess it was true, but I knew nothing of it probably because there were no Jews living in my neighbor and I did not get to know any Jews until I was in high school. I did not think my mother and father were mean and prejudiced, but I knew they did not like Jews. But as I finished high school and started college and working as a reporter for the St. Paul Pioneer Press many of my best friends and colleagues were Jewish.

Anti-semitism in Minnesota and the Midwest goes a long way back to the feelings among farmers that they were cheated on their prices by Jews who controlled the grain warehouses, the railroads and the banks back in New York. Whether this was true or not it was believed.

There is still prejudice against Jews today—it is said they control the big newspapers, Hollywood and television—but I think there is much less anti-semitism than there was fifty or sixty years ago. Some of my Jewish friends agree, but others don't. I have never been a hater and I hope that I am right about this issue.

## Promoting Diversity

Court decisions involving desegregating schools and other institutions have led to what we now call diversity. It is said and often decreed that we all should live and work and learn in inter-racial communities, offices, shops and factories, and schools and colleges.

Fifty or sixty years ago diversity was a rather strange word as it applied to people. Today it is somewhat accepted. But by no means always. It is still difficult to force people of different races and backgrounds to get together. Many people of the same race or background want to be by themselves, as Irish, Italian, German or Polish immigrants were often forced to be segregated when they poured into the United States at the end of the nineteenth century and the beginning of the twentieth. I come away from the diversity issue with mixed feelings. I, for example, am much more comfortable with someone with an educational and intellectual background like my own than I am with, say, a plumber. I think, too, of so often seeing construction workers in Washington taking their lunch break, whites in one group, blacks in another.

## Respect—For Parents and Older People

I certainly respected my parents and my elders such as teachers, ministers, neighbors and of course my bosses when I started working. But I don't think children, youths and younger adults have such respect for their elders today.

I think our institutions are much too youth-oriented. It is said that most movies are made to appeal to an eighteen-year-old boy. So there must be violence, often horrific scenes, and mindless sex and dirty language. Television courts the 18-to-34-year-old audience. Popular music tries to appeal to children as young as twelve. Clothes are designed mostly for the young. Fast-food restaurants seek to wean even five-year-olds to their tasteless and fattening menus.

With such emphasis on the young in our society, it is not surprising that the young think they are all-powerful and all-important and that their elders are not worthy of attention or respect. What is the old saw about how dumb you thought your father was when you were twenty-one and how smart he had become when you reached forty. I deplore this emphasis on youth, and I do think it is a trend damaging to all of society.

## When Smoke Gets in Your Eyes

The picture I still have in my mind of my father going off to work includes the cigarette he always had in his hand as he walked down our front sidewalk. And I still remember when I started working as a newspaper reporter that almost everyone in the city room had a cigarette, cigar or pipe in his mouth or was chewing tobacco. For some reason I never smoked, but liked the smell of burning tobacco.

How things have changed. The number of smokers has declined at least by half in my lifetime. Smoking is banned everywhere today, even in newsrooms and baseball and football stadiums. People are still dying from the cancerous effects of smoking, but in another generation or two the death rate from smoking will decline dramatically.

The changing attitudes towards smoking in my lifetime are largely the result of government—warnings, studies, research, court cases. Some day smoking may be entirely wiped out, and all of society will be better for it. The decline brought about in smoking is a great example of government at its best.

## The Spread of Gambling

While government has discouraged smoking by proving and stressing the health hazards of inhaling tobacco smoke, it has encouraged gambling. Every state except Mormon-dominated Utah has a lottery and Indian casinos are proliferating. Even as staid a state as Iowa has countenanced riverboat gambling on the Mississippi which flows past the state's eastern borders.

I am not a gambler, and I realize that gambling cannot be prohibited because so many people like to take a chance and are beguiled by dreams of instantly becoming millionaires. But I deplore the spread of gambling under government fiat because gambling preys on the poor and can easily destroy families and even lives. This trend is a change in our lives that is all for the worst.

## Violence in Our Lives

When I was a boy, I was quite aware of violence in our society. The nineteen thirties were the age of the gangsters—Al Capone, John Dillinger, Pretty Boy Floyd and all the rest. Chicago was their headquarters and St. Paul was a refuge when the heat was on in the Windy City.

Today the gangsters are gone, but violence at times seems greater than it was sixty or seventy years ago. Movies and television are filled with violent scenes that audiences seem to love. Guns are all too common in our society and the number of murders in our cities is frightening.

I don't know whether violence in movies and on television begets violence in real life, but I feel it does to some degree. I wish we could get guns out of our society, but no one seems to know how to beat down the greedy gun lobby.

## Some Optimistic End Notes

Have I been too pessimistic about many of the changes I have seen in a long life? Perhaps; so I shall try to end on some optimistic notes:

Travel, both at home and abroad, has increased tremendously and has given Americans a broader view of both their own country and foreign places. I did not get out of Minnesota until I had graduated from high school, and my first trip was only to Milwaukee, three hundred miles away. My children have traveled the country and the world, and so have I as an adult. Travel brings with it greater understanding of one's own country and the rest of the world.

I have mentioned but not said enough about computers. I suppose that is because I am a computer illiterate. But here I am writing on a computer, going faster that I ever could on an old-fashioned typewriter. The computer and the Internet have brought many important changes to the world from ease in making reservations for air travel to finding information on everything from health care to legal assistance.

Finally, the camera. When I was a boy a family was fortunate to have a Kodak Brownie camera, a small box-like affair that took pictures if the light was just right and the subjects stood perfectly still and close to the simple lens.

Today we all have high-speed cameras, and are taking both still and moving pictures without a thought. Now there is something called a digital camera that doesn't even use film. And cell phones have cameras attached to them. Smile!

In much the same category are compact discs that have replaced phonograph records, DVDs and VCRs—I don't even know what those initials stand for—that play movies through television sets and who knows what will be next?

## A Further Conclusion

As I have read over what I have written about changes that have occurred in my lifetime, I realize I have forgotten to mention such things as the development of plastics, on the invention of the ballpoint pen which made the fountain pen with its messy ink obsolete, and so many other changes, many mundane but some most significant.

But as I said in beginning this chapter, the most important change is in the quality of life. Whether you are a journalist, as I was, a lawyer or even a truck driver, one's working life is so much better and easier and the rewards—the pay, that is—are much greater than they were seventy-five years ago. Even in difficult times of recessions we Americans are all so much better off than our ancestors were in the booming nineteen-twenties. Pay is better, working conditions are better, there are governmental safety nets available in times of trouble, hours and work weeks are shorter so there is more time to enjoy life. I would not trade my life for my grandfather's life or my father's life.

Despite the complaining we all do, we are all so much better off economically, socially and I suppose even spiritually than almost anyone was seventy-five years ago. And who is responsible for these giant steps forward? The government with programs ranging from unemployment compensation to Social Security pensions and Medicare to help for the inevitable health and medical needs that come with old age. Industry with its innovative practices. Both workers and management with improvements in productivity. Schools and colleges providing better education for most of us. On and on the list could go.

Onward and upward we have gone, and my guess is that life will be even better still after I am gone.

978-0-595-37057-3
0-595-37057-8

Printed in the United States
37347LVS00003B/151-174